CAMBRIDGE
UNIVERSITY PRESS

CAMBRIDGE ENGLISH
Language Assessment
Part of the University of Cambridge

OFFICIAL

Cambridge English

SECOND EDITION

First for Schools

TRAINER

SIX PRACTICE TESTS WITH ANSWERS
AND TEACHER'S NOTES

Sue Elliott, Helen Tiliouine and Felicity O'Dell

Cambridge University Press
www.cambridge.org/elt

Cambridge English Language Assessment
www.cambridgeenglish.org

Information on this title: www.cambridge.org/9781107446052

© Cambridge University Press and UCLES 2014

First published © Cambridge University Press and UCLES 2014
5th printing 2015

Printed in Dubai by Oriental Press

A catalogue record for this publication is available from the British Library

ISBN 978-1-107-44605-2 Practice test with answers with Audio
ISBN 978-1-107-44604-5 Practice tests without answers with Audio
ISBN 978-1-107-44611-3 Student's Pack (Practice tests without answers with Audio CDs (3))

Contents

Introduction

If you are aged between 12 and 16 and want to take **First for Schools (FCE)**, this book is for you!

This book is called '**Trainer**' because it is full of exercises to help you get better and better at doing each part of **First for Schools**.
So, complete all the exercises then do all the practice papers! If you train and work hard, you'll soon be ready to take **First for Schools**.

First, do the grammar and vocabulary exercises on each **Training** page. Then do the task on the **Exam practice** page and check your answers.

On Training pages you will find:

⊙ **Cambridge Learner Corpus**

This shows information about mistakes that some **FCE** candidates make. If you do these useful exercises, you will learn <u>not</u> to make these mistakes when <u>you</u> do **First for Schools**.

Tips!

These are ideas to help you do well in the exam. For example: *You may find that Listening Part 3 options include adjectives to describe the speaker's feelings, which you then have to match carefully to what the speaker says.*

Remember!

These are quick hints about grammar points or vocabulary that you should learn.
For example:
To change **direct questions** to **indirect questions**:
Wh- questions: **What's** the time? → Do you know **what** the time **is**?
Yes/No questions: **Is** John here? → Do you know **if** John **is** here?

On Exam practice pages you will find:

- a **First for Schools exam task** for you to try and complete
- **advice** to help you with different parts of the task.

Tests 3, 4, 5 and 6:

When you finish Tests 1 and 2 you will be ready to do complete **First for Schools practice tests**.

Tests 3, 4, 5 and 6 are just like real **First for Schools** Reading and Use of English, Writing, Listening and Speaking papers. Doing these tests will give you extra help to prepare for the exam.

Keep a record of your scores as you do the tests. You may find that your scores are good in some parts of the test but you may need to practise other parts more. Make simple tables like this to help record your scores.

Paper 3 Listening

	Part 1	Part 2	Part 3	Part 4
Test 3				
Test 4				
Test 5				
Test 6				

Other features of the First for Schools Trainer

• Visual material

In the Speaking test the examiner will give you a booklet with pictures and photographs in it. The visual material in the colour section from pages C1–C24 will help you practise and become familiar with the type of photographs and written questions you will see in the test and help you increase your confidence.

• Answer sheets

Look at these to see what the **First for Schools** answer sheets in the test look like and learn how to complete them. Ask your teacher to photocopy them so that you can use them when you do your practice tests.

• Audio recordings

Listen to these to practise the Listening paper. You will need to listen to these to practise some parts of the Speaking paper too.

Cambridge English: First for Schools

Contents

First for Schools has four papers:

Reading and Use of English: 1 hour 15 minutes

The paper contains seven parts. For Parts 1 to 3, the test contains texts with grammar and vocabulary tasks. Part 4 has separate items with a grammar and vocabulary focus. For Parts 5 to 7, the test contains a range of texts and reading comprehension tasks

Writing: 1 hour 20 minutes

The paper contains two parts. You will have to complete two tasks: a compulsory one in Part 1 and one from a choice of four in Part 2. Each question on this paper carries equal marks.

Listening: about 40 minutes

The paper contains four parts. The text types are *monologues* (answerphone messages, information lines, commentaries, radio documentaries and features, instructions, lectures, news, public announcements, advertisements, reports, speeches, stories and anecdotes, talks) and *interacting speakers* (conversations, discussions, interviews, quizzes, radio plays, transactions). For each correct answer you will receive one mark.

Speaking: 14 minutes

The Speaking test contains four parts: short conversations with one examiner and another student; a one-minute 'long turn' on your own; a task where you speak with the other student; and a discussion. Usually you will take the Speaking test with just one other student, but sometimes students take the Speaking test in groups of three (only when there's an odd number at the end of the session – it isn't an option normally). You will be marked on your performance throughout the test.

Frequently asked questions:

> What level is First for Schools?

At this level you should be able to:

- use the main structures of the language with some confidence
- demonstrate knowledge of a wide range of vocabulary
- use appropriate strategies to communicate in a variety of social situations
- pick out facts from spoken language and written text
- understand the difference between main points and other points
- understand the difference between the main idea of a text and specific detail
- produce written texts of various types showing that you can develop an argument as well as describe or retell events.

> What grade do I need to pass First for Schools?

Results are reported as three passing grades (A, B and C) and two failing grades (D and E). If you don't get a passing grade but show that you have ability in English at a slightly lower level (Council of Europe Level B1) you will get level B1 on your certificate. If you score below level B1 you will get a fail grade.

Basic user		Independent user		Proficient user	
A1	**A2**	**B1**	**B2**	**C1**	**C2**
	Key for Schools (KET for Schools)	Preliminary for Schools (PET for Schools)	First for Schools (FCE for Schools)		

What marks do I need to pass each paper, and to get an A or B in the exam?

You do not have to get a certain mark to pass each paper in the test. The final mark for First for Schools is the total number of marks from all four papers: Reading and Use of English, Writing, Listening, and Speaking. The Reading and Use of English paper carries 40% of the marks, while Writing, Listening, and Speaking each carry 20% of the marks. You will receive a graph showing the results and a score for each paper out of 100. This means that the mark you need to pass the test will always be 60.

Grade A = 80–100   Grade B = 75–79   Grade C = 60–74

How can I find out about how I did in each paper of First for Schools?

Before you get a certificate you will get the Statement of Results telling you how well you did in First for Schools. As well as your result and your score out of 100 it also gives you your 'Candidate Profile'. This is an easy-to-read graph that shows how well you did on all the papers of the test compared to the all the other students taking the same test. If you do not get the score that you wanted, the Candidate Profile will show you which of the skills (reading and use of English, writing, listening or speaking) you did well in and which you need to improve.

Is First for Schools appropriate for students of any age?

First for Schools is more appropriate for students who are at school and aged from 12–16 but it is generally suited to students who are still at school who want to start working in an English-speaking environment or study at an upper-intermediate level. To make sure that the material is interesting for your age group and not too difficult or too easy for the B2 level, all the parts of the papers are pre-tested. This means that different groups of students try the materials for each part of the test first. The material will then only be used in real exams if the results of the pre-test show that it is appropriate for students who want to take First for Schools.

Can I use pens and pencils in the exam?

In First for Schools students must use **pencil** in all the papers. It's useful for you if you want to change one of your answers on the answer sheet.

What happens if I don't have enough time to finish writing?

You can only be given marks for what you write on your answer sheet, so if you do not complete this then you will miss the chance to show the examiner what you can do and how good your English is. Watch the clock and plan your time carefully. Do not waste time writing your answers on other pieces of paper. However, in the Listening test it is a good idea to write your answers on the question paper first. You will have time at the end to move your answers from the question paper to your answer sheet.

If I write in capital letters, will it affect my score?

No. You do not lose marks for writing in capital letters in First for Schools. Whether you choose to use capital letters or not, you should always make sure that your handwriting is clear and easy to read. Remember that the examiners can't mark a piece of writing that they can't read!

Note that different students have different strengths and weaknesses. Some may be good at speaking but not so good at writing; others may be good at reading but not so good at listening. The B2 Level 'Can Do' statements simply help teachers understand what First for Schools candidates should generally be able to do at this level.

For more information on 'Can Do' statements go to:
http://www.cambridgeesol.org/images/28906-alte-can-do-document.pdf

In this part you:

- **read**   a text with eight gaps
- **choose**   from four options (**A**, **B**, **C** or **D**) to fill each gap

Useful language Verbs + prepositions

1   Which prepositions – *on, with, in, of* or *for* – can follow the verbs below? Write the correct prepositions in the gaps. Some of the verbs can go with more than one preposition.

depend ......*on*........	result	participate ....
co-operate	approve	rely ....
succeed	apologise	insist ....
consist	concentrate	believe ....

> **Tip!** Use your vocabulary notebook to record any new words you learn in a short phrase, e.g. *have a good time*, *rely on your friends*. It's easier to remember them that way.

2   Complete the text with the correct form of the verbs from Exercise 1.

> **Tip!** Remember that the prepositions you need to look at to answer a question are not always after the gap. For example, look at number 7.

I try to **(0)** ......*participate*...... in as many sports as I can at school, but to be honest I'm pretty hopeless! Anyway, last week I decided I'd try to get onto the school relay team, as they're considered really cool. And amazingly, after some running trials, I actually **(1)** .... in getting a place – only as a reserve for competitions, but still! Then I realised that was just the beginning. The other team members didn't exactly object to a newcomer, but I could tell they didn't totally **(2)** .... of my being there. As I said, the team **(3)** .... of the best sports people in the school, so joining them was a real honour. And any races they were in usually **(4)** .... in a win. Anyway, the annual school sports day was coming up, so I thought I'd better start practising.

Finally, sports day came, and I was as well prepared as I could be. And I knew my friends all **(5)** .... in me, so that helped a lot. But just then we heard that another team member had been injured, so they'd be **(6)** .... on me to help them win. This was my chance. I started **(7)** .... as hard as I could on the task ahead.

I was incredibly nervous waiting for the runner behind me to pass me the baton. But suddenly there he was – and I was off! And guess what? I ran faster than any other members of the team – and we won! It was fantastic! But the best part was that after the race, the rest of the team **(8)** .... on carrying me round the track on their shoulders. I'll never forget it!

Useful language Verb collocations

3 Which phrases go with the following verbs? Write the phrases on the
correct lines below. Some phrases can go with more than one verb.

Tip! In Part 1, you need to know
common collocations to get the
answers to some questions.

your homework	your time	a good time	fun	a difference
friends	a break	sure	a photo	your best
a noise	an exam	a shower	a party	you good
better	a mess	sense	the washing up	some exercise

do   ....

make ....

have ....

take ....

4 Choose the verbs from the box which go with each group of nouns. Can
you add any more nouns to each group? Some groups can go with more
than one verb. Use a dictionary if necessary.

| pass | spend | miss | go | play | cross | save | catch | move | change | run |

1 .... a cold, a bus

2 .... money, time

3 .... the bus, your friends

4 .... shopping, away on holiday

5 .... an exam

6 .... volleyball, the piano

7 .... the road

8 .... house

9 .... your mind, your clothes

10 .... a company, a computer program

5 Complete the sentences below with the correct forms of the verbs from Exercises 3 and 4.

Example: *Whenever I* ....*go*......... *away on holiday, I really* ....*miss*......... *my friends at home.*

1 I need to .... some money to .... shopping with my friends at the weekend.

2 Luca and Maria .... the road and ran to the bus
stop but they still .... the bus.

3 I'd love to be able to .... the guitar, but I can't
afford lessons.

4 We've just .... house, so I haven't managed to
.... many friends here yet.

5 Ben's teacher told him to .... his time when
.... his maths homework, instead of rushing it.

6 Cristina .... the best she could in the exam, and
as a result she .... !

7 Mum asked me to .... the washing-up before I .... a shower.

8 Eliott .... a mess of building his new bookcase, because the instructions didn't ....
sense.

Useful language Phrasal verbs

6 Use the particles in the box to complete the phrasal verbs, according to the meanings given. Use a dictionary if necessary.

Tip! You will often need to use Phrasal verbs in Part 1 questions.

across	away	by	down	into	off
out of	over	through	up	~~up with~~	

Phrasal verb	Meaning
keep ......*up with*......	understand something that's changing fast
put	discourage
pick	collect
break	stop working
come	find by chance
fall	plans that fail
get	avoid doing something you don't want to
look	investigate, find out more
pull	stop on the side of the road
run	escape
stand	support someone who's in difficulty

7 Complete these sentences with the correct form of the phrasal verbs from Exercise 6.

Example: When Harry had a problem in the sports team, his friends all ......*stood by*...... him.

1 The dog slipped off its lead and .... , but luckily his owner found him.

2 Tom was busy, so his mum .... his new cricket bat for him from the sports shop.

3 It was raining so hard that Jack's dad had to .... on the side of the road for a while.

4 Julian managed to .... helping his mother with the washing-up by saying he had a lot of homework!

5 Our car .... on the way to the match, so we were late getting there.

6 Most people are .... eating this cheese by the smell – it's awful!

8 ⊙ Correct one mistake in each of these sentences written by exam candidates. Underline the wrong word and write the correct word in the space.

1 I would agree to the opinion that keeping animals in zoos is cruel. ....

2 When I am reading and the television is on, it bothers me because I am concentrating in reading my book. ....

3 If you decide to come in my country, I would advise you to visit the capital. ....

4 I am always fascinated of your garden. ....

5 This shows that it should be taken to consideration. ....

6 We could finish by some Spanish lessons. ....

Focus Meanings of words

9 For each group of four sentences (a–d), choose the correct word from the box for each gap. Use each word once only. Sometimes capital letters are needed.

support   assist   co-operate   benefit

a Many people in the town .... the plans for a new supermarket.

b I think I'll really .... from all the travelling I'm planning to do.

c As part of Tom's summer job, he had to .... the manager with various tasks in the office.

d Will people .... with the police to help find the criminal?

surely   absolutely   totally   definitely

e Harjeev .... said he'd be here to help organise the party.

f Unfortunately, I'd .... forgotten I'd agreed to meet Gareth in town.

g The cake that Kate made was .... delicious.

h I'm surprised our friends aren't here yet. .... they'd have called if there was a problem?

accident   confusion   error   fault

i A lot of people were trying to get on the bus and, in all the .... , Samantha lost her bag.

j Robert knew he was at .... and decided to apologise.

k Louis made a basic .... in his maths homework and it cost him five marks.

l Sasha hadn't intended to delete his homework files. He did it completely by ....

achieved   resulted   managed   succeeded

m I've tried baking cakes lots of times, but they've usually .... in failure – no-one wants to eat them!

n I'd be thrilled if I finally .... in passing my exam!

o Alex .... to leave the house just in time to catch the school bus.

p Becky's .... something amazing – she's been accepted for the school relay team!

For questions **1–8**, read the text below and decide which answer (**A**, **B**, **C** or **D**) best fits each gap. There is an example at the beginning (**0**).

Tips! Remember to read the example and title before you read through the task.

Look carefully at the words that come before and after each of the gaps.

Example:

| 0 | **A** support | **B** assist | **C** co-operate | **D** benefit |

| 0 | A | B | C | D |
| | ▢ | ▢ | ▬ | ▢ |

Tip! If you don't know which option is correct, cross out any you know are wrong. This gives you fewer options to concentrate on.

Dolphins

There have been countless stories of dolphins appearing to **(0)** .... with humans. But a recent incident has convinced a group of lifeguards that some dolphins were **(1)** .... attempting to help them – by protecting them from a shark!

The lifeguards were on a training exercise in the sea when the dolphins swam towards them at considerable **(2)** .... , then circled them repeatedly, hitting the surface of the water with their fins. At first, the swimmers were puzzled by the dolphins' **(3)** .... , but then began to fear they'd swum too close to some baby dolphins by **(4)** .... , and disturbed them.

Suddenly, one of the lifeguards spotted a small shark some way off. He realised that the dolphins had been **(5)** .... a lot of noise and causing general chaos in order to **(6)** .... off the shark. And to his relief, they **(7)** .... in doing so, because the shark soon disappeared. However, the dolphins insisted on staying until a colleague's boat safely **(8)** .... the swimmers. What an experience!

1	**A** surely	**B** absolutely	**C** totally	**D** definitely
2	**A** distance	**B** pace	**C** time	**D** speed
3	**A** occupation	**B** behaviour	**C** situation	**D** attitude
4	**A** accident	**B** confusion	**C** error	**D** fault
5	**A** doing	**B** making	**C** having	**D** trying
6	**A** call	**B** set	**C** put	**D** take
7	**A** managed	**B** succeeded	**C** achieved	**D** resulted
8	**A** picked up	**B** came over	**C** got away	**D** caught up

Advice

*0 Only **co-operate** can be followed by **with** in this context.*

*4 Which of these nouns can follow **by**? Look at the training exercises if you are unsure.*

*5 This is part of a collocation. Which verb can go with **noise**?*

*7 Only two of these verbs can be used with **in**. You need to think about the meaning to choose between them.*

In this part you:

- **read** a text with eight gaps
- **think** of a word that fills each gap correctly

Useful language Relative clauses

1 In relative clauses, which of the words in the box are used to describe the things below?

| why which whose where who when |

1 a time	....	**4** a reason	....
2 a person	....	**5** a thing	....
3 a place	....	**6** a possession	....

2 Complete the text with relative pronouns from Exercise 1. One of the gaps can be left blank. Can you see which one?

Anais Marin is a teenager **(1)** .... lives on the coast in the south of France, **(2)** .... the climate is quite mild and the views spectacular. Yet **(3)** .... she and her family go on holiday, they always go to a resort **(4)** .... they can find snow!

Anais finds it difficult to explain **(5)** .... she and her family choose somewhere that's so different from their home town. 'I know there are lots of tourists **(6)** .... absolutely love coming to this town. But it's not the same if you live here – you need a change from time to time!' says Anais.

Anais loves going skiing, and her three brothers, **(7)** .... hobbies range from snowboarding to ice skating, start looking forward to their holiday as soon as the summer's over. 'We know **(8)** .... the temperature starts to drop slightly here that it's time to prepare our winter sports equipment!' she says. 'And the amount of stuff **(9)** .... we take away with us could probably equip the entire resort!'

Which of the gaps could also be filled by the word 'that'?

Useful language Linking expressions

3 Choose a linking expression from the box that has the same meaning as the words in italics in these sentences. There are some expressions you don't need to use.

whereas	despite the fact that	in order to	owing to	as long as	instead of	despite	in spite of

1 *Even though* it was pouring with rain, Ben still cycled to school.
2 Joseph's quite extrovert and sociable, *while* his sister is more reserved.
3 The school trip had to be postponed *because of* the train strike.
4 Leon and Clara decided to walk into town *rather than* going on the bus, as it was expensive.
5 The homework deadline was extended *so as to* give everyone more time to complete it.
6 You can come camping with us *provided that* you get your parents' permission.

4 Choose the correct linking expression from the box to complete these sentences about Anais Marin from Exercise 2.

unless	in view of	in addition	so as to	yet	until

1 The Marin family live near the beach, ... they enjoy taking their holidays somewhere cold.
2 They always travel to a ski resort .... get a complete change of scenery.
3 They wait .... the weather changes before they start preparing their equipment.
4 The family's hobbies are probably quite unusual .... where they live.
5 .... to all the usual winter sports like skiing and skating, her brothers are also good at ice hockey.
6 It's quite hard to do lots of winter sports .... you're reasonably physically fit.

5 Complete the text below about an unusual sea creature. Use relative clauses and linking expressions from Exercises 1–4.

> Have you ever heard of a creature called a blobfish? It hit the headlines **(0)** ....*when*.......... it was voted 'the world's ugliest animal.' The blobfish, **(1)** .... natural habitat is deep in the ocean off Australia, spends its life swimming around in the dark, largely unnoticed. However, various factors have reduced the numbers of blobfish to dangerously low levels and, in **(2)** .... of this, conservationists are trying to take action to save it. **(3)** .... addition, some conservationists have suggested that previous projects have ignored the blobfish **(4)** .... to its ugly appearance, and that people are not keen to protect species **(5)** .... they look cute.
>
> Another such creature is the kakapo, **(6)** .... is the only species of parrot that can't fly. **(7)** .... the fact that there have been many campaigns to save these and other creatures, there are very few left in the wild. So we need to think about creatures such as these, **(8)** .... of just focusing on the more attractive-looking ones, such as pandas.

Useful language Articles, quantifiers and determiners

6 Complete the story below with words from the box. You may need to use some words more than once. Sometimes capital letters are needed.

a	an	both	the	any	many	more	most	some	every	none	one	few

(0) ....*One*.... day (1) .... boy called Matt was walking down (2) .... street when he saw (3) .... girl's bag lying on (4) .... pavement by a bus stop. There weren't (5) .... other people around, so he picked it up and had (6) .... look inside. To his surprise, he found quite a (7) .... coins in (8) .... bag, and even (9) .... money inside a small purse, (10) .... of which was in notes. There were also some books, but (11) .... of them had the name or address of the owner written in them. For a moment, Matt was tempted to keep the bag. But he liked to think he was (12) .... honest person, so he took it to the police station.

There were very (13) .... people inside when he arrived, apart from two girls who were (14) .... looking very worried. As soon as (15) .... of the girls saw (16) .... bag, she rushed over to him. 'That's mine!' she said. '(17) .... time I go out, I leave it behind somewhere! Thanks so much for finding it! You're fantastic! ' Matt felt embarrassed, so he mumbled something in reply – then blushed and left.

7 ◉ Choose the correct word in italics in these sentences written by exam candidates.

1 I'm writing in order to reply to the advertisement in my local paper *who / which* asks for people to help in a summer camp.

2 This is the moment *that / when* we must work fast.

3 They will take you to your hotel *which / that* is called the Loughborough.

4 I'm convinced that zoos, as institutions *that / who* take care of animals, can play a good role.

5 She wanted to see her husband *which / who* she had not seen for over two months.

6 We are a private clinic *who / which* treats all kinds of illnesses.

For questions **9–16**, read the text below and think of the word which best fits each gap. Use only **one** word in each gap. There is an example at the beginning **(0)**.

 Tips! You might find that you can think of several words which could fit a gap. Read the text around the gap very carefully as only *one* word will fit.

Example: | 0 | M | U | C | H | | | | | | | | | | | | | | | |

Water

We all know that water is essential for our health, and that we should drink as **(0)** .... of it as possible. Yet in **(9)** .... of this, many of us still don't drink enough, so bottled water is a good way of **(10)** .... sure we drink clean water while we're on the move.

Unfortunately though, the manufacture of all those plastic bottles can result in a lot of waste, **(11)** .... to the amount of oil required. It's actually **(12)** .... equivalent of keeping a million cars on the road for a year! Also, if empty bottles are **(13)** .... properly disposed of, they can cause a major pollution hazard.

However, there are steps we can take to improve the situation. For example, very **(14)** .... of the plastic bottles we use get recycled. So **(15)** .... of throwing them in the bin, we should send them to a recycling centre where the plastic can be re-used. And in many countries now, the water **(16)** .... comes straight from the tap is perfectly clean and safe to drink so perhaps many of us don't need to buy bottled water at all.

Advice

9 This sentence is **contrasting** with the sentence before it, so it needs a contrasting link.

11 This part of the sentence is giving a **reason** for plastic bottles causing waste. What kind of link is suitable?

13 Will this part of the sentence be positive or negative? Read on to the second half of the sentence before you decide.

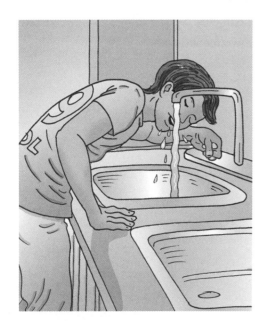

In this part you:

- **read**   a text with eight gaps
- **form**   an appropriate word for each gap from the word in capital letters
              at the end of the line

Useful language Suffixes

1a Add suffixes from the box to the words below to make other words. You may need to make some spelling changes.

- ness	- ly	-ship	-ment	-ive	-ion	- ful	-er	-ish
-hood	-al	- ation	-ance	- able	-en	- less	-ing	-ed

> **Remember!**
>
> The category of a word can change when we add suffixes to the ends of words, e.g. *lucky* (adj) + *ly* = *luckily* (adv). The spelling sometimes has to change too, e.g. with *lucky* the *y* has to change to an *i* to become *luckily*.

Example:

impress   + ive + ly   impressively   impress   + ion   impression

1 child	**4** agree	**7** involve	**10** friend
2 arrive	**5** explore	**8** attract	**11** hope
3 comfort	**6** accept	**9** conscious	**12** threat

b Now put all the words – the base words and new words – into the table. It is not always possible to complete each column for the base word.

base word	noun	verb	adjective	adverb
impress	impression	impress	impressive	impressively
child	child / childhood	–	childish	childishly
arrive				

2 Complete the sentences with a word formed from the word in brackets and a suffix from Exercise 1.

Example: The sea was ....*surprisingly*.... **(surprise)** *warm when we went for a swim.*

1 Finn's father is a very .... **(success)** lawyer.

2 My mum wants to play golf at the local club, but .... **(member)** is very expensive.

3 Conservationists work for the .... **(survive)** of endangered species.

4 The whole family tried to make Dad's 50th birthday as .... **(memory)** as possible.

5 Bram's painting attracted a lot of .... **(admire)**, as it was so original.

6 Judging by Max's .... **(appear)**, he'd walked a long way in the rain.

7 Although my grandmother is in her eighties, she's still very .... **(act)**.

8 There's so much traffic going into the city now that the authorities will have to .... **(wide)** some main roads.

Useful language Opposites

3 Write the opposite of these adjectives using the prefixes in the box.

Example: *relevant*   *irrelevant*

> il-   ir-   im-   in-

1 possible	**3** experienced	**5** polite	**7** patient
2 regular	**4** legal	**6** correct	**8** responsible

> **Remember!**
>
> A prefix is added to the beginning of a word, and can change the meaning of the original word to mean its opposite, e.g. *happy + un = unhappy*.

4 Write the opposites of these words using the prefixes in the box. Use each prefix at least twice.

> dis-   un-   mis-

1 satisfaction	**3** understanding	**5** honesty	**7** certain	**9** behave
2 satisfactory	**4** popular	**6** approve	**8** happiness	**10** organised

Useful language Spelling changes

5 Sometimes you will need to make some spelling changes when you add a suffix to a word. Put each word and suffix together to make a new word.

1 lucky + -ly	**6** responsible + -ity
2 mystery + -ous	**7** finance + -al
3 active + -ity	**8** sense + -ible
4 continue + -ous	**9** maintain + -ance
5 survive + -or	**10** criticise + -ism

> **Remember!**
>
> *easy + -ly = easily*
> *arrive + -al = arrival*
> *possible + -ity = possibility*

Useful language Word families

6a Look at the different words you can make from 'succeed'. Match each word (1–5) with the correct part of speech (a–e).

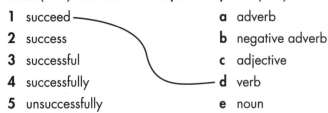

1 succeed	**a** adverb
2 success	**b** negative adverb
3 successful	**c** adjective
4 successfully	**d** verb
5 unsuccessfully	**e** noun

b Now build as many words as you can from the base words in the box. Say what type of word each one is. Use a dictionary to help you. N.B. you may not be able to make all the categories above from each base word.

> compete   courage   act   friend

For questions **17–24**, read the text below. Use the word given in capitals at the end of some of the lines to form a word that fits in the gap **in the same line**. There is an example at the beginning (**0**).

Write your answer **IN CAPITAL LETTERS on the separate answer sheet**.

Tips! Don't worry if you can't understand every word of the text. Read the rubric and title carefully first, then read through the text to see what it is about.

Read the whole sentence before you put a word in the gap.

You have to decide what kind of word fits the gap (noun, verb, adjective or adverb). Read the sentence carefully to check which one is needed.

Example: | 0 | U N U S U A L

Gliding

What's the most **(0)** .... birthday present you've ever been given? How would you feel if your birthday surprise turned out to be an **(17)** .... to gliding? That's exactly what happened to me – when I was only 8 years old!

USUAL

INTRODUCE

I'd never experienced anything like it – absolutely **(18)** .... ! After that I was hooked, so my parents arranged another **(19)** ....for me as soon as they could, and then I started taking lessons. It's been the perfect **(20)** .... for me – I learn a lot and I'm outside too, which I love.

BELIEVE

FLY

ACTIVE

I don't think my friends really understand my **(21)** .... , though. They're more into music and fashion. I enjoy those, too, but there's nothing to beat the **(22)** .... views I get from inside the glider.

ENTHUSIASTIC

DRAMA

Anyway, I finally flew solo on my 16th birthday, which was the **(23)** .... I could possibly do it. And soon I'm due to compete in some national gliding **(24)** .... Wish me luck!

EARLY

CHAMPION

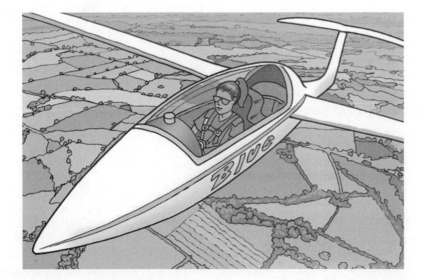

Advice

17 The article before the gap tells you that **one** of the word categories you looked at (noun, verb, adjective, adverb) is likely to be the answer. Why couldn't a verb, adjective or adverb fit here?

18 Should this word be positive or negative?

23 This is a superlative – what changes will you need to make?

In this part you:

- **read**   six sentences
- **rewrite**   the sentences using the word in capital letters so that your answers have a similar meaning

Useful language *-ing* and *to* + infinitive

1   Some verbs are followed by *-ing* and some are followed by *to* + infinitive. Others can be followed by both *-ing* and *to* + infinitive with no change in meaning. Write these verbs under the correct heading.

> **Tip!** You may have to answer questions that test *-ing* or *to* + infinitive in Part 4.

intend	like	~~mind~~	refuse	promise	suggest
finish	pretend	offer	continue	consider	tend
dislike	prefer	avoid	plan	decide	enjoy
deny	risk	fail	start	practise	afford

verbs + *-ing*	verbs + *to* + infinitive	verbs + *-ing* and *to* + infinitive (no change in meaning)
mind		

2   Some verbs can be followed by either *-ing* or *to* + infinitive, but there *is* a change in meaning. Look at sentences 1–5 and try to work out the difference in meaning in each pair, a and b.

1 **a** Jack did some homework and then **stopped to watch** his favourite TV programme.
   b Jack **stopped watching** his favourite TV programme because he needed to do his homework.

2 **a** Even though Maria's lesson had finished, her teacher **went on talking**.
   b Maria's teacher told them all about their new project, and then **went on to talk** about their homework.

3 **a** Why don't you **try taking** lemon and honey for your cough?
   b I **tried not to cough** during the film, but it didn't work!

4 **a** I **need to ask** mum to make an appointment at the hairdresser's for a haircut.
   b My hair really **needs cutting** – it's too long!

5 **a** I **remembered to take** my project to school with me yesterday.
   b I can clearly **remember going** to the seaside for the first time. It was wonderful!

3   ⊙ Underline the correct alternative in italics in each sentence.

1 I look forward *to hear / to hearing* from you.

2 I can't wait *to meet / to meeting* you.

3 I am interested *to apply / in applying* for the IT web design course.

4 Thank you for giving me the chance *to suggest / of suggesting* new ideas.

5 The money will be used *in improving / to improve* our customer services department.

6 I am writing this letter *to asking / to ask* for more information.

Useful language Comparatives

4 Complete the sentences with the expressions for comparison in the box.

the worst	less interested	a lot more slowly	far better
as expensive as	more difficult	the most	much older	~~newer than~~

Example: Your school bag is ......*newer than*...... mine. I bought mine ages ago.

1 Callum is .... than me at history. He gets high scores in all the tests.

2 That was .... film I've ever seen. I wished we hadn't bothered watching it.

3 I'm definitely .... in art than in music – I hate painting and going to galleries.

4 My friend cycles .... than I do, so he's generally late for school.

5 This dress wasn't .... you might think. I bought it in a sale.

6 The harder I try to produce a good drawing, the .... it seems to be.

7 That's ....money I've ever spent on a book. I just hope it's worth it!

8 The last house Sam lived in was brand new, but where he lives now is .... – it was built in the last century!

Useful language Phrasal verbs

5 Match phrasal verbs 1–10 with the correct meaning a–k. Use a dictionary if necessary.

0	clear up	**a**	manage even though you haven't got something you need
1	cut down on	**b**	end in a successful way
2	take care of	**c**	reach someone ahead who's going faster
3	get round to	**d**	improve, get better
4	leave out	**e**	invent
5	do without	**f**	argue and stop being friends with someone
6	work out	**g**	find the time to do something
7	catch up with	**h**	trust someone
8	fall out	**i**	not include
9	rely on	**j**	look after, keep an eye on
10	make up	**k**	reduce

6 Complete the sentences using the correct form of phrasal verbs from Exercise 5.

1 I hope the weather .... soon. We want to go to the beach!

2 I still haven't .... doing my homework. I'd better do it tonight!

3 Tom was a long way ahead, but Sam ran and .... him.

4 Sasha and Jackie have .... again. They're not speaking to each other.

5 Ned has to stay at home and .... his younger sister on Wednesday evenings.

For questions **25–30**, complete the second sentence so that it has a similar meaning to the first sentence, using the word given. **Do not change the word given.** You must use between **two** and **five** words, including the word given. Here is an example (**0**).

Tip! | Make sure the second sentence means *exactly* the same as the first – read it carefully.

Example:

0   Karen didn't really want to go to the party.

FORWARD

Karen wasn't really .... to the party.

The gap can be filled by the words 'looking forward to going', so you write:

Example: | **0** | LOOKING FORWARD TO GOING

Write **only** the missing words **IN CAPITAL LETTERS on your answer sheet**.

---

25   The film wasn't nearly as good as the book.
MUCH
The book ....the film.

26   I haven't had time to tidy up my bedroom.
ROUND
I haven't .... up my bedroom.

27   Jake couldn't carry on cycling along the road until he'd fixed his brakes.
STOP
Jake had ....his brakes before he could carry on cycling along the road.

28   I'd rather watch football than play it.
PREFER
I .... playing it.

29   'I'm sorry I missed your birthday party,' Ben told Sam.
APOLOGISED
Ben .... his birthday party.

30   I can only come if Mum says it's OK.
UNLESS
I can't .... me permission.

Advice

*26 Think of a phrasal verb that includes the word **round**. What construction might you need after it? **-ing** or **to**?*

*27 Do you need **stop to do** or **stop doing**? Which has the right meaning for this context?*

*30 Remember that **unless** often acts as the negative of **if**. You also have to find a verb to go with **permission** that means **says it's OK**.*

In this part you:

- **read**   a long text
- **answer**   six multiple-choice questions
- **choose**   your answer from four options (**A**, **B**, **C** or **D**)

1a Read quickly through the section of the text below, and then cover the text and try to tell your partner about it, in your own words.

> **Tip!** Before you answer the questions, read quickly through the text to get a general idea of what it is about.

b Now try to answer the following questions in pairs about the person telling the story to check your understanding.

1 Who is Anna, do you think?
2 What activity was she planning to do? Who with?
3 How were they feeling? Why?
4 What were they slightly worried about?
5 What were they optimistic about?

Anna's Story

I'd been learning to play the guitar for what seemed like years, without much success. So I'd wanted to go to see rock guitarist Jason perform for ages – and now he was coming to our town. My friends and I were all fans, so 'thrilled' just didn't go far enough to describe how we felt! Our town isn't particularly big or amazing, so we couldn't quite believe he'd included it in his concert tour. But there it was, on the programme. So we spent the weeks before the performance planning what we'd wear and how we'd get there – all the time hoping, of course, that our parents would say we were old enough to go unaccompanied. But then it was an afternoon concert for under-18s, so we reckoned the chances were pretty good!

2a Read this question about the section of text that you have just read.

What was a surprise to the writer about the concert?

Read through the text again and underline the part which gives you the answer.

b Now read the four options below. Which one is the closest to the answer you marked in the text?

A that a well-known musician would perform just for young people
B that her parents had given her permission to go
C that it would be held in such an uninteresting location
D that the rock guitarist was performing alone

3 Read the next section of the text. Check your understanding by answering the following questions. Work with a partner.

1 How did they travel to the concert?

2 What were they wearing?

3 What was the weather like?

4 How did the weather affect them?

> The day of the concert finally came, so off we went to catch the bus in our carefully-chosen outfits – only to find halfway to the bus station that we were caught in a sudden downpour of rain, so we didn't look quite as good as we'd hoped. But then we were only an hour or so away from finally seeing our musical hero perform live, so nothing could really dampen our spirits. We carried on nevertheless, finally taking our seats in the concert hall looking slightly wet, but with big smiles on our faces.

4a Find the answer to the following question in the text. Underline the parts of the text which gave you the answer.

What does the writer mean by *nothing could really dampen our spirits?*

Compare your answer with your partner.

b Now look at the four options. Which one is closest in meaning to the answer that you underlined in the text? Why are the other three options wrong?

A It was impossible to feel any worse than they did already.

B They were disappointed that the rain had soaked their clothes.

C Even the weather couldn't spoil the way they felt.

D They were determined to look happy despite their appearance.

5 Now read the final section of the text. As you read, think about whether the writer is positive or negative about this part of her trip, or whether she has mixed feelings. Which words and expressions reveal how the writer feels?

> Finally, the longed-for moment came, our guitar hero walked out on stage – and we were astonished! He looked absolutely nothing like all the pictures we'd collected of him – in fact, we barely recognised him. But determined not to be put off, we just settled back into our seats and focused on the music – and that certainly didn't disappoint. All the hits were there, the skilful playing, and the way he made 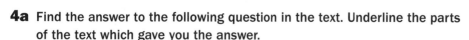 the instrument sing so effortlessly, in just the way I'd always hoped to – but had always failed miserably. It was amazing, and after he'd left the stage we walked out of the concert without speaking, almost as if words would break the spell of what we'd just seen.

6 Now look at the question and options, and underline in the text where you find the answer. Why are the other options wrong? Compare your answers with your partner. How did the writer feel about the musician during the concert?

A envious of his incredible talent

B amused by his extraordinary appearance

C disappointed that he played for only a short time

D surprised that he performed none of his recent compositions

You are going to read a short story by a boy called Dan, who is talking about going out with a group of friends. For questions **31–36**, choose the answer (**A**, **B**, **C** or **D**) which you think fits best according to the text.

| Tip! | Make sure you know who is writing and what they are writing about before you begin answering the questions. |

Mark your answers **on the separate answer sheet**.

It all started when my friends and I booked some concert tickets to go and see *Pulse*, who we considered to be one of the coolest bands around, playing exactly our type of music. But before we went, one of our group suggested we should practise a few dance moves, like the ones the band was so famous for. We were pretty sure everyone else in the audience would be doing exactly that, so we were keen to avoid turning up to the concert only to feel totally excluded, and reduced to the status of mere spectators in front of the stage. So, after a few hopeless attempts at home, we decided to try a dance studio in the city centre.

I set off early that morning – well, 11 am, which is something I don't intend to repeat very often! I'd reluctantly got out of bed, got ready and rushed down to the studio where we'd be learning how to dance along to the kind of stuff that bands like *Pulse* are into. But I have to say, I wasn't exactly overflowing with confidence when we arrived – I'd be the first to admit that I have two left feet when it comes to dancing. And, sadly, the friends I was going with were some way ahead of me at dancing, although the really gifted dancer in our group didn't actually show up in the end.

We walked into the dance studio where we'd be learning the moves, and instantly felt as if, instead of participating in a class, we'd somehow signed up to take part in some high-profile pop band's dance video which was to be expected actually. Luckily, our instructor appeared just then and told us we shouldn't stress if we couldn't do the moves. Instead, we should just concentrate on enjoying it. Apparently it would be an amazing form of exercise and far more interesting than just spending hours on end at some boring hi-tech gym.

Anyway, I was relieved to find that most of the other people in our class weren't anywhere near becoming professional dancers either. That became pretty clear during the warm-up, when it was obvious some of them were even more uncoordinated than I was. Even so, that part of the class was a bit of a shock to the system. I'd assumed we'd be doing some simple muscle-warming exercises like I do at football practice, but evidently not. We were straight into some tough dances and exercises performed along to some rap music I hadn't heard before.

Finally we moved on to what we'd really come for – the kind of moves the band would be performing at the concert, strutting across the stage like true stars. And after doing it for only a short time I really
line 28 began to imagine I'd got the hang of it and would be looking pretty cool at the concert. Then I suddenly caught sight of myself in the studio mirrors, struggling and straining to keep up with the rest of the class, and saw to my dismay that cool was actually the last thing I'd be looking! But never mind...
Anyway, to cut a long story short, by the end of the session I really felt I'd got somewhere. Afterwards, my friends and I stepped out into the street, safe in the knowledge that even if we weren't going to be wowing the concert crowds with our moves, at least we wouldn't be totally left out!

31 What motivated Dan and his friends to go to the dance studio?

   A They thought their favourite singer might be there, too.

   B They were keen to impress at an event they were attending.

   C They hoped they might be invited to dance on stage at a concert.

   D They knew the studio taught dance moves to their favourite band's music.

32 How did Dan feel when he arrived at the studio?

   A nervous that he might not be able to keep up

   B disappointed that one of his friends hadn't come

   C irritated that he'd had to get up so early

   D tired because of a lack of sleep

Advice

*32 What does Dan mean when he says he **wasn't exactly overflowing with confidence** when he arrived?*

33 On entering the dance studio, Dan's impression was that

   A they were going to focus more on exercise than dance.

   B the class was going to be more serious than he'd hoped.

   C it resembled a gym rather than a studio.

   D they had accidentally enrolled for the wrong activity.

34 Why did Dan describe the warm-up as *a shock to the system*?

   A The other students there were even worse dancers than him.

   B The music they danced to was not at all what he'd expected.

   C The moves were far from the gentle introduction he'd imagined.

   D The session was led by some strict professional dancers.

35 What does Dan mean when he says he'd 'got the hang of it' in line 28?

   A He'd progressed as far as he was going to.

   B He'd understood what he was supposed to do.

   C He'd decided he was ready to give up.

   D He'd persuaded himself that he was talented.

36 What would be a suitable title for the story?

   A My talented friends

   B An impossible ambition

   C The best concert I've ever been to

   D A way of joining in

In this part you:

- **read**   a text with six sentences missing
- **choose**   the correct sentence to fit each gap

1 **Work with a partner. Look at the kinds of words that can be useful in Part 6 in the *Remember!* box. Choose the best words and phrases to complete these sentences. Sometimes capital letters are needed.**

1 Nathan had a problem at football practice yesterday, as he hadn't got his sports kit with him. .... , he'd forgotten to tell his mum he'd be home late.

2 If you want to make an omelette, first beat some eggs together. .... put some oil in a pan and heat it up.

3 My sister adores playing computer games. .... is always first in line at the store whenever a new .... comes out!

4 .... I was really keen to try some dark chocolate, but .... I found it tasted far too bitter for me.

5 Watching films on TV is great as it's so comfortable. .... watching them at the cinema lets you see them as the director intended.

6 My older brother's a research assistant. He's .... looking into the effects of certain medicines on different people.

7 Theo likes listening to really loud music in his bedroom. .... seems to be a problem for his sister, as she doesn't share his musical tastes!

8 .... Chloe doesn't usually enjoy classical music, she agreed to go to a concert with me.

2 **What are the words and phrases doing in Questions 1–8? Which sentences:**

a tell us *what time* the writer is talking about?

b *refer back* to something already mentioned?

c add a *similar* or *contrasting* piece of information?

3a **Read the following paragraph and choose the correct sentence (A, B or C) to fit the gap.**

> People often talk about whether living in a city or in the countryside is better. Of course it rather depends on your lifestyle and the things you enjoy doing. If your favourite activity is shopping, say, then this may well restrict your choice. .... And that can be quite hard to achieve without good public transport.

A It means that you're unlikely to be completely happy living miles from anywhere unless you've got easy access to a town.

B A home out in the countryside, on the other hand, might suit you.

C What's more, living in a city can bring all sorts of unexpected disadvantages, like noise and pollution.

b **Compare your answer with your partner. Why are the other two sentences wrong?**

Tip! Look for words and phrases that hold the text together, like pronouns and time words. These can give you important clues when deciding which sentences fit the gaps.

Remember!

Pronouns	Time expressions	Adding/ contrasting information
he / she / it	after that	however
that	next	on the other hand
this	currently	what's more
one	at first	besides this
	then	although

You are going to read an article about diamonds in space. Six sentences have been removed from the article. Choose from the sentences **A–G** the one which fits each gap (**37–42**). There is one extra sentence which you do not need to use.

Tips! Read through each paragraph carefully. What is each one about?

Mark your answers **on the separate answer sheet**.

DIAMONDS IN THE SKY

We're probably all familiar with the feeling of walking out of the door, only to find the weather is miserable. Grey skies hang overhead, it's chilly and it's pouring down. **37** [ ] And believe it or not, this isn't the start of the latest science fiction story from a fantasy magazine.

Research by scientists indicates that's exactly what could be happening around planets like Jupiter and Saturn. There's evidence to suggest that the atmosphere surrounding these two huge planets could be filled with enormous – and priceless – diamonds. **38** [ ] However, the precious objects would have to be collected before they got too near to the planet's surface, as they might be melted by the temperatures there and the extreme pressure in the planet's atmosphere.

And the diamonds in question could be bigger than anyone has ever seen. Some may be not much more than a few centimetres across, which is still enough to make them very valuable. **39** [ ] However, others could have grown to reach a substantial size, which would pose significant problems for anyone trying to collect them.

For anyone interested in chemistry, the science behind the formation of these diamonds is interesting. Apparently, the diamonds may have been formed by storms, in which the flashes of lightning have transformed a gas called methane, present on Jupiter. **40** [ ] It is thought the process is due, among other things, to the intense heat of the lightning. The material then hardens into pieces of graphite – used in pencils – which in turn eventually becomes diamond – the hardest substance known to man.

Advice

37 What is this experience like? Pleasant or not so pleasant?

38 The paragraph is talking about collecting the diamonds. Why might scientists want to do that?

For scientists this has come as something of a surprise. It was previously thought that planets such as Uranus and Neptune might well contain precious stones, but it was believed that Jupiter and Saturn did not have suitable atmospheres. However, after more research into conditions on the two planets, scientists have agreed that diamonds could easily be raining down, on Saturn in particular. They are careful to point out, though, that closer to the planet the temperature is so extreme that the diamonds would be unable to remain in their solid form. **41** [ ] And because of the size of the planets, the quantity of diamonds there could be considerable.

Of course, no-one has been able to actually travel to either Saturn or Jupiter so far to confirm whether this theory is correct. **42** [ ] The same conditions have been recreated, putting liquid methane under intense pressure to observe the result. When intense heat was also applied, diamond dust was formed. Experts agree that such complex chemical reactions may well be taking place on these planets. In the meantime, writers and filmmakers will undoubtedly waste no time in using their imagination to incorporate the findings into fantasy films and books. And who knows – in years to come, scientific advances may mean that these stories no longer appear so fantastic after all!

A This is turned into carbon, which is the element that diamonds are made up of.

B There's even the possibility that they could be brought back here to earth one day.

C However, scientists have set up their own experiments in labs to replicate what may be happening on these gas giants.

D They could certainly be impressive enough to create an eye-catching piece of jewellery.

E It could even be that there's a sea of diamonds on the surface of the planet.

F That means the story may actually be less exciting than everyone imagines.

G But out in space, this experience might be much less unpleasant – because what would be falling might well be precious stones!

In this part you:

- **read** through one long text divided into sections, or up to six shorter texts
- **find** information in the text that matches ten short questions

1 Read through what Maisie says about her first family skiing trip. Then find the part of the text in which she talks about:

1 how optimistic her dad was about how the family would feel regarding the trip.

2 something they did that subsequently proved very useful

3 what her dad had overlooked when calculating whether they could afford it

4 her family's attitude to going somewhere cold for a holiday.

Tip! Make sure you read the instructions and the title of the text, if there is one. Then read through the questions and underline any keys words that may help you find the answer.

I think it was my dad's idea that we should give a skiing holiday a try – despite the fact that, as a family, we've actually never been very keen on chilly weather, snow, and all those other things you have to cope with on trips to places like the average ski resort! But, determined not to be put off, he went ahead and booked it, hoping that our enthusiasm would grow once the departure date drew a bit nearer. Of course, when he was first deciding whether we could pay for it all, he hadn't reckoned on all the extra expense involved – warm clothes, gloves, ski-lift pass. But we were all touched by the fact that he really wanted to give us a special treat, so we put on a brave face, and even went to get in some practice on the dry ski slope near our home before we left – which we were all glad we'd done, in the event.

2a Which one of these sentences matches most closely what Maisie says about the trip?

A They really appreciated what their dad was trying to do for them.

B They feared they weren't going to enjoy skiing, however hard they tried.

C They changed their minds about the trip when they realised skiing wasn't as hard as they'd thought.

b Why are the other two options wrong?

3 Now read what Marko says about his first time out on the ski slopes. Find the part in which he talks about:

1 the discomfort he felt while attempting to ski

2 what he'd imagined himself achieving

3 the sudden change in his level of ability

4 his irritation at the lack of warning from others

Of course, nobody had told me what it would really be like to be on skis, had they? They'd somehow carefully avoided mentioning it would be virtually impossible to stand up on skis initially, never mind gliding skilfully down the slope, doing an amazing jump or turn at the bottom, and hearing gasps of admiration from everyone watching. I spent most of the first hour or so down on the ground, ankles burning with the pain of being twisted over my unforgiving boots. But I was determined to keep going, and it wasn't long before something amazing happened and I actually experienced what it felt like to ski a short distance without crashing over. From then on I didn't look back – and by the end of the week, my instructor had actually promoted me out of the beginners' group. Way to go!

4a Which of these sentences most closely matches what Marko says about his skiing experience? Underline the part of the text where he says this.

A His early attempts made him realise he probably wasn't a natural skier.

B He refused to be put off by his initial lack of success.

C After his poor performance, his instructor's response came as a complete surprise.

b Why are the other two options wrong?

You are going to read an article about four young people taking part in swimming races in open water. For questions **43–52**, choose from the people (**A–D**). The people may be chosen more than once.

Mark your answers **on the separate answer sheet**.

Tip! Read closely when you think you have found the answer to a question. There may be information in more than one paragraph which appears to answer a question, but it won't be *completely* correct in both. Check carefully!

Which person

made a costly mistake about what strategy to use in the water?

43 ___

found they were handling poor conditions more easily than some other competitors?

44 ___

was lucky to have escaped being injured while swimming?

45 ___

was on the way to victory at an early point in their race?

46 ___

felt confident about producing a good performance prior to the race?

47 ___

remained unaware for some time that others in the race were in difficulty?

48 ___

exceeded their own expectations in the initial stages?

49 ___

missed out on winning due to an unfortunate occurrence?

50 ___

received much-needed support at a critical point?

51 ___

felt they'd learned from the race despite not being successful?

52 ___

Advice

44 Look for a reference to poor conditions. B says the water was **rough**, and D mentions conditions were **dire**. Which one found that other swimmers were not continuing with the race?

49 Which person was surprised to keep up with the leaders early on, as they knew those swimmers were better?

A Angela

As I was about to set off, I just kept thinking about what my coach had told me: 'The ones who are ready are the ones who win.' And I knew I'd done everything I possibly could to prepare, even swimming the course a few days previously, so I felt his words really applied to me. On the day of the race, the water was calm but I couldn't see far ahead, and I'd lost sight of the other competitors, so I hoped I was leaving them behind. Then suddenly I felt a huge bang on my chest and realised other people were actually ahead of me – and one had kicked me hard. She apologised and no damage was done, fortunately, but it was a reminder to try and keep my distance, if possible. Anyway, the incident didn't affect the result – I was so far back by then that I couldn't possibly have won anyway!

B Sam

On race day, I was a bit cautious getting into the water as it was rough. And there were a lot of other people swimming the same route, so my plan was to try and keep up with them, while also avoiding them so that I didn't get kicked, difficult though that might be. Once in the water, I actually began to swim a lot harder than I'd ever done in practice and I suddenly realised I was keeping up with swimmers who were clearly stronger than me in training. However, I soon noticed they'd all switched to a more relaxed breaststroke, presumably to pace themselves and conserve their energy, while I'd made up my mind to maintain the faster overarm crawl, and becoming worn out in the process. Anyway, to cut a long story short, I just decided to put this race down to experience. I found myself further and further behind, and in the end realised I'd never be able to win!

C Krista

There were so many swimmers taking part that I knew I'd have to swim tactically. The only problem was, I didn't really know any tactics! But I decided to up my speed to pass the swimmer ahead of me, and then settle into a rhythm before I passed the next one. That'd always seemed to work OK before, as long as I managed to swim wide around them to avoid getting hit. Anyway, I was soon up among the leaders and in with a good chance. The aim of the race was to swim out around a marker, then back to the beach, and run straight to our coach who'd be timing us. The three fastest times would win. However, as I hadn't got my glasses on, I rushed up to the wrong person, sadly ... and dropped out of the first three places as a result. Oh well!

D Tom

The sea conditions were pretty dire on race day, with big waves rolling towards the shore. I decided I'd just let others go ahead of me and simply aim to finish – that in itself would be an achievement. I resolved to see each wave as a challenge and meet each one head on, then go with the current as much as possible. The trouble was, doing that, I couldn't really see what the other swimmers were up to, so I was amazed when I heard some of them call out that it was too rough and they were giving up! I'd been coping OK, so I ploughed on, although I was getting tired. What really got me through, though, was finding my close friend swimming just nearby, so we made a promise to each other then to keep going now we'd come so far – and we did! That's what I call teamwork – even though we didn't win!

In this part you:

- **read** the instructions *and* the main essay question carefully
- **read** the notes that you must include in your essay
- **write** a formal essay that gives your opinion about the main question
- **include** the points you need to cover, and add another point of your own
- **write** between 140 and 190 words

1 Look at the instructions for a Part 1 question below.

> In your English class you have been talking about good places to go on class trips together. Now your English teacher has asked you to write an essay for homework.

This part of the question tells you about the *general subject* you are going to write about.

Focus Adjectives

2a Look at the adjectives below. Check any new words in your dictionary.

peaceful	remote	thrilling	picturesque	accessible
urban	interactive	wild	fascinating	outstanding
dramatic	exhausting	impressive	original	coastal
educational	memorable	breathtaking	remarkable	rural

Tip! In Part 1, you will need to give your opinion about something. Some adjectives can be useful in helping you to say what you think about something.

b Match each definition (1–10) with an adjective from the box. Sometimes several answers are possible.

Example   a long way from any towns or cities   *rural, remote, wild*

1 located in a town or city   ....

2 makes you tired   ....

3 attractive to look at   ....

4 an area by the sea   ....

5 very quiet   ....

6 something good that you will remember for a long time   ....

7 a place that you can get to easily   ....

8 based on a new idea, hasn't been done before   ....

9 designed to help you learn something.   ....

10 e.g. computer games and displays that involve the user   ....

3 Work with a partner. Look at the list of places to visit. Have you been to any of these places?

a museum	a zoo	a beach	an art gallery	a cinema	a forest
a climbing centre	a sports centre	a sailing centre	a castle	a farm	a factory

**When? Who with? Talk with your partner about one place you visited. What was it like?
Use some of the adjectives from Exercise 2 to help you.**

4 Work with a partner. Which of the places in Exercise 3 are more likely to be in the countryside? Which are more likely to be in a city?

5a Look again at the instructions at the beginning of the exam question.

> In your English class you have been talking about good places to go on class trips together. Now your English teacher has asked you to write an essay for homework.

b Now read the next part of the essay question. It tells you exactly what you must write about. Read the essay question and the notes below.

> Write your essay using **all** the notes and giving reasons for your point of view.

It is better for teenagers to visit somewhere in the countryside than somewhere in a city.

What do you think?

Notes

Write about:

1. which has more interesting places to visit

2. which is more convenient to visit

3. .... (your own idea)

c Look carefully at the two points that you *must* write about. Make notes about the ideas you would like to include. Remember you have to say what you think, and give reasons for why you think so.

6 Now read what a girl called Sarah wrote about these two points in her answer. She also included a short introduction at the start of her essay.

> Lots of teenagers go on educational trips, to the countryside or the city, and both places offer different attractions. So which one is better for teenagers?
>
> Even though the city has lots of attractive facilities, the countryside could be more interesting. It's fascinating to go on a nature-watching trip to a forest or a coastal area, with breathtaking views. And that's especially true if an expert there can tell you about important sites, say, and the creatures that live there.
>
> Of course, neither of these places is convenient to visit if they're not very accessible from where you live. It depends on whether students live in a rural location or in an urban area.

7 Look carefully at how Sarah writes about the first two points. Which does she think is more interesting? Which is more convenient?

8 Look at Sarah's own idea that she has added. What is it about?

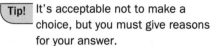

Tip! It's acceptable not to make a choice, but you must give reasons for your answer.

> Another point to consider, though, is how enjoyable these places might be. Teenagers enjoy going to theatres and sports centres in the city, but may not enjoy museums and galleries so much. That's why for them the countryside may be better. They can learn a skill at a climbing or sailing centre in a remote area while doing something fun and energetic.

9 Look at some other ideas to include in this essay. Write a few notes about each idea and then compare your ideas with a partner.

> cost   weather   equipment   age of teenagers

10 Sarah has also added a final sentence to finish off her essay. Remember, though, that you must try to keep within the word limit of the task.

> Class trips can always teach you something new wherever you go, but I think the countryside offers you the chance to discover more about the planet we live on.

Focus Joining words and expressions

11a Look at the words and phrases that Sarah uses to join her points together. Underline them in the text.

even though …

that's especially true if …

another point to consider …

that's why …

it depends …

if …

b Complete the sentences below with suitable words and and phrases from Exercise 11a.

1 Going to an outside activity centre can be fun. And .... you're a real fan of sports such as climbing.

2 The countryside can teach us a lot about our planet. .... it's important to go there.

3 .... the weather can sometimes be poor, it's important to get out into the fresh air as much as possible.

4 .... you don't enjoy history, then museums may not be good places for you to visit.

5 Places in the city can be easy to get to, but of course .... on where you live.

6 .... about the countryside and the city is that people usually find one more enjoyable than the other.

You **must** answer this question. Write your answer in **140–190** words in an appropriate style **on the separate answer sheet**.

 Tip! Make some brief notes about what you are going to include in your answer, especially your own idea that you have to add yourself.

In your English class you have been talking about sport. Now your English teacher has asked you to write an essay for homework.

Write your essay using **all** the notes and giving reasons for your point of view.

Doing sports outside is better than doing sports inside.

What do you think?

Notes

Write about:

1. which is more enjoyable

2. which is cheaper

3. .... (your own idea)

Tip! Remember that you can give your *own* opinion – you don't have to agree with the statement.

Check! Have you:

- [ ] included everything in the notes?
- [ ] written about your own idea?
- [ ] given reasons for your point of view?
- [ ] written 140–190 words?

In Part 2 there may be a question asking you to write a letter or email.

In a letter / email you:

- **need** to open and close your letter in a suitable way
- **may need** to give advice, suggestions, information or opinions, describe something or offer help
- **write** between 140 and 190 words.

1 Work with a partner. Look at the following sentences that can be used in letters and emails. Decide where you would use them – when you open (O) or close (C) a letter.

> **Tip!** Don't spend too much time writing a long introduction. The focus of your letter must be about answering the question.

1 I hope you're OK …

2 Bye for now …

3 Many thanks for your nice letter …

4 Take care and write soon …

5 Drop me another line if you get time …

6 All the best for now …

7 I hope what I've written will help …

8 Let me know all your news.

9 It was really nice to hear from you …

10 I'm looking forward to seeing you / hearing from you …

11 I'd love to hear from you again soon …

12 Sorry I haven't been in touch for a while.

2a Look at the exam task below.

> **Tip!** Look carefully at the question to check who it is you are writing to. Make sure you address the points in the exam question. What is the writer of the letter asking you?

You have just received this letter from Dan, your English-speaking friend.

My best friend has asked me to go away on a camping holiday by the sea with him and his family. It sounds fantastic! The problem is my parents have booked a holiday at the same time, and they want me to go with them and my little sister. What should I do?

Write your **letter**.

b Work with a partner. How would you reply to the letter from Dan? What advice would you give him?

3a Read the letter that a boy called Max wrote to Dan. What functions from the list below has Max included in his letter? Tick (✓) five functions that he has included. Underline examples in the text.

Functions

1 apologising

2 offering an explanation

3 making arrangements

4 saying thanks

5 giving a warning

6 being sympathetic

7 giving an invitation

8 giving advice

9 agreeing

Hi Dan,

Thanks for your last letter. It was lovely to hear from you again and sorry I haven't replied sooner.

Going on holiday with your friend and his family sounds fantastic, doesn't it? I'm sure you'd have a really good time. And camping by the sea is great if you've got a friend to do things with. But I'm sorry to hear it's at the same time as your family holiday. That's a bit awkward, isn't it? I guess they'd prefer you to go with them and spend time together – and your little sister will have company, too.

If I were you, I'd talk to them and see what they think. I don't know whether they'll change their minds, but if you explain, they can at least think about it. Or why don't you ask them if you could spend some days with them and a few days with your friend? That might be possible, so you should certainly give it a try.

Hope all this helps, anyway, and that you have a great time on holiday – whatever you do!

Let me know how it goes!

All the best,

Max

b How many paragraphs has Max included in his letter?

4a Look at the way Max uses questions and *should* and *if* sentences in his letter to give advice and make suggestions.

If I were you, I'd talk to them …

If you explain, they can at least …

Why don't you ask them if …?

You should certainly …

b Give suggestions to a friend about these things.

1 I need a camera to take some good photos.   *If you …*

2 I've left my football kit at home!   *Why don't you …*

3 I've lost my mobile!   *If I were you, I'd …*

4 I'm late – I'm going to miss the bus!   *I think you should …*

5a Look at the way Max uses a question tag to show he agrees with Dan.

Going on holiday with your friend and his family sounds fantastic, doesn't it?

b Add question tags to these sentences.

1 You'll have a great time at the party, ...

2 It was busy in town yesterday, ...

3 This maths homework isn't very easy, ...

4 You should probably help your mum in the kitchen, ...

5 We had a great weekend, ...

6 We need to buy a birthday present for Sophie, ...

6a Indirect questions and statements can be useful in letters. Read this example which Max uses in his letter to Dan.

I don't know whether they'll change their minds …

b Change these questions into indirect questions or statements.

1 Is Mark at home today?

Do you know... ?

2 What homework did our teacher give us?

Do you know... ?

3 There might be a party tomorrow night, but I'm not sure.

I'm not sure ....

4 This answer is wrong, but I don't know why.

I don't know why ....

5 Do teenagers in your country watch a lot of TV?

Can you tell me... ?

6 Are your sisters going on holiday with you?

Do you know .... ?

Test 1 Exam practice Writing • Part 2 (letter)

Write your answer in **140–190** words in an appropriate style **on the separate answer sheet.**

Tips! Don't forget to open and close your letter in a suitable way – but remember you must start answering the exam question as quickly as possible. Don't spend time on too much general information, such as your recent news.

You have received this letter from Maria, your English-speaking friend.

> A school friend of mine has invited me to a party next week. I've got nothing to wear, but my sister has some great clothes I'd really like to borrow. She often borrows my things, but doesn't like it so much when I borrow hers! What should I do?

Tip! You should leave enough time to check through your answer when you have finished writing.

Write your **letter.**

Tip! When you have written your answer, check that you have covered everything in the exam question, and that you have used a good range of language.

Check! Have you:

- [ ] answered the questions in the letter?
- [ ] given your opinions or advice?
- [ ] opened and closed the letter in a suitable way?
- [ ] written 140–190 words?

In Part 2 there may be a question asking you to write a short story.

In a story, you:

- **continue**   your story from the prompt sentence you are given
- **include**   the words or ideas you are given in the prompts
- **need**   to show you can use past tenses – past simple, past continuous and past perfect
- **should**   use good describing words – think of suitable adjectives and adverbs
- **write**   between 140 and 190 words.

1a Look at the exam task below.

You have seen this announcement in an international magazine for teenagers.

> We are looking for stories for our new international magazine for teenagers. Your story must begin with this sentence:
> *Sam and Henry read the letter and then climbed on their bikes and set off along the country road.*
>
> Your story must include:
> - a meeting
> - a prize

Write your **story**.

b Read the task carefully. Before you start writing, you need to spend a few moments thinking, and perhaps making brief notes. Think about these things:

- Who are you writing the story for?
- Who are Sam and Henry, do you think? Friends? Brothers? How old are they?
- What is in the letter?
- Where are they going?
- Who will they meet, do you think?
- What will the prize be? For what?

c Now imagine that you have the letter and you are going along the road on your bike. Look at these describing words that you could use to tell your story. Which could they describe – the letter, the road / countryside, the weather or your feelings? Put them in the best categories below, and then compare your answers with a partner. Some words can go in more than one category.

mysterious	nervous	determined	confusing	stormy	rough	picturesque
confident	bitter	bright	uneasy	stunning	astonishing	optimistic
bumpy	muddy	wild	enthusiastic	eager	coastal	unfamiliar
frosty	misty	puzzled	mild	damp	surprising	

the letter	the road / countryside	the weather	your feelings

2 Complete the story below by putting the verbs in brackets into the correct past tenses. More than one answer may be possible.

Tip! It is important to use narrative tenses correctly when you are writing a story.

It (0) ....was........ (be) a cold day. All Tim's friends (1) .... already .... (arrive) at Victor's house by the time he (2) .... (get) there. It (3) .... (rain) hard for most of his journey, so he (4) .... (be) soaked. As soon as he (5) .... (walk) through the door, Victor's mum kindly (6) .... (take) his wet coat from him and (7) .... (lay) it on a radiator to dry. Then she quickly (8) .... (go) back into the kitchen, as she (9) .... (make) their dinner. Tim (10) .... (wander) into the living room where his friends (11) .... (sit) and (12) .... (chat) , and (13) .... (hand) over the computer game he (14) .... (bring) for them all to play. Tim (15) .... (get) it as a birthday present last month and (16) .... (look) forward to showing it off to his friends. They (17) .... (be) all amazed when they (18) .... (see) it – it (19) .... (be) the very latest version! 'Awesome – thanks, Tim!' they all (20) .... (cry).

3 Look at these time expressions, then use some of them to complete the sentences.

Tip! You may want to use words and expressions to describe time when you are telling your story.

until	finally	as soon as	at first	during
while	gradually	meanwhile	by the time	

1 The film that Mauro and Jess wanted to see was .... coming to their town!
2 They raced down to the cinema .... they saw the advert.
3 They waited patiently in the queue .... the ticket attendant was serving the people in front.
4 The queue in front of them .... got shorter and shorter .... at last it was their turn.
5 Unfortuanately, they'd waited so long that .... Mauro got to his seat, he was feeling tired.
6 In the end, Mauro fell asleep .... the film, and Jess had to tell him what happened!

4 You can use descriptive adverbs in your story to show the *way* people do or say things. Look at these examples.

Rob was waiting impatiently ...   ... Kerry said suspiciously.

Now complete the sentences with an adverb from the box. Sometimes more than one answer is possible.

jealously	excitedly	miserably	crossly
desperately	calmly	enthusiastically	cheerfully
nervously	anxiously	peacefully	confidently

1 'I've practised hard for this race, so I've got a good chance of winning,' Matt said ....
2 The dog was sleeping .... in the living room while we were watching the film.
3 'You shouldn't have borrowed my T-shirt without asking!' Jen said .... to her sister.
4 'I don't suppose I'll ever get a laptop as nice as yours,' said Hugo ....
5 Leo waited .... outside his teacher's door, as he knew he was in trouble.
6 To his mum's surprise, Ralph reacted very .... when he knew he'd won the competition.

5 Read the story that a girl called Lena has written as an answer to the exam task about Sam and Henry in Exercise 1. As you read, underline some examples of these things:

- descriptive adjectives
- time words
- adverbs that describe the way people said or did things
- verbs in the past simple, past continuous and past perfect tenses

Going for a ride

Sam and Henry read the letter and then climbed on their bikes and set off along the country road. They were slightly puzzled by the contents of the letter that had been delivered to Sam's house that morning, but were eager to get to the bottom of what was going on. The road ahead was rough and bumpy, but they were so determined at first that even the bitter wind that they were heading into didn't put them off – until they had cycled some distance without seeing anyone else at all.

'It can't be much further now, can it?' asked Sam anxiously.

'Don't worry,' replied Henry confidently. 'I've worked out exactly where we're going.'

Almost immediately they came across a house right out in the picturesque countryside – with balloons hanging by the gate and an arrow pointing up the drive.

'Here we are!' announced Henry, as he cycled up to the house. The door opened – to reveal all their classmates inside their friend Miriam's house! 'Happy end-of-term, everyone,' said Miriam. 'And thanks for coming! Now, everyone gets a prize for understanding my directions in the letter and finding the house. And Sam and Henry – you've won a special prize for the most difficult journey. Well done! '

Write your answer in **140–190** words in an appropriate style **on the separate answer sheet**.

 Tips! Your story *must* continue from the prompt sentence. Look carefully at the *person* in the sentence – will you need to write your story in the first person – *I* – or is it a story about someone else? Check that the people in your story don't change halfway through.

Your teacher has asked you to write a story in English for the school magazine.

Stories wanted

Your story must **begin** with this sentence:

Nicholas was looking through a dictionary from his school library when he found a photo hidden between the pages.

Your story must include:
*   a friend
*   some money

Write your **story**.

Tip! Your story *must* include the ideas that you are given.

Check! Have you:

☐ used a range of past tenses?
☐ used descriptive adjectives and adverbs?
☐ used a range of time words and expressions?
☐ divided your story into paragraphs?
☐ written 140–190 words?

209.

In Part 1 you:

- **listen**   to eight short recordings, with either one or two people speaking
- **answer**   a multiple-choice question with three options for each recording
- **hear**   each recording twice

Tip! When you read through each question before the recording starts, look carefully at the first sentence. This tells you what the recording will be about – who will be talking, and the topic. The second sentence is the question you have to answer.

1   Read these examples of multiple-choice questions and recording extracts. For each question, choose the correct answer from the three options. Underline the words in the text that give you the answer.

1   You hear a boy talking about a trip he went on to a wildlife park.

What does he say about the experience?

> My family and I headed off to a wildlife park last weekend, some distance from where we live. We hadn't been there for ages, so I guess we'd forgotten just what was in the park, and we were a bit disappointed, to be honest, especially having driven for miles to get there. When we arrived, we had a much-needed rest and drink before we began the visit. There were some fantastic elephants and a big monkey and giraffe house, but there wasn't much else to see, despite the fact that the park was a reasonable size.

A He did not expect to see such a great range of animals.

B Getting there involved a long and tiring journey.

C The park covered a huge area of land.

2   You hear two friends talking about a class they have just had.

What was the class?

> **Boy:** That class was quite difficult, wasn't it? I wasn't even sure where some of those countries were.
>
> **Girl:** Yes. I mean it's interesting to see how people in other countries approached these things years and years ago, even going right back to the ancient Egyptians, but I find it hard enough keeping up with how we're supposed to work things out now!
>
> **Boy:** Yes, I know what you mean! For example, I don't remember doing fractions in that way when I was at school in the States.
>
> **Girl:** No. Well, anyway, now we've got calculators, so that makes it all a whole lot easier.
>
> **Boy:** Absolutely!

A maths

B geography

C history

3   You overhear a girl speaking to a male shop assistant.

Why is she speaking to him?

> **Assistant:** Can I help?
>
> **Girl:** Yes, I've just tried on this sweater in the changing rooms …
>
> **Assistant:** So you'd like to buy it. OK.
>
> **Girl:** Well, I don't suppose you have another one in stock, do you?
>
> **Assistant:** I think that's the last one. Is there a problem?
>
> **Girl:** Well, yes – there's actually a hole in the sleeve of this one – look. So I'm not really keen to have it.
>
> **Assistant:** Oh, in that case, we could reduce the price a bit.
>
> **Girl:** It's fine – I don't really want to get something that's damaged. I think I'll leave it, thanks.

A to pay for something

B to get a refund on something

C to complain about something

4 You hear a boy talking about a film he has just seen.

What did he think of it?

210

I've just been to see an adventure film with a friend of mine. There was a lot of publicity and hype about it, how fantastic it was … best film ever made and so on. So I went in expecting something amazing, and I suppose it was pretty good in some respects, certainly as far as the guy playing the central character went. The music was definitely a new experience for me, couldn't have been better for the film, and the whole storyline kept you on the edge of your seat – until the final few minutes. What a let-down! I feel like writing to the director to complain.

A The ending was not as good as he had expected.

B The main actor's performance was disappointing.

C The soundtrack did not really suit the story.

5 You hear two friends discussing hiring some bicycles.

What do they agree about?

Girl: Look, John. We could hire bicycles here for the day and cycle along the coast road.

Boy: Mm, that'd be great, but look at how much they cost. Quite a lot.

Girl: That's for the whole day, so we could save on bus fares if we cycle instead.

Boy: True. Let's see – they've got a couple left – but are they big enough?

Girl: Let me try. Hm – these aren't really made for people our age, I don't think.

Boy: And it looks as if these are the only ones left. Oh, well … We can always come back again tomorrow!

A The roads may be unsuitable to cycle on.

B The only cycles available are too small for them.

C The hire price is more than they can afford.

2 **Look at the options below. A girl is talking about how she feels about a T-shirt she received as a present. Is she being positive or negative when she says the following? Or does it depend on the context?**

a My friends must have spent ages choosing it.

b Why on earth would I want a picture of a dog on it?

c I've never come across anything like it in the shops.

d I didn't even say it was my birthday, but they still remembered.

e It could be a bit looser round the arms.

f I doubt if I'll be able to exchange it for another one now.

Tip! Look carefully at any questions that ask you about the *feelings* of the speakers. You may have to match what the speakers say to an adjective in one of the options.

3a 1 02 **Now listen to the recording and answer the question below.**

How does the girl feel about the T-shirt she was given for her birthday?

A surprised that so much thought went into buying it

B disappointed that it does not fit her well enough

C pleased that it has a favourite image on it

b **Which is the correct answer? Why are the other two wrong?**

Test 1 Exam practice   Listening • Part 1

(1 03) You will hear people talking in eight different situations. For questions **1–8**, choose the best answer (**A, B** or **C**).

1   You hear a girl talking about a running race she is going to compete in soon.
     What does she say about the race?
  A   She hopes the spectators will be supportive.
  B   She has prepared for it as well as she can.
  C   She thinks her chances of success are poor.

2   **(1 04)** You hear the beginning of a radio programme for teenagers.
     What is today's programme going to be about?
  A   conservation
  B   climate change
  C   pollution

3   **(1 05)** You overhear a boy phoning a friend.
     Why is he calling?
  A   to ask a favour
  B   to pass on some news
  C   to confirm travel arrangements

4   **(1 06)** You hear two friends talking about a school photography exhibition.
     What is the girl trying to do?
  A   persuade the boy to display his photos
  B   suggest how the boy could improve his photos
  C   encourage the boy to go and see the photos with her

5   **(1 07)** You hear two friends talking about a shopping trip they've just been on.
     How does the girl feel about the trip?
  A   sorry that she did not buy an item she saw
  B   disappointed that she could not find what she was looking for
  C   relieved that she did not spend too much money

6   **(1 08)** You hear a girl talking about her class trip to the theatre to see a play.
     She thought the play was
  A   more frightening than she had expected.
  B   surprisingly different from the version she had studied.
  C   very difficult to understand when performed on stage.

7   **(1 09)** You hear two friends talking about a canoeing lesson they have just had on the river.
     What do they agree about?
  A   how risky the activity seemed at times
  B   how painful their muscles felt
  C   how difficult it was to paddle properly

8   **(1 10)** You hear a teacher telling a class about a science project they are going to do.
     Which place is the class going to visit for the project?
  A   a science laboratory
  B   the city library
  C   a museum

> **Tip!** Try to use the first listening to answer the question, and then check your answer during the second listening. If you're still not sure, have a guess – don't leave the answer blank.

> **Advice**
>
> **3** If you are not sure of the answer, try to eliminate each option, e.g. Alfie is asking Jake something – but is it a favour or does he need advice? He is also telling Jake something – does Jake know about it already? And is he confirming travel arrangements or making new ones?
>
> **5** For this question, you need to look carefully at the **feelings** adjectives. The girl says she **would've regretted it** if she had bought something expensive she saw. What does she mean?

In Part 3 you:

- **hear**   five different people talking about related things
- **match**   what they say with one of eight options

1 These adjectives describe people's feelings. Complete the sentences below with adjectives from the box. Sometimes more than one answer is possible.

> **Tip!** You may find that Part 3 options include adjectives to describe the speaker's feelings, which you have to match carefully with what the speaker says.

thrilled	~~surprised~~	annoyed	bored	grateful
relieved	impressed	confident	sorry	shocked
disappointed	embarrassed	uncomfortable	discouraged	disgusted

1 Michal was ......**surprised**...... that he'd done so well in the test, as he hadn't really studied.

2 I was so .... when I finally found my new watch in the bottom of my bag – I was worried I'd lost it!

3 The coach was very .... when he saw Jack score at basketball, as he'd never played before.

4 The team were quite .... by their poor score in the first half of the match, but they tried harder in the second half – and won!

5 Zofia was .... when she found out she'd got the prize – it was 500 euros!

6 Anna gets a lot of ideas from her dad for her school art projects, which she's very .... for.

2a 🎧 15 Listen to Matthew talking about a long train journey he went on with his family. How did he feel about it? Choose one letter.

A worried about missing the train

B thrilled at the thought of the journey

C surprised at how quiet the train was

D pleased to be given food during the journey

E impressed by the view outside

F disappointed with the seating arrangements

G relieved at the space available

H bored by the length of time it took

> **Tip!** In the recording, you may hear words or ideas that are similar to several of the options, so you need to listen carefully to decide which option is correct.

b Look at where the answer comes in the audioscript below. Which options also contain similar words or ideas? Why are they wrong?

> My family and I had planned to travel by train the length of the country for a holiday. It involved a four-hour train journey, plus a drive to the station first. My family usually does everything at the last minute, but this time at least we left home in plenty of time to avoid missing the train. I'd got lots of magazines to stop myself getting bored, as I knew the view from my seat by the window wouldn't be very inspiring – I'd seen it loads of times before, from the car. But what I hadn't expected was to be presented with a tray by the attendant – sandwiches and drinks for the trip. Great!

3 🎧 16 Now listen to Maria talking about a similar journey by train. How did she feel about it? Choose one letter (A–H) from Exercise 2. What does she say? Does she use the same words as A–H, or different words? Which other options are also referred to? Why are they wrong?

🎧 17 You will hear five teenagers talking about their hobby, collecting different things. For questions **19–23**, choose from the list (**A–H**) how each speaker feels about their hobby.
Use the letters only once. There are three extra letters which you do not need to use.

Tip! Before the recording begins, read quickly through the options so that you are familiar with them. Remember, you will not need to *use* all of them.

A   I'm grateful to family members for expanding the collection.

B   I'm thrilled to have met so many other people through it.

Speaker 1 [   ] 19

C   I'm discouraged by the cost of adding to it.

Speaker 2 [   ] 20

D   I'm aware it no longer has the same appeal for me.

Speaker 3 [   ] 21

E   I'm proud of the size of the collection.

Speaker 4 [   ] 22

F   I'm disappointed at other people's lack of interest in it.

G   I'm surprised how many other people have similar collections.

Speaker 5 [   ] 23

H   I'm impressed at how it has increased in value.

Advice

*Look carefully at the **feelings** adjective in each option, A–H, and check that this is how the speaker says they feel.*

*19 What does the speaker mean when she says she has begun to **wonder why [she is] doing it**?*

*21 The speaker says when she talks to other people about the collection and how many dolls she has, it **makes [her] appreciate [it] more**. What does she mean?*

In Part 4 you:

- **listen**   to a recording of two people speaking
- **answer**   seven multiple-choice questions, each with three options

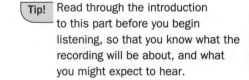

Tip! Read through the introduction to this part before you begin listening, so that you know what the recording will be about, and what you might expect to hear.

1   Work with a partner. Look at the topics (1–4) below. Decide which key words from the box you might hear for each topic. Some key words can be used for more than one topic.

1 buying something expensive

2 going into the countryside on a wildlife trip

3 trying something for the first time

4 taking photos of a watersport

| nervous | weather forecast | thrilled | lens | shot | weather conditions | look forward | |
| spectators | action | equipment | creatures | credit card | uncertain | identify | wetsuit |

2   ⌂ 18 **Listen to a boy called Jack being interviewed about doing a sport called *wakeboarding* (similar to waterskiing). Then answer this question:**

How did Jack feel about going wakeboarding?

A worried that he would not be any good at it

B curious to see why his friend liked it so much

C content to go along and try it

3a   ⌂ 19 **Now cover options A–C and the extract from the audioscript below, and just look at this question. Listen to the next part of the interview and write down the answer as you listen.**

What does Jack say about his first attempt at standing on the wakeboard?

b   **Now look at the three options below. Which one matches your answer the most closely? Compare your answer with a partner. Then look at the audioscript and underline the part that gives you the answer.**

A He was embarrassed by the response of people watching.

B He was taken by surprise by the sudden speed of the boat.

C He was disappointed that his careful preparations did not pay off.

Anyway, we arrived at the lake, got our wakeboarding kit on, and before long it was my turn. I crouched down in the water on the wakeboard, as I was supposed to, holding tightly onto the rope while the boat driver waited for me to give him the signal that I was ready. But almost as soon as I did, he opened up the engine and roared off, and the pressure on my legs to keep the wakeboard in front of me was suddenly immense! I hadn't been prepared for that, so what do you know? I fell into the water to the sound of laughter from my spectators, which I joined in with … and, apparently, my friend's father had managed to get some good shots of it all!

4   ⌂ 20 **Now listen to the final part of Jack's story. Read the question below and choose the correct option, A, B or C.**

How did Jack feel during his second attempt to stand on his wakeboard?

A ready to improve on the technique he had used previously

B sure of his ability to succeed this time

C prepared not to make the same mistake again

21 You will hear an interview with a boy called Jamie Davidson, who has just tried rock climbing for the first time. For questions **24–30**, choose the best answer (**A, B** or **C**).

Tips! Look carefully through the questions and options before you begin to listen.

Listen carefully for the interviewer's questions to help you keep your place in the recording. They signal when you need to move on to the next question.

24 Jamie says that the climbing centre he went to

   A   specialised in courses for beginners.
   B   was situated near the coast.
   C   offered other sports as well.

25 How did Jamie feel when he had got his climbing equipment?

   A   confused by all the things he was given
   B   determined to make sure he dealt with everything correctly
   C   confident once he was wearing it all

26 Jamie was doubtful at first that

   A   he would know how to check the ropes as the guide had taught him.
   B   the guide had enough experience to take them climbing.
   C   he would enjoy the climb as much as his guide expected.

27 When they started to climb, Jamie began to

   A   feel envious of his guide's climbing skills.
   B   ask himself whether he was up to the trip.
   C   worry about possible bad weather.

28 When Jamie was told to let go of the rock, he

   A   felt relieved to see other climbers doing the same thing.
   B   remembered his training about using ropes safely.
   C   found it hard not to panic.

29 Jamie says that the view from the top of the rocks

   A   wasn't quite what he had expected.
   B   seemed hard to appreciate after the difficult climb.
   C   reminded him of another view he'd seen.

30 At the top of the rock, Jamie regretted

   A   being unable to take any pictures.
   B   leaving his lunch behind.
   C   wearing clothes that were too warm.

Advice

*25 Jamie reports that he **felt ready to tackle whatever lay ahead** when he got his climbing gear on. What does he mean?*

27 Jamie reports that it had begun to rain when they started to climb. Was he worried by it? Did he feel he couldn't manage the climb? And what did he wish about his guide, Max?

29 Jamie mentions once being at the top of a castle. What was his experience there?

In Part 1 you:

- **talk**   to an examiner
- **answer**   questions about yourself and your life, e.g. your name, free-time activities, family, future plans, etc.

Understanding the task

1   **What happens in Part 1 of the Speaking test? Write letters a–g under the correct photo.**

1    □ □

2    □ □ □

3    □ □

a   The first examiner asks you to sit down, and says 'Good morning / afternoon / evening'.

b   You are given a piece of paper – your mark sheet – with your name on it.

c   The first examiner asks you for your names then takes your mark sheets.

d   You wait outside the exam room with your partner.

e   The first examiner asks you questions about yourselves for about two minutes.

f   The first examiner introduces herself / himself and her / his colleague.

g   You go into the exam room and meet two examiners. The first examiner will talk to you, and the second one will only listen.

> **Tip!** The examiners are experienced teachers and will always be friendly. Try to be relaxed and smile if you can.

Useful language   Answering the questions well

2   **Most of the following answers are good, but three are not so good. Put a cross (X) next to the answers that are not so good. Why are they less good answers than the others?**

What's your name?

   1 Barbara.   **2** I'm Barbara Lario.   **3** My name's Barbara Lario.

Where are you from?

   4 Italy.   **5** I'm from Italy – from a small town called Modena.
   6 Well, I live in Rome now but I was born in Genoa.

> **Tip!** Give full answers, but don't give too much detail. You'll have an opportunity to talk for longer in Parts 2, 3 and 4.

How do you travel to school?

   7 By bus.   **8** By bus, bicycle sometimes, and I walk.
   9 I take the bus because I live quite far away so I can't get to school on foot.

Useful language Asking the examiner to repeat the question

3 Put the words in the right order to make sentences.

1 you / again, / that / Could / please? / say

2 catch / said. / I / what / didn't / Sorry, / you

3 repeating / please? / you / that, / Would / mind

Tip! Always ask the examiner to repeat anything you don't understand.

Useful language Linking your ideas together

4 Complete the sentences with words or phrases from the box.

but	because / as	like / such as	also
but sometimes	That's because	so	and anyway

Tip! Never just reply *Yes* or *No*. Try to give reasons for your answers and link your ideas together. You get extra marks for doing this well.

1 I play a lot of football .... all my friends like it too, and I .... enjoy playing basketball.

2 Maths and chemistry are probably my favourite subjects, ... I'm not very good at writing essays, ... I find subjects .... history more difficult.

3 My friends and I don't go to the cinema much. .... the tickets are quite expensive, ... , we all like watching DVDs together at each other's homes.

4 Most of the time, I'm glad I have lots of brothers and sisters, ... I wish they'd be a bit quieter when I'm trying to do my homework!

Test 1 Exam practice   Speaking • Part 1

1 Work with a partner. Take turns to ask and answer these questions. Ask the questions in any order.

Tip! Listen carefully to the questions. Practise asking and answering questions before the test, but don't learn answers because you won't sound natural.

Part 1   2 minutes [3 minutes for groups of three]

Interlocutor First, we'd like to know something about you.

- Where are you from?
- What do you like best about living here? (Why?)
- What do you spend most of your time doing at home? (Why?)
- How are you going to spend next weekend?
- How did you spend your last school holiday? What did you enjoy most about it?
- What is your favourite subject at school? (Why?)
- Where do you do your homework? (Why?)
- Have you got any brothers or sisters? Tell me about them.
- Where do you enjoy going with your family in your free time? (Why?)
- What sort of job would you like to do in the future? (Why?)
- What was the last film you saw? Was it good? (Why? / Why not?)

2 🎧 22 Now listen to the recording and answer the questions you hear.

In Part 2 you:

- **talk**   about two photos on your own
- **compare** your photos and answer a question about them
- **answer**   one short question about your partner's photos

Focus Understanding the task

1 What happens in Part 2 of the Speaking test? Write letters a–f under the correct photo.

1
 ☐ ☐

2
 ☐ ☐ ☐

3
 ☐ ☐

a Then Student A answers a question about the photos – this question appears on the task sheet in the booklet.

b When Student A has finished, the examiner asks Student B a short question about one or both of Student A's photos.

c The first examiner gives Student A a booklet which shows two photographs.

d Student A is asked to talk about the photos for about one minute in total, while Student B listens without saying anything.

e Student A should talk about similarities and differences between the two photos.

f Student B listens to her / his partner but doesn't interrupt.

g The examiner gives Student B their photographs and question.

Useful language Talking about similarities and differences

2 Look at photos A and B on page C1, then complete the sentences with words from the box. The words can be used more than once.

while / whereas / but   look / seem / appear   could / might / may   perhaps / maybe   both

1 The people are .... using cameras outside, though they are in very different situations.

2 Photo A shows someone taking a picture of friends .... photo B shows someone taking a photo of a landscape.

3 The people in photo A .... very relaxed; .... they are celebrating something.

4 The person in photo B is concentrating hard. She .... be taking part in a photography competition.

Useful language Answering the follow-up questions

3 Complete the sentences with phrases from the box.

> I prefer to / I'd rather   would choose   it would be   more enjoyable

1 Taking photographs of friends and family is .... because it's a good way of sharing happy times. It's a great way of remembering special events, too, and I love looking at the pictures afterwards with other people.

2 I think .... great to be able to take photographs of beautiful places and I'd like to do that one day, because I'd like to show them to other people. I don't think I could actually be a professional photographer, but I'd still like to try and take very good pictures.

3 To be honest, ... take photos of my friends for fun because I don't have the patience to take artistic photos. It's really just a way of remembering what happened when.

4 I .... to take a photograph of the countryside, because I already have hundreds of pictures of my friends. It's a good idea to take photographs of lots of different things, I think, and I haven't taken many pictures of landscapes. That's why I'd like to do that.

Tip! Don't interrupt your partner. When s/he has finished speaking, listen carefully to the follow-up question the examiner asks you, because you don't see this question.

Focus Instructions

4 Look at the exam instructions below and photos A and B on page C2.

a What two things does candidate A have to do?

b What does candidate B have to do?

Work with a partner. Look at the photos and write down four things you could say about the photos.

Tip! You have time to answer the question *and* give reasons for your answer, so don't limit yourself to a one-sentence answer.

5 🎧 23 Jana and Fernando are two students. Listen to them talking about the photos and tick (✓) the expressions from Exercises 2 and 3 that they use.

Tip! Say what is similar and different about the photos, without describing each photo in detail. Always give reasons.

> (*Candidate A*), it's your turn first. Here are your photographs. They show **people doing different activities in their free time**.
>
> I'd like you to compare the photographs, and say **why you think the people have chosen to do these activities**.
>
> (*Candidate B*), **which of these situations would you prefer to be in? Why?**

6 🎧 23 Listen again. Write down any other expressions you notice that would be useful for Speaking Part 2. Compare your notes with your partner.

Look at the exam instructions below and
photos on pages C3 and C4, then do this exam task in pairs.

Tip! Get your partner to tell you when you have spoken for one minute, so you know what it feels like to speak for that long.

Part 2

Interlocutor In this part of the test, I'm going to give each of you two photographs. I'd like you to talk about your photographs on your own for about a minute, and also to answer a question about your partner's photographs.

(*Candidate A*), it's your turn first. Here are your photographs on page C3 of the Speaking appendix. They show **people singing in different places**.

I'd like you to compare the photographs, and say **why the people are singing in these situations**.

All right?

Candidate A
🕐 1 minute ....

Interlocutor Thank you.

(*Candidate B*), **which place would you prefer to sing in? (Why?)**

Candidate B
🕐 *Approximately 30 seconds* ....
Interlocutor Thank you.

Task B

Interlocutor Now, (*Candidate B*), here are your photographs on page C4 of the Speaking appendix. They show **people doing different jobs**.

I'd like you to compare the photographs, and say **what you think the people enjoy about doing these jobs**.

All right?

Candidate B
🕐 1 minute ....

Interlocutor Thank you.

(*Candidate A*), **which of these jobs would you prefer to do? Why?**

Candidate A
🕐 *Approximately 30 seconds* ....

Interlocutor Thank you.

In Part 3 you:

- **exchange** ideas with your partner
- **read** a question and five ideas
- **talk** about different possibilities, give opinions, agree or disagree, make suggestions, and try to decide something with your partner

Understanding the task

1 What happens in Part 3 of the Speaking test? Write letters a–f under the correct photo.

1

2

☐ ☐ ☐   ☐ ☐ ☐

- **a** You discuss the topic with your partner for about two minutes.
- **b** The examiner gives you a booklet with a question and five prompts around it.
- **c** The examiner asks you to make a decision related to what you have been discussing.
- **d** The examiner asks you to start the discussion with your partner.
- **e** You and your partner have about one minute to try to reach a decision.
- **f** The examiner gives you time to read the question and the prompts.

Useful language Suggesting, agreeing and disagreeing

2 Choose the correct heading from the box for each set of expressions.

> **Tip!** Have a conversation with your partner, agreeing and disagreeing with the points they make.

| Agreeing | Expressing an opinion | Disagreeing politely | Starting the discussion |

A	B ....
Are we ready? Shall I start? Shall we talk about this one to start with?	I'd say … Personally, I think … In my opinion, …
C	**D** ....
That's right. Well, I agree with you. Yes, I think that's true.	Well maybe, though… I'm not sure I agree… I know what you mean, but…

3 Add one expression from the box to each set.

| Good point.   I believe …   Shall I go first?   Yes, that's true, but … |

Focus Instructions

4 Look at the ideas and a question to discuss on page C5 and the exam instructions below.

Tip! Use the question in the middle to help you focus on the task.

a What is the discussion topic?

b What two things do you have to do?

Interlocutor Now, I'd like you to talk about something together for about two minutes.

Here are some reasons why teenagers might want to do sport and a question for you to discuss. First you have some time to look at the task.

Now, talk to each other about **whether it's important for teenagers to do sport**.

Candidates

🕐 *2 minutes (3 minutes for groups of three)*

Interlocutor Thank you. Now you have about a minute to decide **which two are *not* good reasons for teenagers to do sport**.

Candidates

🕐 *1 minute (for pairs and groups of three)*

Interlocutor Thank you.

---

5 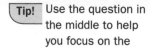 **Listen to Jana and Fernando doing this task. Choose T for True or F for False after each of the following sentences.**

1	They give reasons for their opinions.	T / F
2	They discuss all the ideas.	T / F
3	They disagree with each other politely.	T / F
4	They give each other opportunities to speak.	T / F
5	They listen to each other.	T / F
6	They agree on two things that are not good reasons for teenagers to do sport.	T / F

6 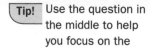 **Listen to Jana and Fernando again, and tick (√) the expressions in the table in Exercise 2 that they use.**

Do this exam task with a partner.

Tip! Listen carefully to hear what decision you have to make, because this is not written down. It doesn't matter if you don't reach a decision. Always try to give reasons for what you say.

Part 3   4 minutes [5 minutes for groups of three]

Interlocutor Now, I'd like you to talk about something together for about two minutes.

I'd like you to imagine that a teacher is planning a school trip for her class. Here are some reasons why teachers might take students on school trips and a question for you to discuss. First you have some time to look at the task on page C6 of the Speaking appendix.

Now, talk to each other about **whether it's a good idea for teachers to take students on school trips**.

Candidates

🕐 *2 minutes (3 minutes for groups of three)*

Interlocutor Thank you. Now you have about a minute to decide **what the two best reasons are for taking students on a school trip**.

Candidates

🕐 *1 minute (for pairs and groups of three)*

Interlocutor Thank you.

In Part 4 you:

- **speak**   with an examiner and one or two other candidates
- **answer**   questions that are related to the topic in Part 3, but the questions focus on more general aspects of the topic

Focus Understanding the task

1   Complete the sentences with words from the box.

> different   three   see   list   first   topic   agree

> In Part 4, the examiner asks you questions that are related to the **(1)** .... in Part 3. You or your partner may be asked a question **(2)** .... You do not **(3)** .... these questions. The examiner has a **(4)** .... of questions to choose from, but may only ask you two or three of them.
>
> This part lasts about **(5)** .... or four minutes. After your partner has answered a question, the examiner may ask you if you **(6)** .... with your partner, or ask you a **(7)** .... question.

Useful language Giving and justifying opinions

2   Complete the sentences with words from the box.

> seems   way   reckon   point   actually

1   I .... think everyone should do more sport at school.

2   One .... of looking at it is that students might focus better in class if they also did more sport.

3   I .... if people did more sport at school, they wouldn't have enough time to study important subjects.

4   It .... to me that sport is not really something that students should spend much time doing.

5   From my .... of view, it's always better to have as many opportunities to take part in sport as possible.

3 Read questions and opinions 1–6. Then match them with reasons a–f.

Tip! You can also use examples from your own experience to extend your answers.

1 Should people do more sport at school?

I don't actually think that's necessary.

2 Do you think sports stars are good role models for teenagers?

It seems to me that some of them are, and we can learn a lot from them.

3 Do you think people talk about sport too much?

I reckon they do. Some people just talk about it non-stop.

4 Is sport the best way of keeping healthy?

I don't think so.

5 How important do you believe it is to take part in sports competitions?

Well I think it's a very good idea.

6 Are there enough sports facilities near where you live?

Yes, sure, there are plenty.

a You'd think they'd like to discuss other things too, wouldn't you?

b After all, there are enough opportunities to do sport outside school if you want to.

c It motivates people, but of course you shouldn't have to if you don't want to.

d That's because there are other things to consider, like what you eat, for example.

e But then, I'm not very interested in sport, so I wouldn't use more facilities if they were built.

f I mean, they don't all behave well, do they?

4 🎧 1 25 Listen to Jana and Fernando answering questions 1–3 in Exercise 3. Do they express similar opinions to those in the exercise?

Tip! Give a reason for your opinion, and use some of the expressions you have practised.

5 Answer Questions 4–6 in Exercise 3 and discuss them with your partner.

Test 1 Exam practice   Speaking • Part 4

Work in pairs. Ask and answer these questions.

| Part 4 | 4 minutes [6 minutes for groups of three] |

Interlocutor

- What can students learn from going on school trips? (Why?)

- Do you think students should go on school trips? (Why? / Why not?)

- Should students decide where they go on school trips? (Why? / Why not?)

- Some people say students learn more outside the classroom than in lessons. What do you think?

- Where would be good to go for a school trip in your area? (Why would it be good?)

- Some students go on school trips to other countries. Do you think this is a good thing to do? (Why? / Why not?)

Thank you. That is the end of the test.

What do you think?
Do you agree?
And you?

Tip! You never see the questions in Part 4, so listen carefully to the examiner. If you don't understand a question, ask the examiner to repeat it. Use the expressions on page 56.

Tip! If you're not sure how to answer a question, say something like *I'm not too sure about that, but I reckon ...* or *I've never thought about that before, but I suppose ...*

- How many questions do you have to answer in Part 1?
- How many options do you have to choose from in each question?

Useful language Phrases and collocations

1 Circle the correct word or phrase in each sentence.

Example: *We need to* (raise) */ rise enough money for the new project.*

1 *From / At* first, I thought the test would be easier, but I quickly realised that in fact it wasn't.

2 Ben is very kind-hearted, but some people tend to *take / get* advantage of him.

3 Una isn't the sort of person who enjoys *receiving / attracting* attention to herself.

4 Mr James welcomed the three new students on behalf *of / from* all our class.

5 If Noel doesn't like what we're talking about, he just changes the *subject / topic*.

6 You shouldn't go out in the rain without a coat – that's just *common / normal* sense.

7 When you're choosing a career, you need to *take / put* a lot of things into consideration.

8 Our plans for next weekend depend on the weather to a great *extent / part*.

9 I need to *keep / hold* an eye on the dog while we're walking through the park together.

10 I've *got / put* rid of so much rubbish from my room that there's much more space now!

11 It *gets / goes* without saying that Karl will come top in maths this term!

12 Alex's house is noisy as it's on a main road, but on the *other / another* hand it's close to the town centre.

Tip! Build up your knowledge of set phrases, like these. Sometimes choosing the right option of four choices depends on knowing these kinds of phrases.

Focus Meanings of words in context

2 Complete the sentences below with a suitable word from the box. Use the correct form of the word. Use each word once.

> settle   establish   plant   uncover

1 George's mum has .... a lot of flowers in the garden of their new house.

2 While the archaeologists were digging in the ruins, they .... a wonderful mosaic.

3 Some artists are planning to .... a centre for young people's art activities in the city.

4 After my sister got married, she .... in the city centre with her new husband.

tell	consider	mention	say

5 I daren't .... Jack the news for fear of upsetting him.

6 Alissa .... her ideas to her teacher, who thought they were excellent.

7 There's a lot to .... when you're thinking about what career to go in for.

8 Andrei .... goodbye to everyone and left the party.

contact	influence	link	touch

9 TV programmes have a lot of .... on people's behaviour.

10 There's a direct .... between doing some exercise and being fit.

11 'I promise I'll keep in ....!' said Tereza when she moved away from our town.

12 Ali's phone is down, so Robert hasn't been able to make .... with him.

spite	view	order	bear

13 Students always have to .... in mind that academic success means working hard.

14 Max had to stay up late in .... to get everything finished.

15 Dan still went off to play football in .... of having a bad cold.

16 In .... of the forecast for bad weather, the coach thought it best to cancel the match.

Useful language More prepositions

3 Prepositions can also occur *before* certain phrases. Look at the phrases below. Which of the prepositions in the box goes with each phrase? Sometimes more than one preposition is possible with the same word or phrase.

at	by	for	in	on	out of	under

.... speed   .... my own   .... chance

.... accident   .... a hurry   .... time

.... nothing   .... control   .... purpose

.... order   .... once   .... a change

4 Complete the sentences with a suitable phrase from Exercise 3.

Example: The driver didn't notice the road sign as he was driving ......*at speed*......

1 If you don't want to come into town with me, I'm quite happy to go ....

2 The train left the station exactly .... – 5.15 pm!

3 Sam hadn't arranged to see Julia last Saturday. They met purely .... in the street.

4 We arrived just .... to catch the beginning of the film.

5 Dan and his friends always eat in burger bars, so yesterday they went to a pizza place ....

6 Oh no! I've deleted all my birthday photos .... and now I can't get them back.

7 That café's got a special offer – you pay for one ice cream, and you get another one ....

8 We'll have to climb the stairs – the lift is .... again.

For questions **1–8**, read the text below and decide which answer (**A**, **B**, **C** or **D**) best fits each gap. There is an example at the beginning (**0**).

Mark your answers **on the separate answer sheet**.

Tip! If you don't know the answer to a question, look carefully at the options and cross out the ones that you know are wrong, then make a guess. You should never leave an answer blank – the guess you make may be correct.

Example:

| 0 | **A** recommend | **B** suggest | **C** volunteer | **D** submit |

| 0 | A ▭ | B ▭ | C ▬ | D ▭ |

Life on Mars

Are you the kind of person who'd happily **(0)** .... to go and live on Mars? In fact, plans were recently revealed to **(1)** .... a human base on Mars in 2023, and when an opportunity came up to go and help build it, over 200,000 people **(2)** .... their names down. However, money still needs to be raised to fund the project – a cool £3.8 billion!

So what would the job **(3)** .... for the astronauts? To begin with, they'd need to have **(4)** .... intensive training during the months **(5)** .... up to departure. In addition, they'd need to learn how to live in close **(6)** .... with other crew members, both during the eight-month journey, and on the surface of Mars. There'd be very few facilities such as showers, not to **(7)** .... a diet of freeze-dried and canned food.

So in **(8)** .... of everything you'd have to put up with, you may decide a trip to Mars is not really for you after all!

1	**A** settle	**B** establish	**C** plant	**D** uncover
2	**A** signed	**B** gave	**C** put	**D** noted
3	**A** concern	**B** involve	**C** consist	**D** intend
4	**A** gradually	**B** consequently	**C** increasingly	**D** additionally
5	**A** moving	**B** running	**C** going	**D** leading
6	**A** contact	**B** influence	**C** link	**D** touch
7	**A** tell	**B** consider	**C** mention	**D** say
8	**A** spite	**B** mind	**C** order	**D** view

Advice

2 This is part of a phrasal verb. Read ahead – which verb will go with **down**?

5 Which of these verbs fit with **up to** to mean the period before something takes place?

- Are you given words to choose from in Part 2 questions?
- Why is it important to read the text very carefully before you start to answer the questions?

Useful language Prepositions

1 **Complete the phrase with the correct preposition from the box. Use a dictionary to help if you are not sure.**

| at | to | in | by | out of | on |

according ....

.... turns

.... account of

thanks ....

.... risk

.... general

.... heart

.... brief

.... least

.... due course

.... favour of

.... petrol

.... far

.... all costs

.... other words

.... place of

> **Tip!** Getting the answer right in Part 2 often depends on knowing which is the correct preposition to use, or which words go with prepositions to complete a phrase.

2 **Complete the sentences with a suitable phrase from Exercise 1.**

1 My brother said he wasn't keen to take the dog for a walk. .... , he couldn't be bothered!

2 My grandfather knows lots of poems .... and he recites them to me sometimes.

3 There were .... a hundred people at the party last night.

4 Susie is .... the best skier in our family. She beats everyone.

5 My dad watches the news .... before he goes out, then reads the full stories later.

6 Oscar and his sister had to take it .... to hold the puppy's lead.

7 No-one knows the election result yet, but the country will find out ....

8 .... Matt, tomorrow's classes are cancelled!

9 We're completely .... bread, so I'll go and buy some.

10 We knew we had to win .... Losing just wasn't an option.

> **Tip!** When you use a set phrase, make sure you have got it *completely* right, and that it is spelt correctly. A small mistake, such as omitting an s, could lose you a mark.

Useful language Passives

We form the passive from the verb *to be* + past participle, e.g. *takes* → *is taken*.

Remember!

We form the passive from the verb *to be* + past participle, e.g. *takes* → *is taken*.

3 Turn the following into passive or active sentences.

1 Someone cleaned the windows at school yesterday.

The windows at school .... yesterday.

2 You will be told the results as soon as we get them.

We'll .... the results as soon as we get them.

3 The storm has destroyed most of the big trees.

Most of the big trees .... the storm.

4 Someone must have left the door unlocked last night.

The door .... unlocked last night.

5 They're fixing my dad's car at the moment.

My dad's car .... at the moment.

6 The letters are delivered to the office every morning.

Someone .... the office every morning.

7 You mustn't take drinks onto the school bus.

Drinks .... onto the school bus.

8 No-one has seen Class 2A's CD player for ages!

Class 2A's CD player .... for ages!

Tip! You may be tested on passive forms in Part 2. Make sure you select the correct *tense* when answering a question.

4 ⊙ Cross out the spelling mistake made by candidates in each of these sentences. Then write the word correctly.

1 You can choose *wich* film we go and see tonight. ....

2 My new bike isn't much faster *then* my old one. ....

3 Seb had to run home *becouse* he was late for dinner. ....

4 You shouldn't *belive* everything you see on TV. ....

5 My Grandma has lots of *beutiful* flowers growing in her garden. ....

6 This book on science is the most *intresting* I've ever read. ....

For questions **9–16**, read the text below and think of the word which best fits each gap. Use only one word in each gap. There is an example at the beginning **(0)**.

Write your answers **IN CAPITAL LETTERS on the separate answer sheet**.

> **Tip!** You may find that a phrase containing more than one word might fit the gap – but remember, you can only write *one* word, so think carefully.

> **Tip!** Don't leave any of the gaps blank. Always try to write something, as your answer may be correct.

Example:

0	Y	O	U	R														

Solar-powered cars

Have you heard the car drivers in **(0)** .... family complaining every time they have to fill up the car at great expense at the local petrol station? Well, now a solar-powered family car has **(9)** .... developed that's producing very promising results.

The new car is what is known as 'energy positive', **(10)** .... means that it actually produces more energy than it consumes. Thanks to the large solar panels on its roof, the car can travel up to 250 miles even if **(11)** .... is no sunshine. And on a sunny day, when it is fully charged, it can travel a much longer distance **(12)** .... that – nearly 420 miles. That's nearly twice **(13)** .... distance that an electric car can travel **(14)** .... it is out of fuel and needs to be plugged in!

Further models of the solar-powered car are still **(15)** .... tested, according to the designers, who are in **(16)** .... doubt that solar-powered cars could eventually replace all petrol vehicles!

> **Advice**
>
> **9** This is testing passives. What *tense* is needed here?
>
> **12** This is testing a comparison. Which part of the comparative phrase is missing? Make sure you spell it correctly!

- Which kinds of words do you need to form in Part 3?
- Why do you need to read the text around each question carefully before you decide which word to form from the word on the right?

Useful language Suffixes

1a Use the suffixes in the box to form words that can be used to refer to people. Look at the example. Use a dictionary if necessary. You may need to add more letters, take letters away or change letters.

Tips!	Look carefully at each gap in the sentence. What *kind* of word is needed (noun, verb, adjective, adverb)?

Does the sentence need the word in the gap to be *positive* or *negative*? *Singular* or *plural*?

-ant   -(e)r   -ist   -ive   -or   -(i)an

Example: music   musician

1	relate	6	supply
2	assist	7	inhabit
3	photograph	8	detect
4	economy	9	deal
5	politics	10	compete

b Complete these sentences using the words in brackets and a suitable suffix from Exercise 1a. You may need to add more letters, take letters away or change letters.

1 Jihoo's father is an .... **(economy)** and works at the university.

2 There were more .... **(compete)** in his race than Felix had expected.

3 The .... **(photograph)** who took these pictures didn't do a very good job.

4 Seb's sister is working as a shop .... **(assist)** during her holidays.

5 Tristan's mum is a .... **(politics)** and often appears on TV.

6 We spent the public holiday with all our friends and .... **(relate)**.

2 Complete each sentence using the words in brackets and the correct suffixes from the box. You may need to add more letters, take letters away or change letters.

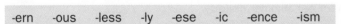

-ern   -ous   -less   -ly   -ese   -ic   -ence   -ism

Example: The maths questions were fairly ....*basic*........... **(base)** so Tom had no difficulty with them.

1 The story was about a girl who receives a .... **(mystery)** letter.

2 Adam's computer was faulty, and was making a .... **(continue)** buzzing noise.

3 The .... **(Japan)** food we had for lunch was delicious.

4 Justin's always been very .... **(athlete)** so no-one was surprised when he was chosen for the Olympics.

5 The .... **(south)** part of the country is much greener than other areas.

6 Yesterday our geography class looked at which cities were very .... **(dense)** populated.

7 There's quite a .... (**differ**) in age between me and my brother.

8 The vase that got broken at the museum was said to be absolutely .... (**price**).

9 .... (**tour**) is an important source of income in many countries.

10 Kim's mum told her that she needed to have a bit more .... (**patient**) with her younger brother.

Useful language Forming nouns

3 Some base words look quite different when they are changed to form nouns. Make nouns from these base words.

Example: high   height

1 wide   ....

2 strong   ....

3 long   ....

4 hot   ....

5 destroy   ....

6 behave   ....

7 anxious   ....

8 free   ....

9 divide   ....

10 admire   ....

Exam skills Words in context

4a Which kind of word (noun, adjective, verb or adverb) is needed to fill the gap in each of these sentences?

1 Swans .... to countries with warmer temperatures every winter.

2 Some .... in the UK are particularly popular with migrating swans.

3 One such centre is always .... full of swans once winter arrives.

4 Many of the swans are so .... when they first arrive that they sleep for 24 hours.

5 Most .... agree that the swans are an amazing sight.

6 It's .... that swans should attempt to fly so far just for the winter.

b Now think of a suitable word for each gap.

5 ⊙ Correct one spelling error written by exam candidates in each of these sentences.

1 My parents still haven't booked any accomodation for our summer holiday. ....

2 There's an advertisment in the local newspaper for a job at the sports centre. ....

3 I suddenly saw someone I recognised on the other side of the road. ....

4 We've been studying the enviroment in our science classes this month. ....

5 Karl will definately be back at school tomorrow. ....

6 Sarah was dissapointed that the cake she made wasn't very successful. ....

For questions **17–24**, read the text below. Use the word given in capitals at the end of some of the lines to form a word that fits in the gap **in the same line**. There is an example at the beginning (0).

Write your answers **IN CAPITAL LETTERS on the separate answer sheet**.

Tips! Depending on the context, you may have to make only one change to the word, or more changes.

Don't spend too long thinking about answers you're not sure of. Complete as many answers as you can, then return to the ones that you haven't done. You may have a better idea of those answers as you become more familiar with the text.

Example:

| 0 | N | O | R | T | H | E | R | N | | | | | | | | | |

Swans

For many people in **(0)** .... Europe, the start of autumn marks the beginning of the swan migration season, and the promise of a truly amazing **(17)** ....

The **(18)** .... of thousands of birds at their winter homes is prompted by the **(19)** .... of dropping temperatures and cold winds in their summer habitat in places like Arctic Russia.

As the winter progresses, the number of swans **(20)** .... increases. As many as 9,000 swans **(21)** .... make the journey every year to one favourite spot in England. Once they land, they need a period of rest and **(22)** .... after their flights of up to 2,500 miles. They spend time sleeping and **(23)** .... on plants to build up the energy they have lost on the way. **(24)** .... , the coming of spring signals the end of the swans' stay, and they soon begin preparing for their incredible journey back. However, by then hundreds of visitors will at least have had the chance to see them during their stay.

NORTH

SEE

ARRIVE
COMBINE

STEADY
SUCCESS

RECOVER
FOOD
FORTUNE

Advice

17 The article **a** before the gap tells you the answer is a noun. What is the noun that comes from the base word **see**?

20 This needs an adverb to qualify the verb **increases**. What changes will you need to make to **steady** to add an -**ly** suffix?

24 Look carefully at the gap. This needs an adverb. What changes will you make to **fortune**? Also, look carefully at the sense of the sentence. Is **the end of the swans' stay** positive or negative? The word **however** in the next sentence also gives you a clue. If you decide it is negative, what prefix should you add to your answer?

- How many sentences do you have to rewrite in Part 4?
- After you have done each question, you should read the first sentence again and the sentence you have just written. What do you need to check?

Tip! Part 4 questions can test both grammar *and* vocabulary. You may need to use phrasal verbs, for example, or know set phrases to answer the questions.

Useful language Wishes and regrets

1 **What does each sentence mean? Circle the correct letter, a or b.**

1 I wish I didn't feel so tired.

   a I feel tired today, which isn't good.

   b I felt tired yesterday, which wasn't good.

2 If only my best friend would come to the party with me!

   a My best friend didn't come to the party with me.

   b My best friend probably won't come to the party with me.

3 I'd prefer it if you came on Monday evening rather than at the weekend.

   a It's better if you come on Monday, not at the weekend.

   b You shouldn't have come at the weekend.

4 I'd rather we'd gone swimming than come to the cinema!

   a I really didn't want to come to the cinema.

   b Come to the cinema instead of going swimming!

Useful language Conditionals and past modals

2 **Circle the correct words in each sentence.**

1 If I *wouldn't have / hadn't missed* the bus, I *would be / wouldn't be* in my lesson by now.

2 Liam's not here yet. He *might have / might have been* held up in the traffic.

3 I *can't have / couldn't have* won the race if I hadn't trained so hard.

4 Maisie *wouldn't have gone / wouldn't go* there if she had known what it was like.

5 We ran to the station but the train was late leaving, so *we needn't have hurried / needn't hurry*.

6 Josh *can't forget / can't have forgotten* about the party. He's got it in the diary on his phone.

7 Ryan is never late, so he *must be / must have been* on his way here now.

8 Otto *should have / might have* told his football coach that he couldn't play, but he forgot.

9 Andy *wouldn't be able / wouldn't have been able* to call me yesterday if he hadn't borrowed a phone.

10 Emil *didn't need to / needn't* take any money into town as his Dad paid for everything.

3 ◉ **Choose the correct words in italics in these sentences written by exam candidates.**

1 If I were you, I *will / would* visit the city centre.

2 If they had come by car, they *should / would* have had to wait for their parents.

3 I hope you *will / would* not continue like this.

4 You'd better buy a car so that you *could / can* travel anywhere you want.

5 I think we *must / should* meet outside the city stadium.

6 I was sure that I *will / would* pass the exams.

For questions **25–30**, complete the second sentence so that it has a similar meaning to the first sentence, using the word given. **Do not change the word given.** You must use between **two** and **five** words, including the word given. Here is an example (**0**).

Tip! It is especially important not to leave any answers blank here. Each answer is worth two marks, so even if your answer is not completely correct, you might still get a mark.

Example:

0   Karen didn't really want to go to the party.

   FORWARD

   Karen wasn't really .... to the party.

The gap can be filled by the words 'looking forward to going', so you write:

Example:	**0**	LOOKING FORWARD TO GOING

Write **only** the missing words **IN CAPITAL LETTERS on your answer sheet**.

---

25   I ran all the way to the bus stop, but it wasn't necessary as the bus was late.
   HAVE
   I .... all the way to the bus stop as the bus was late.

26   If Max isn't interested in what we're talking about, he just starts talking about something else.
   SUBJECT
   Max just .... if he's not interested in what we're talking about.

27   I'm sure that Paul has remembered his mum's birthday today.
   CAN'T
   Paul .... his mum's birthday today.

28   The strong wind blew down some tall trees during the night.
   BY
   Some tall trees .... the strong wind during the night.

29   Ilona took her mobile, so she was able to call her mum.
   HAVE
   Ilona .... to call her mum if she hadn't taken her mobile.

30   Please don't stroke the dog, as he's very nervous.
   RATHER
   I'd .... stroke the dog, as he's very nervous.

Advice

26 *Think of a phrase using* **subject** *that means you are no longer talking about the same topic.*

28 *This needs a passive construction. What tense do you need? And will the verb* **be** *be singular or plural?*

- How many questions do you have to answer in Part 5?
- What kind of questions are they?
- How many options do you have to choose from?

Tip! As you begin the task, try to get a feel for what the text is about. Read the rubric, look at what sort of text it is, the topic, any title and any artwork. Then think about what you might expect to read in the text.

1a Read through the following text about a boy called Jack. Where might you find a text like this? Compare your answers with a partner.

> Jack had never been on a wildlife trip into the countryside before, so when the idea was suggested by his teacher, and welcomed by the rest of the class, he was immediately alarmed. Having spent his whole life in the centre of one of the world's busiest cities, he regarded the countryside with some suspicion, as a place where his parents had once taken him on a camping holiday, when it poured with rain. Apart from that, even though his class had had nature trips into the city parks, Jack was far more into computers and technology.

b Now read the question, and choose the best answer (A, B, C or D).

Why does the writer mention that Jack had spent his whole life in a city?

A to emphasise what a different experience the proposed trip might be for him

B to show the contrast between the subject of the trip and Jack's own interests

C to explain why Jack had had little opportunity to get involved with wildlife

D to suggest that his teacher's plan might not be a very successful one

Tip! When the questions are in the form of incomplete sentences, remember to read both parts of the sentence together, not just choose your answer from the four options. Information in the incomplete sentence may determine which option you choose, and make the others wrong.

c Compare your answer with a partner. Why do you think the other options are wrong?

2a Read the next section of the text, and decide the most suitable way to complete the sentence below.

Once Jack got to the countryside, he felt...

> However, despite his doubts, Jack reluctantly agreed with his parents that he would go on the trip. On the day, the coach driver dropped them at a campsite in the middle of a forest – next to the most enormous stretch of water that Jack had ever seen, apart from on family trips to the beach. Jack couldn't help wandering down to the water's edge, where he immediately spotted a number of tiny fish darting around in the shallows, together with a variety of small wingless insects *skittering* over the water, making barely a ripple as they touched the surface of the lake with their tiny legs. And in spite of his initial hostility, Jack thought it was one of the most absorbing sights he'd seen – for a while at least ...

b Now look at the four options below. Which one is closest to your answer?

A determined to prove to his parents that the trip was a mistake.

B more interested in what he found there than he had originally expected.

C concerned that the place they were camping in wasn't very suitable.

D surprised to discover that he would be staying on the coast.

Tip! When meeting unknown words in a text, look carefully at the context to try and work out the meaning.

3 There is a word underlined in the text – 'skittering'. Read the section carefully. What do you think the word means? Now look at the question below. Which of the four options matches your idea most closely?

What does the writer mean when describing the insects as 'skittering' in line 5?

A They were diving into and out of the water.   **C** They were swimming through the water.

B They were flying close to the surface of the water.   **D** They were moving lightly across the water.

You are going to read an article by a girl who has taken a trip across the desert with her family. For questions **31–36**, choose the answer (**A, B, C** or **D**) which you think fits best according to the text.

Mark your answers **on the separate answer sheet**.

DESERT TREK

by Kara Lane

My family and I are from the US, but we're currently living in China. And last year we undertook an incredible trip across the country! My dad's a busy but very successful architect, working in one of the country's biggest cities. However, we were all in need of a break, so he decided we'd do a nature trip into the countryside, which we often did. And for him, because he was always keen to push himself to the limits, this time that had to be a trip to some of the country's remotest areas. He knew we'd look back and remember it as the adventure of a lifetime. But as always, he did check it met with our approval too – which of course it did! After all, who'd turn down the chance of a trip like that?

Dad's dream was a trip across the desert where we could experience its raw wildness, and spot some wild animals such as camels that had become endangered. The dream sounded awesome – but the practical arrangements turned out to be incredibly complicated. In all his enthusiasm, dad hadn't particularly considered the practicalities, even though in his professional life he has to do exactly that all the time. To start with, getting someone to accompany us was a challenge, as few tour companies had the right experience for this kind of trip. So my parents were left trying to find the right team, and sort out the equipment they planned to take. Gathering it all took weeks, and we ended up taking far too much stuff. But finally we were ready.

Personally I couldn't wait for the off, and certainly didn't think twice about going on the trip or what risks might be involved. To me, it was yet another adventure I'd be having with my parents. However, they finally very reluctantly admitted to me that they'd come in for some harsh criticism for taking a teenager along on a challenging and potentially dangerous trip. That was hard for me to hear. But those critics clearly just hadn't taken in the fact that I'd been totally at home with trekking through the toughest of terrains from a young age, and that their interference wasn't needed. Trips like this had become a way of life.

Anyway, off we went into the desert, and before long we'd had some spectacular sightings of amazing wild horses. At first, though, I found it really hard to take in the sheer size and isolation of it all. But I just kept reminding myself we'd got plenty of supplies, and were with an experienced team – who'd hopefully get us out again! No amount of planning or training, though, could have prepared us for what happened one day – a day that brought home to me how powerless we were in the face of the forces of nature. A huge storm suddenly blasted across the area and transformed the desert from a dry wasteland to a winter wonderland. It was a timely reminder not to take anything for granted out there in the wilderness, and to remember our limitations.

Finally we had to start preparing for the long journey home to our busy, bustling city. But then the night before we set off, our guide admitted he'd once got stuck in the desert when a sandstorm swept over everything and his group were unable to travel for days. Luckily they'd all survived, and I guess it demonstrated how skilled a guide he was, and that we were in safe hands. But I remember wishing he hadn't mentioned it until we were back home again. It just reminded me of the dangers we were still facing, and wasn't exactly the kind of story I'd imagined I'd be telling all my friends. Anyway, despite my enthusiasm to get home, I still wasn't completely ready to say farewell to it all, and I knew a small part of me would always remain in the free, open spaces of the desert, with its vast skies and total silences.

31 The impression we get of Kara's father in the first paragraph is of someone who

A wants his family to be high achievers like him.

B makes decisions that his family don't always agree with.

C puts his family's needs above his own whenever possible.

D considers whether his family will benefit when making plans.

32 Why does Kara make reference to her father's professional life in the second paragraph?

A to explain why he paid such careful attention to some aspects of the trip

B to emphasise how different the trip would be from his own personal experience

C to suggest that his initial approach to preparing for the trip was surprising

D to say why he was just the right kind of person to take such a trip

33 In Paragraph 3 what does Kara mean when she says she 'didn't think twice about going on the trip'?

A She knew she didn't have much choice.

B It never occurred to her that she shouldn't go.

C She tried to put it out of her mind until it was time to leave.

D It was better not to think too much about the dangers.

34 What was Kara's attitude towards people who criticised her parents?

A She was irritated because it was unjustified.

B She was worried that the critics might be right.

C She was sad that her parents were upset by it.

D She was grateful that her parents hadn't told her earlier.

35 What seems to have particularly made an impression on Kara during her time in the desert?

A the skills of the team of people travelling with them

B the fact that they were able to survive on just the supplies they'd taken

C the realisation that they had no control over certain events

D the range of rare and unusual wildlife they managed to see

36 The night before they were due to return home, Kara felt

A saddened at having to leave the quiet of the desert.

B unprepared to resume her normal life again.

C reassured by something she heard from their guide.

D excited about all the stories she would be able to tell.

Advice

*32 What was her father's **professional life** that Kara refers to? What kind of skills would he need to use in his job? And how is that different from the way he started preparing for their trip?*

*35 If something **makes an impression** on you, is it a good or bad thing? Generally it is something positive that you notice and remember. Go through each option carefully. Can you find evidence to support them? If there's a reference to them, did they **make an impression** on Kara? Look especially for an **event** that occurred.*

- What do you have to do in each paragraph of Part 6 texts?
- What are some examples of things to look out for when trying to find sentences that fit the gaps?

1 You are going to read about art. With a partner, check that you know the meaning of the following words. Choose a word and explain the meaning to your partner. Your partner must guess which word you are describing.

exhibition	drawing	image	portrait
landscape	abstract	sculpture	cartoon
illustration	graphics	scene	model

> **Tip!** You may find there is related vocabulary and expressions linking the missing sentence to the rest of the paragraph – but don't just match the same words together. That may not give you the answer.

2 Read the text about a visit to an art gallery. Then read the sentences below. Which sentence fits the gap? Why do the other two *not* fit?

As part of our theme for the term, our art teacher was keen to take us to visit an art gallery in the city. As it happened, there was a major exhibition by an abstract artist, so she thought that would be ideal. And as I hadn't had much experience of seeing abstract paintings in real life, I was quite looking forward to the exhibition – but I also wondered what to expect. **(0)** .... Imagine my surprise, then, when we actually had to queue round the block to get in. But it was worth putting up with the boredom for what we saw in the exhibition rooms. There were so many wonderful images that I didn't know where to look first. And of course, I've been back by myself a few times since!

A I'd seen plenty of abstract paintings in art books, but I realised that would be nothing like seeing the real thing.

B I knew, though, that the paintings were by one of the most famous abstract artists of the 20th century.

C I guess in the back of my mind, I'd thought it wouldn't be very well attended.

You are going to read an article written by an art student. Six sentences have been removed from the article.
Choose from the sentences **A–G** the one which fits each gap **(37–42)**. There is one extra sentence which you do not need to use.

Mark your answers **on the separate answer sheet**.

Tip! Underline any words in sentences A–G which might link the sentence with a particular paragraph, for example pronouns, tenses or linking words. Look carefully to see if any of the sentences are adding a similar or contrasting idea.

Tip! Remember that words in the sentences might refer to something before or after the gap.

Art is good for you – it's official!

Did you know that looking at a painting you really love can be very beneficial for the brain? According to recent experiments by scientists, it can actually increase the blood flow to your brain by as much as 10%! And the more you like the painting you're looking at, the better the effect.

Art has always been my passion, so I was really pleased to read that. And I've always believed that actually doing some art is really beneficial too. It's a great way to express yourself and cheer yourself up when you feel fed up. **37** And that's an important positive effect.

But apart from making you feel better, creating art can also teach you numerous different practical skills. For example, many of the actions involved in making art, such as holding a paintbrush, are essential for building what are called 'fine motor skills' at an early age. So children may well think that their teachers just want them to have fun drawing a circle or painting a face. **38** And talking about shapes and colours helps increase vocabulary by using descriptive words.

What's more, learning how to make art can also help you with problem-solving and critical-thinking skills. Just think, for example, of all the times you've decided on a project you really want to get started on. **39** But making art helps you learn the skills to deal with them. And the experience of making decisions and choices when you're working on a piece of art can carry over into other areas of life. That experience will help you become a thinking, inventive person who'll come up with new ideas and not just follow instructions.

I have to admit, though, I hadn't really appreciated how much the formal study of art, such as art history helps you to interpret what you see. **40** But we also need to be given the opportunity to develop those skills through actually doing some art, too, to help us understand that images have a meaning. Otherwise we might find it hard to operate in the real world, where we're constantly having to respond to graphics and symbols, for example on a computer.

And in addition to all of these benefits, my art tutor also maintains that research has shown there's a link between studying art and doing well in other other areas of study. She says that someone who regularly does art is more likely to get really good academic results. **41** And even if not everyone makes it to the top, doing art gives many talented young people the chance to at least shine at something that they're good at.

Finally, I should say something about the sheer beauty that art brings into our lives. **42** Taking time to study paintings – really study them, and not just glance at them as you pass by – is what helps us understand what the artist was trying to say, and to have the chance to look closely at something beautiful. And that's certainly essential to my life.

A I had always thought that understanding pictures just came naturally to everyone.

B Just imagine how grey the world would be if there weren't works of art to look at.

C There's also evidence to suggest it can really help if life becomes hectic.

D Then suddenly problems arise that have to be sorted out.

E It's easier said than done to produce the kind of work that's needed.

F In fact, though, the aim is to develop the coordination needed for writing.

G There's a tendency to go on and achieve in all sorts of different fields.

Advice

38 Why might a teacher encourage children to draw or paint? What useful skills might they be learning?

42 The writer mentions **beauty**. Which of the options links best to this?

- What kind of text do you need to read in Part 7?
- How many questions do you need to answer?
- What do you need to do in order to answer the questions?

Tip! Use skimming and scanning techniques – read quickly through the text to get an idea of what it is about, then read in more detail to find the answers you want.

1a Work with a partner. Read quickly through the text, written by a boy called Nathan, to get an idea of what it is about. Then cover the text and talk with your partner about what you can both remember.

> For my birthday this year my parents decided to hold a big family barbecue and invite relatives that we hadn't seen for ages and owed a visit to. While I could see that it would be a good idea, and it was really nice of them to go to all that trouble, I couldn't help thinking that my party had somehow been taken over and I wasn't getting a say in what it would be like. But then I felt guilty for being ungrateful and put those feelings to one side. Anyway, on the day of the party, the temperature outside was about 10 degrees lower than it should have been at that time of year, so the barbecue was off. But it didn't matter at all, because what my parents hadn't mentioned to me was that the party was in a hall in our village – and all of my friends were there too! Great surprise!

b Now try answering these questions without looking back at the text. Work with a partner and compare your answers. What do you learn about:

a what kind of event it was?   **c** who was there?
b where the event was held?   **d** what the weather was like?

2 Read the text in more detail. Nathan mentions a lot of different feelings about the party. Which of these options match most closely how Nathan felt about it? Underline where you find the answer in the text.

A Nathan was relieved that the plans for the barbecue had to be called off.

B Nathan was hesitating over whether to suggest to his parents that his friends should come too.

C Nathan was disappointed that he didn't have any control over the party arrangements.

3a Now read quickly through the text below, written by a girl called Sarah, to get an idea of what it's about.

> Our annual family beach holidays are always fantastic – once we've finally arrived! The actual preparation, though, is always a complete nightmare. I wouldn't say my parents are disorganised exactly, but they do seem to have an amazing talent for leaving everything until the last minute – a talent which I'm relieved to say I haven't inherited! And I can remember one year we had everything packed, and we had to leave immediately for the airport if we were going to catch the plane. But then Dad suddenly noticed his mobile was missing. We searched everywhere, and then finally rang the number – only to hear the ring tone coming from inside his suitcase ... But I'm pleased to say that after unpacking and then repacking the case, rushing to the airport by taxi and then finally collapsing into our plane seats, we had the most wonderful family holiday ever!

b Now try answering these questions without looking back at the text. What do you learn about:

a the kind of holidays Sarah's family usually have?
b the means of transport they've used?
c what Sarah's parents are like?
d what Sarah thinks of the holiday preparations?

You are going to read a magazine article about teenagers' experiences of cooking and eating a special family dish. For questions **43–52**, choose from the teenagers (**A–D**). The teenagers may be chosen more than once.

Mark your answers **on the separate answer sheet**.

Tip! Try beginning by reading the questions. Then read the texts. The more you can *remember* about each text as you are working, the more quickly you will be able to find the answers.

Which teenager

feels the fact that they have collected the ingredients for the dish makes it very special?	43
is proud of the fact that their food is so popular among friends and relations?	44
finds the food they make is a useful remedy for the effects of being outside?	45
mentions arguing over the right to be in charge of the final stage of preparing a dish?	46
enjoyed one way of seeing if the food they were preparing was ready to eat?	47
is reminded of a particular season by the dish they make?	48
has developed an expertise in using a certain piece of equipment?	49
earns special benefits due to their role in producing the food?	50
admits that the current version of the dish they make is an improvement on the previous one?	51
says there are generally very few leftovers from the dish they help to make?	52

Advice

44 Look at which of the four teenagers mentions that the dish was eaten by family and people they know.

52 Which of the four people mentions that the food is eaten very quickly by their family?

Favourite Family Dishes

A Oliver

I think one of the best memories I'll have of my teenage years will be the times I've spent horse-riding with my dad, wandering along through the countryside. Sometimes my sister comes along, but we usually end up fighting, so it's quieter when she doesn't! On winter rides I'm always absolutely freezing by the time we get home again, and it takes me ages to defrost. So the only cure for that is to make a soup from whatever we can gather together from the fridge or the garden, which I somehow manage to chop up using our enormous kitchen knives. And I'm pleased to report, the delicious smell wafting out generally summons the rest of the family into the kitchen. But as I am the one assisting the chef, I'm always allowed the first taste, and the first bowlful – and the choice of what we watch on TV while we're sitting around eating it!

B Eve

Spaghetti with sauce is the meal that will always have the strongest family associations for me. I used to spend dark chilly evenings experimenting with recipes, even when I was quite young. And after dad had told me that you could check whether spaghetti was cooked if it stuck to the ceiling, I had endless fun testing out the theory! But the sauce I used to do then was dismal, with just a few tomatoes, onions and a bit of cheese found in the back of the fridge, made in a very posh pan! Since then I've got much more into cooking and my culinary skills have progressed. I've discovered a fantastic recipe that never fails – probably because it takes over three hours to be thoroughly cooked! I have to say it's become quite a celebrated dish among my extended family – and anyone else who happens to drop by!

C Alfie

One meal my family loves at weekends in the freezing depths of winter is the roast meat that my mum cooks – and then the meals we create in the following days from the meat we didn't manage to finish. One such dish is a minced meat pie, which usually gets demolished in a fraction of the time it took to make. We use an ancient mincer that belonged to my great-grandmother – it's just become part of the tradition. And I've slowly improved on my technique in handling it until somehow I've become the family specialist. We top the minced meat with potatoes dug from our garden, cooked and mashed and decorated with a fork – at which point I generally fall out with my younger sister. Being older, the privilege of drawing the patterns on top should definitely be mine! Anyway, when it finally comes out of the oven, all bubbling and crispy, you know it's ready to eat. Delicious!

D Josie

There's one dish that I'll always associate with weekend evenings with my family, and that's a dessert with apples that my father has showed us all how to cook. It's a dish his mother used to make for him, so it has fond memories for him too – although he maintains that his version is much better than hers! But the very thought of it instantly makes me think of our warm kitchen with its big shiny saucepans, at that point in the year when the temperature's beginning to drop outside, and we're preparing for the really cold weather to come. The fruit has often been picked from the trees in our neighbour's garden, and just the fact that I've contributed by being involved in that activity increases the pleasure of eating what we've made, somehow. That's my feeling, anyway – I can't speak for the rest of the family, of course!

You *have* to answer the question in Part 1 of the writing paper. Unlike in Writing Part 2, there is no choice here.

What do you have to write in Part 1?

- **Who** are you writing it for?
- **What** do you have to include?
- **How many** words do you have to write?

1 Read through the instructions for an exam task below. What is the general topic that you are going to write about?

> In your English class you have been talking about protecting the environment. Now your teacher has asked you to write an essay for homework.
>
> Write your essay using **all** the notes and giving reasons for your point of view.

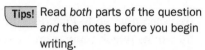

Tips! Read *both* parts of the question *and* the notes before you begin writing.

Remember that you *must* plan your answer to include what is given in the notes. You must also include another idea of your own, *and* give reasons for your opinions.

2 Look at some examples below of environmental issues that are often in the news.

air pollution	plastic waste	food waste	flooding
water pollution	wildlife conservation	global warming	climate change

Work with a partner. What does each of these mean? Explain them in your own words. Can you add more examples to the list?

3a Now look at the question included in the exam task:

> School is the best place to learn about (protecting) the environment.
> Do you agree?

b Read the essay that a boy called Ben wrote for his answer.

Young people are usually taught about protecting the environment at school – but is school really the best place to learn about it?

There is no doubt that we need to learn about protecting the environment. In fact, many people think it's an essential topic to study at school. We have teachers who may be experts in areas such as climate change or wildlife conservation, so they're the perfect people to teach us about the environment.

Learning about the environment can also be fun. Many schools have up-to-date technology to help us, and there are hands-on experiments we can do such as monitoring weather changes or plastic waste.

4 Now look at the notes below. Which two points do you think Ben had to include in his essay about protecting the environment?

- the cost of studying it
- how important it is as a topic
- other ways of learning about it
- how enjoyable it is to study
- how interesting it is
- the amount of time available at school

5 Ben also needed to include a third idea of his own in his essay. Read what he wrote. Which topic from Exercise 4 did he write about in this paragraph?

> On the other hand, although schools are good places to learn about the environment, there are other things we can do to find out more. There are huge amounts of information available on the Internet, for example. Personally, though, I feel the best way is just to go outside, whether you live in the city or the countryside. In that way, you can see for yourself any changes taking place, for example with wildlife or weather, and then think about what you might do to help protect the environment.

6 Look at the different words and phrases that Ben uses to make points and say what he thinks. Underline them in Ben's essay.

- there is no doubt …
- many people think …
- on the other hand …
- … although …
- … for example …
- personally …
- in that way, …

7 Choose the best words or phrases from Exercise 6 to complete the sentences. Add any punctuation that is needed. There is one word or phrase that is not needed.

Example: *We need to put more money into research about wildlife. ....In that way...., we can find out more about how we can help to save wild animals.*

1 .... that the climate has changed in many areas – there's plenty of evidence to prove it.

2 Many insects are disappearing because their habitat has changed. There are butterflies that we don't see any more, ...

3 .... that we have plenty of time to save the environment, but I don't agree with them.

4 We should spend more money on conservation. .... , we also need money to help improve our environment, and maybe we can't do both.

5 I'd say that .... protecting the environment can feel very difficult for us as individuals, we still have to try.

6 .... , I feel that there are many things we could do.

Follow the instructions below.

You **must** answer this question. Write your answer in **140–190** words in an appropriate style **on the separate answer sheet**.

Tip! Allow enough time after you have finished writing to check that you have included the ideas in the notes *and* your own idea.

In your English class you have been talking about ways of improving the environment. Now your English teacher has asked you to write an essay for homework.

Write your essay using **all** the notes and giving reasons for your point of view.

Recycling waste is the best way to improve our environment.

What do you think?

Notes

Write about:

1. how easy it is to recycle waste

2. how useful it is to recycle waste

3. .... (your own idea)

Check! Have you:

☐ included everything in the notes?

☐ written about your own idea?

☐ given reasons for your point of view?

☐ written 140–190 words?

In Part 2 there may be a question asking you to write a review, for example for an English-language magazine, newspaper or website.

In a review you:

- **give**   a brief description of what you are reviewing
- **include**   your opinion – what you liked and what you didn't like about it
- **usually**   give a recommendation – say if you think other people would like it
- **should**   try to use good describing words – think about what adjectives and adverbs you could use
- **write**   between 140 and 190 words.

1 Look at the following points you might want to include in a review. Put them into the different categories below. Some words can go in more than one category.

| prices | staff | actors | atmosphere | range of goods | location | music |
| story | sound quality | musicians | service | ending | instruments | |

shop	music venue	film

Language focus Positive and negative adjectives and expressions

2 Look at the words and phrases below that can be used to give an opinion. Which are positive? Which are negative? Which could be either, depending on the context?

original	fast-moving	impressive	weird	scary	awful	fashionable
complex	outrageous	dramatic	helpful	up-to-the-minute	welcoming	dull
colourful	friendly	confusing	limited	absorbing	efficient	good value for money

3a Work with a partner and follow instructions 1–3.

1 Choose from the following to talk about:

a shop   a music venue   a film

2 Make notes before you begin. Be prepared to describe what you're going to review, say what you liked or didn't like about it, and whether you would recommend it to other people in your class.

3 Write your review. Use some of the points and vocabulary from Exercises 1 and 2.

b Now add a conclusion to your review. As part of your conclusion, trying using a sentence with a superlative, like this:

I've never heard **such** fantastic music in my life so I'd definitely say that other people should go and listen to music here. *or*

It was definitely **the most** absorbing book I've ever read so I would recommend it to other people my age.

4a When you are writing your answer, you will need to use words and
expressions that can link your ideas. You will need linkers for when you are
adding a similar point or a contrasting point about the same thing. Look at
these examples:

Adding a similar point	Adding a contrasting point
One further point …	Yet …
Besides that …	However …
What's more …	On the other hand …
In addition …	Despite this …

Example: *What I specially liked about the shop was that it had a really
wide range of clothes.* **What's more**, *the staff were very friendly.*
On the other hand, *it's quite often crowded because it's so popular.*

b Complete these sentences about a waterpark in a suitable way.

1 The staff at the waterpark were really helpful. Besides that, ……………………………………………… .

2 The changing rooms were very spacious. However, ……………………………………………… .

3 There were plenty of different activities to do. What's more, ……………………………………………… .

4 It wasn't very expensive to get in. On the other hand, ……………………………………………… .

5a Read the exam task below.

You have seen this announcement in an international music magazine.

Do you have a favourite place where you can go and listen to live music? It could be a
concert hall, or a café with a local band – or somewhere else! Write us a review, telling us
why you like it so much, and whether there's anything you don't like about it. Would you
recommend it to other people your age? The best reviews will be published next month.

Write your **review.**

b Now read the review on page 90 a girl called Jodie wrote for her answer. While you are
reading, underline examples of the following things:

opinions   describing words and phrases   linking words

City Hall

My parents love classical music, so we sometimes go to concerts at City Hall near my home. The Hall is by the river, with a beautifully decorated ceiling, and massive glass lights shining like diamonds. At the concerts, there's an orchestra, and a conductor I always find absolutely fascinating. What's more, the audience always dresses up in amazing clothes, so it's a very colourful event.

However, my musical tastes have recently developed a bit and, although I still love classical music, I go to City Hall now to watch rock concerts – which are very different! No-one dresses up or sits in the lovely red velvet seats. Everyone dances and, because the hall is specially built for music, the sound quality is amazing. Besides that, there's a wonderful café that serves delicious food – which we often don't have time to eat, sadly!

On the other hand, the Hall does get very crowded during popular concerts, which I'm not keen on. But the atmosphere there is so amazing and welcoming that I know people of any age would just love to go there!

Test 2 Exam practice — Writing • Part 2 (review)

Follow the instructions below.

Write your answer in **140–190** words in an appropriate style **on the separate answer sheet**.

You see this announcement in an educational magazine for teenagers.

Reviews needed!

Do you have a favourite website that helps you learn? It could be a site that you use for school work, or to find out more about subjects that you're really interested in. Send us a review of the website, telling us how you found out about it, what you use it for, anything that isn't so good about it, and whether you'd recommend it to other people of your age.

The best reviews will win a prize!

Write your **review**.

Check! Have you:

- [ ] given your review a title?
- [ ] included points which will interest your readers?
- [ ] included your own opinions?
- [ ] made your recommendation?
- [ ] used suitable linking words to add similar or contrasting points?
- [ ] written 140–190 words?

In Part 2 there may be a question asking you to write an article.

In an article you:

- **write** in a lively and engaging style, as the article is usually aimed at teenagers
- **include** some of your own opinions in your writing
- **write** 140–190 words

1a **Read the task below carefully.**

You have seen this announcement in an international teenage magazine.

> ## Articles wanted!
>
> We are looking for articles about what young people do to help other people! Which people do you try to help? What kinds of things do you do to help? Is there anything you've found difficult about trying to be helpful?
>
> We will publish the best article next month!

Write your **article**.

b **Start thinking about what you could include in your article about helping people.**

Look at the notes below which may give you some ideas. Work with a partner and add more points of your own.

Who I help	What I do to help
my parents	housework
my friends	homework, money, being a good listener
....	....

2a **Now you need to add some detail – to *expand* on your main points. Look at these examples:**

Main point	Detail
<u>my parents</u> – housework	walking the dog, doing the washing-up, trying to keep my room tidy
<u>my friends</u> – homework, money, being a good listener.	helping with maths homework ....

b **Work with a partner. Look at the points you added and put in more detail about them.**

 Tip! Think about who you are writing the article for. Usually it is for other teenagers to read, so try to make your article lively and interesting.

 Tip! Try to answer any questions that you are asked in the announcement.

3 Now make some notes on the things you find difficult about helping other people. Work with your partner and add another idea of your own to the notes below.

> I'm sometimes too tired.   I don't always have time.
>
> I'd rather be doing something else.

4 Now read the article that a girl called Rosemarie wrote for her answer. Has Rosemarie answered all the questions in the task?

I'm sure many people think that teenagers aren't keen on helping others. But I have to say, I've no idea where that idea has come from, because my experience is exactly the opposite.

Personally speaking, I really try to help my parents with housework because they're often tired after work. I walk the dog, which is better than it sounds, as it gives me plenty of time to think. And sometimes I even get round to tidying my room!

Friends often need help, too, so I really try to be there for them. Whether it's maths homework or help in class, I'll do it if I can. And if they run out of money, which sometimes happens, I'll always lend them some.

It goes without saying, though, that helping other people isn't always easy. Sometimes I'm just too tired to do it, or feel I really can't be bothered, if I'm honest. Some evenings I'd rather sit and watch TV than do the washing up. But then I remember that's probably exactly how Mum and Dad feel – so I make the effort!

5 Rosemarie uses the expressions below to grab the reader's interest, and to make her article more exciting to read. Find and underline where these expressions appear in Rosemarie's article. Then complete sentences 1–8 using Rosemarie's expressions in the correct form. Add punctuation if necessary.

I've no idea where …

… exactly the opposite

personally speaking …

… better than it sounds …

… get round to …

… in need of some help …

it goes without saying …

I can't be bothered …

1 I always thought housework was easy, but I've recently discovered it's .... !

2 I sometimes .... tidying up and putting my clothes away!

3 I know my parents are always .... with the dinner when they get home, as they're tired.

4 Our new puppy is very energetic, so .... that he needs regular walks.

5 .... , I've always quite liked doing the washing up, even though it's not always very easy.

6 My friends always want me to go into town with them, but .... tonight – I'm just too tired.

7 My friend Nadia thinks I hate cooking, but .... she got that idea from!

8 I'm helping out by looking after my little sister tonight, which is ...., as I just get paid for watching TV!

6 Rosemarie also uses *which* to link her sentences together:

... if they run out of money, which sometimes happens, I'll always lend them some.

Complete the sentences with phrases from the box.

... meant it got soaking wet!	... was annoying for her.
... often happens in his village.	... was really thoughtful of them.
... they found a bit scary.	... he was very happy about.

1 She didn't get her sweater back from her sister, which ....

2 Jan's grandparents bought her a new dress for the party, which ....

3 My parents took our dog for a walk in the rain, which ....

4 Karl had to sit and wait for an hour until the bus came, which ....

5 Zac and Will had to walk some of the way home in the dark, which ....

6 Uri got £100 for his birthday, which ....

Test 2 Exam practice Writing • Part 2 (article)

Follow the instructions below.

Write your answer in **140–190** words in an appropriate style **on the separate answer sheet**.

Tip! Try making a few brief notes before you start writing, to answer the questions in the announcement. You have seen the following announcement in an international magazine for young people.

Articles wanted!

Setting a good example

We're looking for articles about people who are great examples to young people. It could be someone famous, or someone you know personally.

Write us an article telling us who the person is, the kind of things they have done, and why you think this person is a good example to young people.

We'll publish the best article next month.

Check! Have you:

 developed your points as fully as you can?

 used expressions to make your writing engaging to the reader?

 checked through your work for the kind of mistakes you often make?

 written 140–190 words?

Write your **article**.

- How many short recordings do you have to listen to in this part?
- How many times do you hear each recording?
- What kind of question do you need to answer about each recording?

1a **Work in pairs. Look at the dialogue. Two teenagers are talking about going to a sports centre with their friends soon. Read through the audioscript before you look at the options below.**

> **Boy:** So are you coming with us to the sports centre on Saturday, Jasmine?
>
> **Girl:** I am, yes, but some of our friends don't seem very enthusiastic about it. I thought we were supposed to be going to have fun!
>
> **Boy:** Well, that's the general idea, and actually one or two people are really keen. They've heard there's a new skate park there and they want to try it out. The problem is, the skate parks we've been to so far have been awesome, and I'm just not sure this one'll match what we've seen elsewhere.
>
> **Girl:** Well, if you're right, we can always go for a swim instead. The sports centre's got a great pool.
>
> **Boy:** Mm – but I go there a lot, and I was hoping to do something different … It *is* very hot at the moment, though …

b **Now look at the options. What does the boy feel about their trip?**

A It will be a waste of time.

B It may offer new opportunities.

C It could prove disappointing.

c 🎧 26 **Listen to the recording.**

2a 🎧 27 **Now listen to two classmates talking about climbing trees. Read the three options below. What do you think the *question* is?**

A Don't start climbing without any preparation.

B Don't stand on any weak branches.

C Don't climb too high up the tree.

b **Look at the options again. Which one matches what they *both* think?**

> **Tip!** Before the recording starts, use the time to look carefully at the options in each question. What *differences* are there between them? This will help you decide which one is correct once the recording starts.

> **Tip!** Some questions focus on the opinion of both speakers.

🎧 28 You will hear people talking in eight different situations. For questions **1–8**, choose the best answer (**A, B** or **C**).

---

1 You hear a girl leaving a message for her brother.
Why is she calling him?
A to apologise for something
B to persuade him to do something
C to promise to do something for him

> **Tip!** It's important to be ready to move on to the next question as soon as the recording starts. If you are unable to answer a question during the first listening, make a guess and move on. Then listen particularly carefully during the second listening.

2 You hear a girl telling her cousin about a music festival they are both going to.
How does her cousin respond?
A He is concerned about the long journey there.
B He is impressed by the bands that are going to perform.
C He is surprised at the difficulty involved in getting tickets.

3 You hear a teacher giving her students advice about writing application letters.
She stresses that the key point when writing their letters is to
A be confident about describing their strengths.
B mention positions of responsibility they have held.
C give full details of their practical skills.

> **Advice**
>
> **1** The girl does all of these things in her message – but which of them was her **reason** for calling?
>
> **4** The question is about what impressed them both. Which of the options do they **agree** about?

4 You hear two classmates talking about a stage performance they have just seen at their school.
What impressed both of them?
A the evidence of teamwork
B the high standard of performing
C the attention to detail

5 You hear the principal of a school talking about a teacher who is leaving.
Which subject has she been teaching?
A sport
B biology
C cookery

6 You hear a girl talking about a ski resort she recently went to.
What does she say about it?
A She met very few people her own age.
B It was not suitable for beginners like her.
C There was less snow than had been forecast.

7 You hear a brother and sister talking about new drinks at their local café.
What does the girl think of the drinks?
A Not many teenagers will be able to afford them.
B They do not taste as good as they look.
C People will buy them just for the decoration.

8 You hear two schoolfriends talking about a book they have just read.
They both agree that the book
A captures the atmosphere of the location.
B accurately describes the behaviour of wolves.
C appeals to the nature lover in everyone.

- How many speakers might you hear in this part of the test?
- How many words might you need to write in each gap?

1   Imagine you are going to listen to a recording about a family holiday. What kinds of places have you visited with your family? Work with a partner. Look at the list and talk about what sort of places you have been to, and what your visit was like and what you saw there.

> the mountains   the beach   the countryside
> a city centre   a lake   a theme park   a ski resort

Tip! Look carefully at the details about the speaker, and the title of the task. They can help you to work out what *kinds* of words you might be looking for in the gaps.

2a   You are going to listen to a boy called Harry talking about a trip he did with his family to a theme park. Before you hear the recording, look at the sentence below and think about the kind of word that might fit the gap. Read the words before and after the gap to help you decide.

Harry wasn't very keen to have a ride on a .... which he saw at the theme park.

b   🎧 29 Now listen to the recording and write the correct word(s) in the gap. Compare your answer with a partner. Do you agree? What other theme park rides are mentioned? Why aren't they correct?

3a   🎧 30 Now listen to Harry talking about the next part of his trip. Look at the sentence below and fill in the missing word(s).

Harry hoped his dad would get him a drink that was .... flavoured.

b   Compare your answers with your partner. Do you agree? What other drinks were mentioned by Harry? Why are they wrong?

4a   🎧 31 It's important to practise your spelling for Part 2, so that your intended answer is clear. Listen and write down correctly the ten words you hear.

1 ....   6 ....
2 ....   7 ....
3 ....   8 ....
4 ....   9 ....
5 ....   10 ....

b   Which words do you find difficult to spell? Keep a record of the words that you misspell in your writing tasks.

1 32 You will hear a girl called Karen talking to her class about an activity she did with her family. For questions **9–18**, complete the sentences with a word or short phrase.

Tip! Read the rubric, title and questions before the recording starts. If you have time, think about words that could fit the gaps. Check the words before and after the gap to make sure your answer makes sense in the sentence.

Dog-sledding in Canada

Karen says the place where the family stayed was a **(9)** ....
so it had good facilities.

Karen took a lot of pictures of the **(10)** .... where the
dog-sledding centre was.

Karen uses the word **(11)** .... to describe the characters
of the dogs that pulled the sleds.

Karen was grateful to be given a **(12)** .... before they set off.

The minimum age for driving the sled was **(13)** ....

Karen became alarmed when crossing a **(14)** .... on the sled.

Karen quickly learnt that she shouldn't **(15)** .... while she was
driving the sled.

Karen was disappointed that she didn't manage to see any **(16)** ....
during her ride.

The family were particularly glad that they got **(17)** .... to wear
in the freezing and slippery conditions.

Karen was thrilled to get the chance to see some **(18)** .... after
the family had finished sledding.

Advice

9 What does the word **facilities** mean? Why might a small village have good facilities?

11 The question is asking for a word that **describes**, so you are looking for an **adjective**. There are several in this section – but the one you are listening for describes **character**.

13 You hear several numbers in this section. You are listening for a **minimum age**, so listen carefully for a phrase that means this, such as **at least**.

- How many short extracts do you listen to in Part 3 of the listening test?
- How many options do you have to choose from?

1   **Work with a partner and look at the list of options below. Talk about what speakers might say about each option.**

   A   preparing for a fancy dress party

   B   wearing the wrong kind of clothes for a party

   C   turning up too late for a party

   D   meeting someone at a party

   E   doing something embarrassing at a party

   F   saying goodbye to someone at a party

   G   arriving at the wrong party

   H   being given something special at a party

> **Tip!** Read quickly through the eight options before the recording starts. If you are not sure of the answer after the first listening, you might find it useful to note down some key words or phrases that may indicate an answer. Then wait until the second listening before you make a final decision.

2a   🎧 33 **Read what Speaker 1 is saying about a party. Which of the options A–H above is she talking about? Underline the words that give you the answer, then listen to what Speaker 1 says.**

> **Speaker 1**
>
> It was my friend's birthday party, which her parents had organised for her. It was quite a posh party, so I'd gone out and bought an expensive dress, which I was relieved to see was exactly the kind of thing everyone else was wearing! Anyway, we'd just got to the point where a few people were making speeches, and the family were giving out drinks, when I ran into a person I recognised, that I hadn't seen for years as she'd moved away. We've been best mates ever since!

b   **Compare your answer with a partner. Which words and phrases are used in the recording that have a similar meaning to the key words in the option? Which words and phrases are used that are similar to other options?**

3a   🎧 34 **Now listen to Speaker 2 talking about a party. Choose from options A–H above, then answer the questions.**

   1   Which words help you decide what the speaker is talking about?

   2   Which other options did you consider as possible answers? Why?

b   **When you have listened, work with a partner and summarise what you heard.**

4   **Work with a partner. You are briefly going to describe to each other a situation in which you did one of the things listed above in options A–H. Try to avoid using the same words as the options you've chosen!**

   Write some brief notes to help you, then talk to your partner. Try to keep talking for about 30 seconds! Your partner should then try to work out which of the options you are talking about. Did you include references to any of the other options too?

🎧 35 You will hear five teenagers talking about helping to organise a surprise birthday party for a family member. For questions **19–23**, choose from the list (**A–H**) the advice each speaker gives to ensure the party will be enjoyable for the family member. Use the letters only once. There are three extra letters which you do not need to use.

Tip! Be careful not to choose your answer too quickly. You may hear something in the recording that sounds like one of the options, but you should listen to the end of each speaker's turn to be sure that your answer is correct.

A   Invite people they get on well with.

B   Find an interesting party venue.

Speaker 1 ☐ **19**

C   Make sure they will appreciate the idea of having a surprise.

Speaker 2 ☐ **20**

D   Be sure you can keep all the party details secret.

Speaker 3 ☐ **21**

E   Don't leave the planning to the last minute.

Speaker 4 ☐ **22**

F   Check they are free to attend the party.

Speaker 5 ☐ **23**

G   Organise party activities that they will enjoy.

H   Don't mention their birthday at all.

Advice

19 The speaker mentions being **less than honest** about the party arrangements, and having to **hide your party things.** Which option do these things suggest? Listen carefully to the recording to confirm your answer.

21 The speaker talks about what happened with their brother's party. What **other arrangements** had the brother made for the day of the party?

- How many speakers are there in Part 4?
- How many questions do you have to answer? What kind of questions?

1 Work with a partner. The people in sentences 1–8 are all talking about different hobbies. Which verb from the box best describes each sentence? Sometimes more than one verb is possible.

Tip! In Part 4, verbs are sometimes used in the options to summarise or report what a speaker has said. Look up in a dictionary any verbs below that you don't know.

inspire	spot	praise	encourage	
intend	plan	describe	prefer	impress
advise	warn	(dis)agree	~~deny~~	
approve	insist	claim	persuade	criticise

Example: 'It definitely wasn't me that broke the frame on the painting.'   ....*deny*.......

1 '*Please* come and see my photos in the school exhibition. You will? Great!'   ....

2 'Don't try to run too far without warming up, or you'll hurt yourself.'   ....

3 'You should have added more blue to that painting.'   ....

4 'I'd rather go swimming than go to the gym tonight, to be honest.'   ....

5 'It's wonderful the way you've captured that bird flying on film!'   ....

6 'I'm making a short red dress with long sleeves and a bow.'   ....

7 'If I were you, I'd try doing some weight training to build up your strength.'   ....

8 'OK, so first we'll buy the ingredients, then we'll bake some cakes, followed by some bread …'   ....

2a Look at this example from an interview with Dan, who loves taking photos.
On the exam paper, you see the words:

Why didn't Dan want to continue with photography when he first tried it?

A He was discouraged when his attempts were criticised.

B He realised his brother was much better at it than him.

C He suspected he had no talent for it.

🎧 1 36 **Cover the script below and listen to the recording.**

Interviewer: Now, you've won some photography competitions, Dan, but you didn't really like photography when you were younger, did you?

Dan: No, I was a bit slow in getting started, really! I did a few pictures with my older brother's camera, which my mum thought were great, and I didn't think they were too bad, either. But when my brother saw the results, <u>he immediately started telling me what I'd done wrong!</u> He hadn't done much photography himself, but I knew he was probably right, and just trying to help me improve, <u>but it wasn't a good start, and I gave up for a while</u>. But then a few months later my brother tried again to help me, and I was more ready to accept it then, as we'd started doing photography at school. Or probably I just wanted to know more and be better than my brother!

b Look at the words which give the correct answer (A). Why are B and C wrong?

You will hear an interview with a boy called Andrew Carpenter, whose hobby is making pots. For questions **24–30**, choose the best answer (**A, B** or **C**).

> **Tip!** While you are waiting for the recording to begin, read carefully through the rubric, questions and options so that you have a clear idea of what you will be listening for. If you can't answer one question during the first listening, you should still be ready to move on to the next question. If you don't, you may lose your place. You still have a second listening when you can confirm your answers.

> **Tip!** If you are not sure after the second listening, make a guess. Don't leave any answers blank!

---

24 What first made Andrew become interested in pottery?
- **A** some work his teacher did with him
- **B** an artist who visited his school
- **C** a film he happened to see

25 What did Andrew particularly like about one piece of pottery he saw?
- **A** He was able to handle it.
- **B** It had a practical use.
- **C** It was carefully thought out.

26 What does Andrew say about his experience of using a potter's wheel?
- **A** It was a much dirtier activity than he expected.
- **B** It greatly increased his enjoyment of making pots.
- **C** His family was prouder of what he produced than he was.

27 Andrew thinks his friends may have stopped attending pottery class because
- **A** it was more difficult than they had expected.
- **B** there was something else they preferred doing.
- **C** they did not find the experience very enjoyable.

28 What does Andrew say about the 'coiled' pot he made?
- **A** It particularly impressed his classmates.
- **B** It took him a long time to learn the technique.
- **C** It was the most successful thing he did.

29 When he received praise for one pot he had made, Andrew
- **A** realised he had not been serious enough in his attitude until then.
- **B** wished people had been more encouraging about all his pieces.
- **C** wondered if people really meant what they had said.

30 Andrew advises other young people interested in pottery to
- **A** be prepared to take their time when trying to make something.
- **B** have a definite plan for what they want to make.
- **C** adopt a determined approach to their work.

Advice

*24 Andrew mentions a **video clip** he saw. What does he mean? What was it about? What happened as a result of his watching it?*

*27 What did Andrew's friends **really** want to be doing at lunchtime?*

- What are the questions about in this part of the test?
- Who do you speak to?

1 Work with a partner. Choose the correct option in the following sentences.

1 Part 1 of the test lasts *one / two / three / four* minutes when there are two candidates.

2 Each candidate answers *the same / different* questions.

3 The candidates *see / don't see* the questions.

2 🎧 1 38 Listen to two students doing Part 1 of the test, and check if your answers were correct.

3 🎧 1 38 Listen again to answer these questions:

1 What was the topic of the questions in Part 1?

2 Which of the following words and expressions do Jana and Fernando use? Tick (✓) the words and expressions you hear.

a **linking ideas:** as well as ☐ and ☐ then ☐ so ☐ also ☐

b **giving an example:** like ☐ such as ☐

c **giving a reason:** as ☐ because ☐

d **asking the examiner to repeat a question:** Sorry, what did you say? ☐

Could you say that again, please? ☐ I'm sorry, I didn't quite catch that. ☐

> **Tip!** Examiners listen carefully for good, appropriate use of linkers.

1 Work with a partner. Take it in turns to ask and answer these questions. Ask them in any order.

> **Tip!** Remember that these questions will all be about you and your everyday life.

| Part 1 | 2 minutes [3 minutes for groups of three] |

Interlocutor First, we'd like to know something about you.

- Where did you go yesterday after school? (What did you do?)
- What are you going to do with your family next weekend? (Why are you going to do that?)
- Do you play any sports? (Why do you enjoy it / them?)
- What do you enjoy doing with your friends in your free time? (Why?)
- Who is your favourite actor? (Why?)

2 🎧 1 39 Now close your books, listen to the examiner and answer the questions.

> **Tip!** The interlocutor will only use the questions in brackets if you have not answered the question fully enough.

- How many photos do you talk about in Part 2?
- What do you have to do when you talk about the photos?
- Do you only answer questions about your own photos?

Useful language Comparing pictures and photos

1   Look at the two pictures below and complete the sentences. You can use the Useful language in Test 1, page 57.

1   The people in .... pictures are at the seaside.

2   .... people are probably on holiday.

3   The person in the .... picture is relaxing on the beach.

4   The person in the .... picture is waterskiing, which is a more exciting activity.

5   I think the person reading on the beach likes being calm and quiet, ... the person waterskiing enjoys a challenge.

Useful language Making guesses about the pictures

2   Complete these sentences about the pictures. Again, you can use the Useful language in Test 1, page 57.

1   The person on the beach .... be tired and that's why he is having a rest.

2   The person water-skiing .... as if she's having a lot of fun.

3   It .... me that the people in the pictures are on holiday at a beach resort.

4   .... they are staying at the seaside with their families.

5   It looks .... a pleasant place to go for the day.

6   I have the .... the girl is very happy, possibly because she's doing so well.

> **Tip!** Always say which picture you are talking about, or make it clear you are talking about both the pictures.

3 The person listening is asked a short question after their partner has talked about the two pictures. Complete these sentences with expressions that the second candidate might use in their answer.

Tip! You will get a better mark if you use a variety of expressions to speculate about the pictures.

Interlocutor [*Candidate B*], which activity would you prefer?

1 I think .... more fun to go waterskiing, because I've never tried it before.

2 I suppose .... prefer to be on the beach reading, because I only have time to read during the holidays.

3 I love sport, ... my choice would be to go waterskiing. I think it looks like a really exciting thing to do.

4 Rewrite the sentences using the words and phrases in brackets.

Tip! The examiner may use a follow-up question (usually *Why?*) if they would like you to say a bit more.

Example: The people in the two pictures are on holiday at the beach. **(seem to be)**

The people in the two pictures ......seem to be.... on holiday at the beach.

1 It's sunny in the two pictures. **(both)**

It's …

2 I think the girl in the second picture is feeling very happy. **(looks as if)**

The girl …

3 The boy appears to be enjoying the book he's reading. **(have the impression)**

I …

4 The girl's doing something thrilling, and in contrast the boy's just relaxing. **(whereas)**

The girl …

5 In my opinion, reading on the beach would be more enjoyable, because I don't like sport very much.

In my opinion, … **(it would be)**

5 🎧 40 Now listen to someone talking about the two pictures, and check whether the sentences you wrote for Exercise 4 are correct.

Look at the exam instructions below and photos on pages C8 and C9, then do this exam task in pairs.

Tip! If you can't remember a word, use other words to explain what you want to say.

Part 2 4 minutes [6 minutes for groups of three]

Interlocutor In this part of the test, I'm going to give each of you two photographs. I'd like you to talk about your photographs on your own for about a minute, and also to answer a question about your partner's photographs.

(*Candidate A*), it's your turn first. Here are your photographs on page C8 of the Speaking appendix. They show **people spending their free time in different ways**.

I'd like you to compare the photographs, and say **why you think the people have decided to do these things in their free time**.

All right?

Candidate A

🕐 *1 minute* ....

Interlocutor Thank you.
(*Candidate B*), **Which of these things would you prefer to do? (Why?)**

Candidate B

🕐 *Approximately 30 seconds* ....

Interlocutor Thank you.

Now, (*Candidate B*), here are your photographs on page C9 of the Speaking appendix. They show **people talking to friends in different situations**.

I'd like you to compare the photographs, and say **why you think people enjoy talking to friends in these ways**.

All right?

Candidate B

🕐 *1 minute* ....

Interlocutor Thank you.

(*Candidate A*), **do you spend a lot of time talking to your friends on the phone / online? (Why / Why not?)**

Candidate A

🕐 *Approximately 30 seconds* ....

Interlocutor Thank you.

- Who do you speak to in Part 3?
- How long does this part last?
- What do you see in the booklet?
- Which question **don't** you see?

Useful language Practice in paraphrasing

1a Look at these question ideas to discuss like the ones you see in Part 3 .

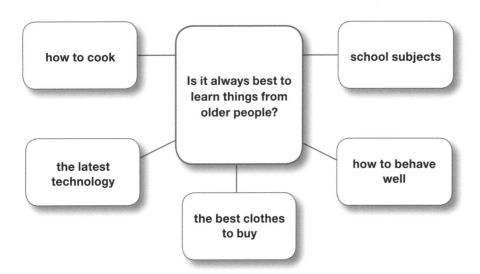

how to cook

Is it always best to learn things from older people?

school subjects

the latest technology

how to behave well

the best clothes to buy

b 🎧41 Listen to Jana and Fernando doing Part 3 of the speaking test and number the ideas in the order you hear them. Which idea is *not* discussed?

> **Tip!** Try to use your own words as much as possible, rather than just read out what is in the booklet.

Focus Keeping the conversation moving

2 🎧41 Listen to Jana and Fernando again. Tick (✓) the expressions you hear.

How about …?	☐
What do you think about …?	☐
This suggestion looks good, doesn't it?	☐
What about this idea here?	☐

3 🎧42 Now listen to Fernando and Jana trying to reach a decision and answer these questions.

1 What question does the examiner ask them?

2 Do they make a decision?

> **Tip!** Make sure your partner also has a chance to speak, and do this by asking a question – for example: *What do you think?*

4 🎧42 Listen again and write down the expressions you hear for:

1 agreeing with your partner ....

2 disagreeing politely with your partner ....

> **Tip!** Don't worry if you don't make a decision, the important thing is to talk and try to reach one.

Look at the exam instructions below and the question and ideas on page C12, then do this exam task in pairs.

Part 1   4 minutes [5 minutes for groups of three]

Interlocutor Now, I'd like you to talk about something together for about two minutes.

I'd like you to imagine that a teacher wants to celebrate the end of the school year with her students. Here are some ideas and a question for you to discuss. First you have some time to look at the task on page C12 of the Speaking appendix.

Now, talk to each other about **whether it is a good idea for teachers to celebrate the end of the school year with their students.**

Candidates

2 minutes (3 minutes for groups of three)

Interlocutor Thank you. Now you have about a minute to decide **which two suggestions are the most important things for the teacher to consider.**

Candidates

🕐 *1 minute (for pairs and groups of three)*

Interlocutor Thank you.

Tip! It does not matter if you don't discuss all the ideas, but try to talk about three or four of them if you have time.

- Do you see the questions in Part 4 written down?
- Do you answer the same questions as your partner?

1 Think about the topic of the Part 3 exam practice task that you heard Jana and Fernando discussing (whether it is always best to learn things from older people). What do you think the examiner might ask them about in Part 4?

2 🎧 1 43 Listen to Jana and Fernando being asked questions in Part 4. What questions does the examiner ask?

1 ....

2 ....

3 ....

Test 2 Exam practice   Speaking • Part 4

Work in pairs. Ask and answer these questions.

| Part 4 | 4 minutes [6 minutes for groups of three] |

Interlocutor

- Do you enjoy talking to older people? (Why? / Why not?)

- Why do you think older and younger people sometimes have difficulty understanding each other?

- Should young people always do what older people tell them to? (Why? / Why not?)

Thank you. That is the end of the test.

> **What do you think?**
> **Do you agree?**
> **And you?**

Tip! Answer the question as fully as you can, and listen to what your partner says, because the examiner may ask you if you agree.

For questions **1–8**, read the text below and decide which answer (**A**, **B**, **C** or **D**) best fits each gap. There is an example at the beginning (**0**).
Mark your answers **on the separate answer sheet**.

Example:

0   **A** hear   **B** listen   **C** sound   **D** ring

0	A	B	C	D
	▭	▭	▬	▭

A dress made of paper

Would you ever wear something made with paper from your old schoolbooks? It might **(0)** .... like a crazy idea, but Kara Koskowich, a high school student in Canada, became front-page **(1)** .... when she made herself a dress out of her maths homework.

The dress was for her school 'prom', or leaving party, and she decided to have some fun creating this amazing and **(2)** .... dress, as well as help the environment at the same time by recycling 75 pages from her maths exercise book. It was also an affordable **(3)** .... compared to buying a new dress at **(4)** .... expense; apart from the thread she bought, the dress was **(5)** .... free.

Kara's best friend **(6)** .... in the creative fun too, making her own recycled dress for the occasion using plastic shopping bags. Other teenagers have also made unusual **(7)** .... of party dresses. Coffee filters, chewing gum wrappers and crisp packets have all **(8)** .... out to be viable materials.

1   **A** news   **B** article   **C** press   **D** report

2   **A** sole   **B** only   **C** unique   **D** single

3   **A** selection   **B** course   **C** preference   **D** option

4   **A** extensive   **B** substantial   **C** considerable   **D** exceptional

5   **A** certainly   **B** basically   **C** definitely   **D** principally

6   **A** joined   **B** involved   **C** concerned   **D** linked

7   **A** alternatives   **B** models   **C** replacements   **D** versions

8   **A** pointed   **B** set   **C** turned   **D** got

For questions **9–16**, read the text below and think of the word which best fits each gap. Use only one word in each gap. There is an example at the beginning (**0**).

Write your answers **IN CAPITAL LETTERS on the separate answer sheet**.

Example:

0	A																		

New dinosaur exhibit at Wigdale Zoo

We're all used to seeing **(0)** .... great many different kinds of animals at a zoo. But now, at Wigdale Zoo, you can also have a look at **(9)** .... very different: dinosaurs. But how on earth could that **(10)** .... possible? Dinosaurs have been extinct for 65 million years **(11)** .... the very least and so surely there is **(12)** .... way they could actually have come back to life.

But Wigdale Zoo is indeed now offering visitors the chance to see those ancient creatures, or, **(13)** .... I'm honest, to see some extraordinarily realistic models of them. **(14)** .... that you need to do is take a walk through a large wood, known **(15)** .... Wigdale Old Forest. By the side of a signposted track there are 19 enormous 'animatronic' dinosaurs. They move, they roar and **(16)** .... of them even spits water. It's an experience not to be missed!

For questions **17–24**, read the text below. Use the word given in capitals at the end of some of the lines to form a word that fits in the gap in the same line. There is an example at the beginning (**0**).

Write your answers **IN CAPITAL LETTERS on the separate answer sheet**.

Example: | 0 | M O T I V A T E D

Training for a long-distance running race

The secret of success when preparing to run in a long-distance race
is to remain extremely **(0)** .... , to train sensibly, and to   **MOTIVATE**
focus on proper nutrition. It takes more than willpower alone to run
several kilometres. There is some **(17)** .... over the best   **AGREE**
way of training, however, and studies have not reached any universal
conclusions.

Nevertheless, successful **(18)** .... tend to approach   **RUN**
their training in similar ways. They focus on staying healthy and,
(19) .... , you may think, are careful not to overtrain.   **SURPRISE**
It is **(20)** .... to train slightly less, but remain strong   **PREFER**
and full of **(21)** .... , than to train too hard and face   **ENTHUSIASTIC**
(22) .... or injury.   **SICK**

The **(23)** .... of a healthy diet can never be stressed   **IMPORTANT**
too much, of course, and you should always eat a good helping of
carbohydrates soon after exercising. Another crucial **(24)** ....   **CONSIDER**
is the need to remain hydrated at all times. Listen to your body: if you
feel thirsty, then you need a drink.

For questions **25–30**, complete the second sentence so that it has a similar meaning to the first sentence, using the word given. **Do not change the word given.** You must use between **two** and **five** words, including the word given. Here is an example (**0**).

Example:

0   Karen didn't really want to go to the party.

FORWARD

Karen wasn't really .... to the party.

The gap can be filled by the words 'looking forward to going', so you write:

Example: | **0** | LOOKING FORWARD TO GOING |

---

25   Nadia left her phone on the bus, and she got to school late, too.
LEAVE
Not .... her phone on the bus, but Nadia got to school late, too.

26   People can't cycle here if they don't wear helmets.
ALLOWED
People aren't .... they wear helmets.

27   They didn't cancel the outdoor theatre performance despite the rain.
EVEN
The outdoor theatre performance wasn't .... was raining.

28   Dan played games on his computer all evening.
WHOLE
Dan .... games on his computer.

29   My grandmother says she remembers her childhood when we come here.
REMINDS
My grandmother says this place .... her childhood.

30   Do you think your mum could take us to school in her car?
LIFT
Do you think your mum would mind .... to school in her car?

You are going to read an article about a teenage writer called Beth Reekles. For questions **31–36**, choose the answer (**A, B, C** or **D**) which you think fits best according to the text.

Mark your answers **on the separate answer sheet**.

Teenage novelist Beth Reekles

Our reporter interviewed a teenage writer and her father.

Aged 15, British teenager Beth Reekles spent hours alone in her bedroom, tapping away obsessively on her laptop. Reekles was writing a bestselling novel. 'All that time, I thought she was messing around on social networking sites, like other teenagers,' her dad told me, shaking his head. Reekles wrote her book as a serial, uploading a chapter at a time onto the Internet — the first chapter alone got a million hits — until her inbox was deluged with emails that she said typically began 'upload faster!' The three-book deal she signed with a publisher only came after her book had been read online for free 19 million times. Through instinct, luck or cleverness, she had discovered the secret to global appeal that had eluded those three or four times her age.

'I wrote it because I was looking for something to read,' says Reekles, with disarming calm simplicity. 'I couldn't find it, so I wrote it.' This is typical of Reekles, making it sound easy. Her writing flows out of her unstoppably and when I ask her, for instance, how she finds the time to study while maintaining her career as an international publishing phenomenon, she looks at me and laughs politely. 'A lot of my friends say that. Some of them don't even take Saturday jobs because there's too much homework now. I suppose I see this as like my Saturday job now.'

The strange thing about her rise to fame is that almost all of her fans have no idea how young she is. Teen fiction is mostly written by adults. But if you look closely enough, there are a few indications of Reekles' age. Not many books end with quite such a specific message to staff at a Welsh school: 'A big thank you to my English teacher, Mr Maughan. Your enthusiastic teaching and interest in my writing was a huge motivation.' Adults always struggle to write the teenage detail – things like how to keep on listening to music even when you're in the shower – but Reekles gets it just right.

Despite these giveaways, the main reason few would guess at the fact that when she wrote the book Reekles was even younger than her teenage heroine is that her writing is so impressive. It is never introspective or pretentious. The pace is controlled, the chapters end on cliffhangers. You might be forgiven for thinking that the book was written by a highly experienced American scriptwriter with an eye for a movie deal.

line 37

Reekles says she wrote addictively from the first moment her father gave her a laptop at the age of 11. She never told or showed anyone for a very long time. She worried she was weird: 'I mean, it didn't seem like the average hobby.' Then a friend recommended she read a book on a free online novel-sharing platform for amateur writers. 'All my stories were squirrelled away in a folder on my laptop. But I saw that on this site I could be anonymous, and I liked that. I was self-conscious about the quality of my writing. I saw that here no one would know me, and I eventually worked up the courage to start posting my own books.'

Her writing soon became very popular on the site, and a year later, she got an email from a publisher offering to publish her latest online novel as a paper book. '"What's this?" I thought. I read it a few times, yanked the charger out of the laptop and ran across to my parents, the noise that came out of my mouth was not human. I was so excited.' Her dad chips in proudly: 'Although it's easy to upload books online, and there are a lot of people doing it, there aren't that many people who can do it well.' I ask him what he thinks of the book. 'Oh, I haven't read it.'

31 What do we learn about Reekles in the first paragraph?

    A She is easily distracted while trying to write novels.
    B She adapted her writing in response to readers' comments.
    C She took care to avoid mistakes made by other novelists.
    D She manages to please a wide range of readers.

32 What does Reekles suggest about her writing in the second paragraph?

    A She has little trouble fitting it into her life.
    B She finds it easier to do than schoolwork nowadays.
    C She does it to boost her income from other part-time jobs.
    D She realises that few people are able to do it as well as she does.

33 What does the reporter say about Reekles' age?

    A It is hard for her to hide it from her readers.
    B It allows her to write in a realistic way.
    C It explains her need to please her teacher.
    D It can sometimes put off adult readers.

34 What is meant by 'giveaways' in *line 37*?

    A slightly irrelevant parts of the book
    B pieces of advice Reekles has received
    C clues giving information about Reekles
    D opportunities to read the book for free

35 According to Reekles, the online novel-sharing site was important for her because

    A it allowed her to compare her writing to that of others.
    B other users gave her positive feedback about her work.
    C she could display her work on it without embarrassment.
    D it proved that she was less unusual than she had thought.

36 How does Reekles' father feel about her success?

    A proud that he recognised her talent when she was younger
    B relieved that her book has become a bestseller at last
    C impressed by his daughter's achievement in a competitive field
    D keen to discover for himself why so many people admire the book

You are going to read an article about baby sea turtles being helped by humans. Six sentences have been removed from the article. Choose from the sentences **A–G** the one which fits each gap (**37–42**). There is one extra sentence which you do not need to use.

Mark your answers **on the separate answer sheet**.

Baby sea turtles get to the water safely

Volunteers on a Caribbean Island and a police officer in the US have something in common: helping baby turtles to reach the sea.

Although human beings are responsible for many of the problems faced by animals worldwide, there are times when people try to make up for it. Recently, in both the Caribbean and the US, people came to the aid of baby sea turtles confused by man-made light.

Though loggerhead sea turtles spend most of their lives in water, they are born on land. Adult females come ashore onto beaches to lay their eggs in the sand. There are around 100 eggs in a nest, and they incubate for about 55–65 days, depending on the temperature. Adult loggerhead turtles weigh up to 140kg and have few predators. **37** This, along with pollution and the loss of nesting habitats due to development, has resulted in these animals being placed on the threatened species list.

On the Caribbean island of Bonaire, conservation volunteers regularly help to ensure that the hundreds of loggerhead sea turtles that hatch on the beaches of the island make it to the sea each year. **38** This time, however, they had to do something they had never done before: create a human wall for some of the little ones that were confused as to the path to the ocean.

It all began when volunteers on Bonaire Island noticed that a turtle had laid her eggs a little further away from the sea than usual, on a beach close to the airport. This was a problem because the babies usually hatch at night, and then use the moonlight to guide them to the sea. However, when turtles are born close to a place that is brightly lit at night, they get confused between the artificial light and the natural light of the moon. **39** In this case, that would be away from the sea and towards the bright lights of the airport terminal. When some turtle eggs were laid close by a few years ago, it caused a lot of problems for the baby turtles.

40 Then came the big day when they began to hatch, and the little hatchlings – as the tiny baby turtles are called – were ready to make their long trek to the water.

In order to ensure the hatchlings were guided by the moon and did not set off towards the airport, the volunteers came together and created a human wall around the turtles. **41** As a result, all 112 turtles scrambled over the sand in the right direction and made it safely to the sea.

And in Florida, in the United States, some baby turtles were similarly confused. A police officer was on patrol at 1 a.m. when he spotted some sea turtle hatchlings crawling towards a hotel. A passer-by told him that several other baby turtles were wandering around the hotel car park. **42** This may explain why they were heading for the hotel's front door. 'I began collecting hatchlings from the street and stopped traffic several times to do so,' said the officer. Helped by some of the hotel guests, the officer scooped up nearly 100 little turtles in a box and released them into the sea near the hotel.

A   Determined not to let the same thing happen again, the volunteers kept a close eye on the turtle eggs.

B   The Bonaire turtle eggs had also been buried near the sea.

C   The task usually involves just keeping an eye on them.

D   Like the loggerhead turtles in the Caribbean, their instinct was to move towards the brightest light.

E   The eggs and young ones, however, are much more vulnerable.

F   This effectively blocked out all the artificial light.

G   As a result they can end up heading in the wrong direction.

You are going to read an article about a summer camp for teenagers where they can learn about a prehistoric animal. For questions **43–52**, choose from the sections (**A–D**). The sections may be chosen more than once.

Mark your answers **on the separate answer sheet**.

Which section

includes praise for the learning environment provided?	43
says a discovery has been long awaited?	44
explains why the mastodon may have been in the area?	45
mentions that the students are carefully supervised?	46
mentions a physical feature of mastodons that was related to their diet?	47
demonstrates the great impact the camp has had on certain people?	48
says someone's initial belief later turned out to be mistaken?	49
shows that difficult conditions failed to put people off?	50
describes how suitable places to dig are chosen?	51
points out that something was hardly unexpected?	52

Summer camp for teenagers – looking for prehistoric animal bones!

A special summer camp in the US gave high school students the chance to look for the remains of mastodons – a prehistoric relative of the elephant.

A

Lying on her stomach, Victoria Bochniak kept digging until she hit something hard. She tapped the object with her trowel, assuming it was a piece of wood. She was wrong. 'We were like: "Wait a second. This is bone!" said Bochniak. In fact, what she found this week nearly 60 cm beneath a boggy prairie was the bone of a mastodon, an extinct relative of the elephant, believed to be more than 11,000 years old. Bochniak was excited but not entirely surprised. After all, this is why she attended Mastodon Camp. With about 30 other high school students, she has been given the hands-on opportunity to help excavate a mastodon. Under the watchful eyes of experts, students have not only unearthed pieces of mastodon, they've also discovered their inner paleontologist, inspiring them to pursue their newfound curiosity about Ice Age secrets.

B

Mastodon Camp is meant to help students and teachers improve their understanding of scientific inquiry and research and their familiarity with scientific technology and tools, as well as teach them about evolution and changes in the ecosystem over time. 'We've changed some folks' lives,' said Tom Pray, education outreach manager at the camp. 'They've decided: "I'm not going to do art history anymore. I'm going to go into archeology."' This fall, Bochniak, 18, plans to study geology and anthropology at university and do field work at a nearby nature reserve. Kaitlyn Hornik, 16, said Mastodon Camp is more engaging than a typical classroom setting. 'Textbooks are boring,' said Hornik, 'You come out here and you find things out for yourself.'

C

American mastodons stood 2.4 to 3 m tall at the shoulder, similar to elephants, but were stockier and covered with thick hair. A ground-penetrating radar was dragged over the area to pinpoint where the students would excavate, Pray said. Soil surveys of the site by the Illinois State Geological Survey have determined that the mastodon was discovered at the shoreline of a glacial 'kettle lake'. These were formed when chunks of ice broke off and melted during the glacial retreat. 'Whether he came down for a drink or fell through the ice, we don't know,' said Jack MacRae, a naturalist with the Forest Preserve District. Pollen samples in the lake demonstrate that plant species in the region were in a time of transition from a spruce forest ecosystem containing trees like pines to the deciduous trees that lose their leaves in winter prevalent today. Mastodons, which had teeth strong enough to crush pine cones, preferred spruce forests as their habitat, experts say. So the site may provide clues as to why the beasts became extinct in North America about 10,000 years ago: possibly disease, human overhunting or loss of habitat caused by climate change.

D

Although this year's camp was plagued by heavy rains, the weather did little to dampen the students' enthusiasm. On Tuesday, Pray arrived at the site at 6:30 a.m. to pump water out of the trenches and was joined a few hours later by students who helped by bailing water. Then they continued digging, using shovels, trowels and their own hands. On Tuesday, the piece of bone that Bochniak had discovered protruded from the black mud. Pray said it could be a rib or the top of a femur. 'This could be what we've been looking for over the last few years,' he said. A discovery like this makes all the hard work worthwhile. 'This gives people the idea that anybody can do science,' Pray said.

---

1   You **must** answer this question. Write your answer in **140–190** words in an appropriate style **on the separate answer sheet**.

In your English class you have been talking about cooking. Now your English teacher has asked you to write an essay for homework.

Write your essay using **all** the notes and giving reasons for your point of view.

All teenagers should learn how to cook.

Do you agree?

Notes

Write about:

1. whether teenagers need to cook

2. whether cooking is enjoyable

3. .... (your own idea)

Write an answer to **one** of the questions **2–5** in this part. Write your answer in **140–190** words in an appropriate style **on the separate answer sheet**. Put the question number in the box at the top of the answer sheet.

---

2   You have received an email from your English-speaking friend Tom.

> ○○○
>
> Hi,
>
> I'm doing a school project on dancing in different parts of the world and I wonder if you can help me. Can you tell me about a dance that is popular in your country? Do people of all ages enjoy it? Do you know anything about the history of the dance and what makes it special?
>
> Thanks,
> Tom

Write your **email**.

3   You see this announcement on an English-language website for teenagers.

> ***Reviews wanted!***
>
> # Cafés
>
> Do you know a café that you could review for us? We'd like to know where it is, what sort of food and drinks people can have there and what the atmosphere is like there. Say whether you would recommend this café to other people your age.
>
> The best reviews will be published on our website.

Write your **review**.

4   You have seen this announcement in an English-language magazine for young people.

> ## We want your story!
> We are looking for stories for our magazine. Your story must begin with this sentence:
> *Jim knew it would be a long journey, but he couldn't wait to set off.*
> Your story must include:
> - a mobile phone
> - a new friend

Write your **story**.

5   Answer the following question based on the set text.

You have been talking about the set text in your English class. Now your teacher has given you this essay for homework:

The characters in the set text have a number of problems in the story. Which character has the most difficult problem to deal with? What do you think about the way this character solved the problem?

Write your **essay**.

---

01 You will hear people talking in eight different situations. For questions **1–8**, choose the best answer (**A, B** or **C**).

---

1   You hear two friends talking about a science website.
     What do they agree about?
     A   The information on the website is useful for homework.
     B   The graphics are better than on similar websites.
     C   The website is easy for everyone to use.

2   You hear a teenager talking to her mother on the phone.
     What is she doing?
     A   asking her mother for some money
     B   telling her mother about a bargain
     C   persuading her mother to do something

3   You hear two classmates discussing a history project.
     The boy thinks that the project will
     A   be easy to complete on time.
     B   involve some interesting research.
     C   prove useful for his future studies.

4   You hear part of a radio programme.
     What is the programme about?
     A   a song
     B   a concert
     C   a singer

5   You hear a brother and sister talking about a party they organised.
     How does the girl feel now?
     A   relieved that it is over
     B   glad so many people came
     C   proud to have organised it so well

6   You hear a teacher talking to some students on a geography trip.
     The teacher wants the students to
     A   follow a specific route.
     B   take notes while he is talking.
     C   photograph some unusual rocks.

7   You hear a teenage tennis player talking about her new coach.
     She says her coach
     A   understands the pressures she faces.
     B   has given her more confidence.
     C   wants her to change her technique.

8   You hear a brother and sister talking about a long car journey they are going to go on.
     What does the boy say about it?
     A   He expects it to be rather dull.
     B   He hopes they will set off early.
     C   He wishes they could go by bus instead.

02 You will hear a teenager called Harvey Mellor talking to younger students at his school about a school play he was involved in. For questions **9–18**, complete the sentences with a word or short phrase.

The school play

Harvey heard about the school play from his **(9)** .... teacher.

Harvey ended up helping with the **(10)** .... as well as acting
in the play.

Harvey and his classmates were asked to design a **(11)** .... for
the play.

Harvey was glad he was asked to play the part of a **(12)** ....

The rehearsals were held in the school **(13)** .... as well as in the
school hall.

Harvey found it helpful to practise with his **(14)** .... at the
weekends.

The food offered to the audience included some **(15)** .... that
Harvey made.

Shortly before the first performance, Harvey realised he had left his black
(16) .... at home.

The fact that a lot of **(17)** .... came to see the play surprised Harvey.

Harvey says he would like to become a theatre **(18)** .... in the future.

(2 03) You will hear five short extracts in which teenagers talk about their best friends. For questions **19–23**, choose from the list (**A–H**) what each speaker says about how they met their best friend. Use the letters only once. There are three extra letters which you do not need to use.

A   We were in the same class at primary school.

B   We were hoping to go to the same concert.

Speaker 1 | 19 |

C   We were sitting next to each other on a bus.

Speaker 2 | 20 |

D   We were at the same party.

Speaker 3 | 21 |

E   We were introduced to each other by a friend.

Speaker 4 | 22 |

F   We were in a sports competition together.

Speaker 5 | 23 |

G   We were doing a project together at school.

H   We were in the same sports team.

24 Why did Stella decide to try surfing?
   A It was something she had always wanted to do.
   B Someone she knew inspired her to have a go.
   C There was little else for her to do on holiday.

25 How did Stella feel the night before her first surfing lesson?
   A worried she might miss the lesson
   B excited to be doing something new
   C nervous that she might get injured

26 What was Stella's first impression of the people in her surfing class?
   A They all looked younger than her.
   B They all seemed to know each other.
   C They all appeared to be sporty.

27 What does Stella say about the surfing instructor?
   A He lost patience with some people in the class.
   B He spent too much time teaching the basic moves.
   C He didn't always explain everything clearly.

28 Stella thinks she was able to keep her balance on the surfboard because
   A She practises yoga regularly.
   B She's good at skateboarding.
   C She does a lot of gymnastics.

29 What was Stella given at the end of the lesson?
   A A certificate saying she had been surfing.
   B A photograph of her on the surfboard.
   C A card offering her a discount in local shops.

30 What did Stella do in the evening after her surfing lesson?
   A went out for a meal
   B went to bed early
   C went to a party

Interlocutor First, we'd like to know something about you.

Family life

- Do you have any brothers or sisters? (Are they younger or older than you?)
- What do you enjoy doing with your family in your free time? (Why?)
- Which person in your family do you spend the most time with? (Why?)
- Have you been anywhere interesting with your family recently? (Tell us about it.)
- Does all your family live near you? (Is there a member of your family you often visit?)

Interlocutor In this part of the test, I'm going to give each of you two photographs. I'd like you to talk about your photographs on your own for about a minute, and also to answer a question about your partner's photographs.

(*Candidate A*), it's your turn first. Here are your photographs on page C13 of the Speaking appendix. They show **people watching a film in different places.**

I'd like you to compare the photographs, and say **why you think the people like watching films in these different places**.

All right?

Candidate A
🕐 *1 minute* ....

Interlocutor Thank you.

(*Candidate B*), **in which of these places would you prefer to be? (Why?)**

Candidate B
🕐 *Approximately 30 seconds* ....

Interlocutor Thank you.

Now, (*Candidate B*), here are your photographs on page C14 of the Speaking appendix. They show **people travelling in different ways.**

I'd like you to compare the photographs, and say **why the people have decided to travel in these ways**.

All right?

Candidate B
🕐 *1 minute* ....

Interlocutor Thank you.

(*Candidate A*), **which way would you prefer to travel if you were on a long journey? (Why?)**

Candidate A
🕐 *Approximately 30 seconds* ....

Interlocutor Thank you.

Part 3

4 minutes [5 minutes for groups of three]

Interlocutor Now, I'd like you to talk about something together for about two minutes.

I'd like you to imagine that there are plans to build new facilities in your area to encourage teenagers to take part in community life. Here are some ideas for the new facilities and a question for you to discuss. First you have some time to look at the task on page C15.

Now, talk to each other about **what the advantages and disadvantages of these suggestions might be**.

Candidates

⏱ *2 minutes (3 minutes for groups of three)*

Interlocutor Thank you. Now you have about a minute to decide **which two suggestions would be the most interesting ones to choose**.

Candidates

⏱ *1 minute (for pairs and groups of three)*

Interlocutor Thank you.

4 minutes [6 minutes for groups of three]

Interlocutor

- How important do you think it is to have special facilities for young people in a town? (Why?)

- Do you think adults and teenagers always enjoy the same leisure activities? (Why? / Why not?)

- Some people say that teenagers have too much free time. Do you agree? (Why?/ Why not?)

- What are useful ways to spend free time?

- Is it better to take part in organised activities during your free time or to just relax at home? (Why?)

- Should older teenagers help look after younger children during the holidays? (Why / Why not?)

- How important is it to take part in community activities with people in your neighbourhood (for example tidying up the local park)?

> **What do you think?**
> **Do you agree?**
> **And you?**

Thank you. That is the end of the test.

For questions **1–8**, read the text below and decide which answer (**A, B, C** or **D**) best fits each gap. There is an example at the beginning (**0**).

Mark your answers **on the separate answer sheet**.

Example:

0 **A** made **B** done **C** had **D** found

0	A	B	C	D
	▬	▭	▭	▭

Dolphins have their own names

Scientists studying a species of dolphin called bottlenose dolphins have **(0)** .... an interesting discovery. Individual dolphins in the group the scientists studied each have their own name, **(1)** .... of a series of whistles. **(2)** .... many animals can copy and learn complicated sequences of sounds, few species are **(3)** .... of associating particular sounds with specific individuals or things. Dolphins use sounds to communicate with one another for a variety of reasons, including **(4)** .... other dolphins to places where food is available and showing how friendly or aggressive they are feeling.

Dolphins mainly use their names (known as 'signature whistles') when they are travelling, to **(5)** .... other dolphins in their group know where they are. And when a group of dolphins **(6)** .... across another group while out at sea, they appear to use them as a **(7)** .... of greeting each other, exchanging information about who is present before the groups join. Mothers and their young also use the whistles if they get **(8)** ....

1	**A** containing	**B** including	**C** consisting	**D** involving
2	**A** However	**B** Although	**C** Despite	**D** Even
3	**A** competent	**B** talented	**C** skilled	**D** capable
4	**A** indicating	**B** leading	**C** signalling	**D** heading
5	**A** allow	**B** permit	**C** let	**D** cause
6	**A** goes	**B** puts	**C** gets	**D** comes
7	**A** manner	**B** form	**C** means	**D** process
8	**A** split	**B** divided	**C** separated	**D** detached

For questions **9–16**, read the text below and think of the word which best fits each gap. Use only **one** word in each gap. There is an example at the beginning (**0**).

Write your answers **IN CAPITAL LETTERS on the separate answer sheet**.

Example: | **0** | Y | O | U | R | | | | | | | | | | | | | |

International pillow fight day

Do you think that pillows are just things you rest **(0)** .... head on at night? It may or may not come **(9)** .... a surprise to you to hear that for several years now, in parks and squares around the world, large groups of people **(10)** .... been meeting on the same day to take part **(11)** .... a massive pillow fight. To make sure everyone stays safe, the rules are that people should use soft pillows and never hit anyone too hard, **(12)** .... should they swing their pillows at anyone with a camera, or anyone not carrying a pillow themselves.

At some pillow-fighting events the organisers ask participants not **(13)** .... use any pillows stuffed **(14)** .... feathers, because they make too much mess. Groups of volunteers usually help clear up after the fight, and the pillows **(15)** .... often donated to charities that help homeless people. And why **(16)** .... so many people take part? Well, it really is just for fun!

For questions **17-24**, read the text below. Use the word given in capitals at the end of some of the lines to form a word that fits in the gap **in the same line**. There is an example at the beginning (**0**).

Write your answers **IN CAPITAL LETTERS on the separate answer sheet**.

Example: | 0 | H | E | A | L | T | H | Y | | | | | | | | | | |

What happens to the body in space?

Human beings will only be able to explore space if astronauts remain **(0)** .... HEALTH

while they travel and work there. Scientists are therefore very **(17)** .... in INTEREST

gathering **(18)** .... about what happens to the human body in space. EVIDENT

The body is a complex system that **(19)** .... detects changes in its AUTOMATIC

(20) .... and responds to them. When astronauts become SURROUND

weightless, the **(21)** .... of them suffer from space motion sickness. MAJOR

The body soon adapts, however and, although some astronauts can feel

very **(22)** .... at first, the effects do not usually last long. COMFORT

In zero gravity, liquids in the body move towards the head, so astronauts have

thinner legs while in space, and slightly swollen faces. The heart has to work

less hard to pump blood, and astronauts do not need the full **(23)** .... of their STRONG

skeleton and muscles to support them. **(24)** ...., astronauts need to do CONSEQUENCE

plenty of exercise in space in order to maintain body tone and bone density.

For questions **25–30**, complete the second sentence so that it has a similar meaning to the first sentence, using the word given. **Do not change the word given.** You must use between **two** and **five** words, including the word given. Here is an example (**0**).

Example:

0   Karen didn't really want to go to the party.

FORWARD

Karen wasn't really .... to the party.

The gap can be filled by the words 'looking forward to going', so you write:

Example:	**0**	*LOOKING FORWARD TO GOING*

---

25   Daisy regretted eating so much cake.
WISH
'I .... so much cake,' said Daisy.

26   Luis managed to fix the bicycle on his own.
SUCCEEDED
Luis .... the bicycle on his own.

27   Bring your swimming things because it might be warm enough to go swimming.
CASE
Bring your swimming things .... warm enough to go swimming.

28   Our teacher said we should use the information available on the Internet.
ADVANTAGE
Our teacher advised us .... the information available on the Internet.

29   When Anne got back from holiday, I called her immediately.
SOON
I called Anne .... back from holiday.

30   My brother's trainers cost a lot less than mine.
FAR
My brother's trainers .... expensive than mine.

You are going to read an extract from a book about an American teenage girl who has moved to a new town. For questions **31–36**, choose the answer (**A**, **B**, **C** or **D**) which you think fits best according to the text.

Mark your answers **on the separate answer sheet**.

We used to live in New York City, in this great old building on the Upper West Side, but last year my mother moved us to a ranch house in the quiet sleepy suburb of Dellwood (or as I affectionately call it, Deadwood), New Jersey. New Jersey! At first I thought she must be joking.

But I have a positive nature. I believe in making the best of even the worst situation. I mean, you have to, don't you? There's no point being negative about things you can't change, you only make them worse. And the upside of moving to Deadwood was that it gave me a chance to re-create myself a little. Back in the city at least half the kids I went to school with were kids I'd gone to school with most of my life. Dellwood, however, was an empty stage as far as I was concerned. An empty stage to which I was allowed to bring my own script. I could choose whatever role I wanted – be whatever I wanted to be – and no one would know any better. A legend was about to be born.

I think it's safe to say that no one at Deadwood High School had ever seen anyone quite like me. And this, of course, was to my advantage. They didn't know what to expect. My first few weeks were devoted to showing them what to expect: the unexpected; the unusual; the individual; the unique. One week I'd dress only in black; the next my colors would be vibrant and bright. One week I'd be quiet and remote; the next I'd be gregarious and funny. It was a demanding part, but it took my mind off other things. Like how difficult it was to be a beacon in the subterranean, wind-swept and coal-black abyss that is Dellwood, New Jersey.

I'd pretty much thought that all I had to do was appear on campus like an incredible sunset after a grey, dreary day, and the starving young souls of Dellwood would immediately abandon their videos and glossy magazines, and flock to me, begging for shelter from the storm of meaningless trivia that made up their lives. But I was wrong. The youth of _line 18_ Dellwood probably wouldn't have noticed a huge storm, never mind a messenger of hope from the greater world. In my first year in the clean air and safe streets of Dellwood (two of my mother's reasons for moving), I've met only one truly kindred spirit. That's my best friend, Ella Gerard.

There was nothing about Ella to suggest that here was my spiritual kin the first time I saw her. She looked like most of the other girls – expensively if dully clothed, well fed, perfectly groomed, their teeth gleaming and their hair bouncing because they use the right toothpaste and shampoo. The girls in Deadwood get their fashion ideas from teenage magazines and television. They don't wear clothes as a statement of their inner selves, as I do; they wear labels.

If New York is a kettle of soup, where tons of different spices and vegetables swim around together, all part of the whole but all different at the same time, then Deadwood is more like a glass of homogenized milk. Ella was wearing a nondescript pink A-line dress and white-and-pink sneakers. Although Ella shops in the same stores as most of her classmates she always goes for what Mrs Gerard calls 'the classic look', which means that everyone else dresses like the dedicated followers of fashion that they are, and Ella dresses like her mother.

Anyway, Ella sat near me in my first class. The kids in Dellwood not only dress the same and talk the same; when they think, they pretty much think the same, too. But I sensed almost immediately that even though she looked like them, Ella was different in that last, crucial respect.

line 33

31 What point is the writer making about Dellwood in the second paragraph?

A Very little of interest is going on there.
B She'll be able to make a fresh start there.
C She doesn't expect to make new friends there.
D Few people from New York have ever been there.

32 During her first few weeks at Deadwood High School the writer

A tried to control her unpredictable moods.
B imitated the different styles of the students there.
C devoted time and effort to making an impression.
D worried that she might never fit in with the other students.

33 Why does the writer say 'I was wrong' in line 18?

A The other students ignored her.
B She managed to make a friend.
C The weather failed to affect people in Dellwood.
D She realised that Dellwood was a pleasant place to live.

34 According to the writer, the clothes worn by the other girls in Dellwood reflect

A how good their taste is.
B a desire for wealth.
C their individuality.
D current trends.

35 What does the writer say about Ella in the sixth paragraph?

A Her appearance demonstrates her independence.
B She has been advised to dress in a particular way.
C She looks old-fashioned compared to people her age.
D Her mother would like her to learn from her classmates.

36 'that last, crucial respect' in line 33 refers to the way kids in Dellwood

A dress.
B talk.
C think.
D look.

You are going to read an article about ice cream produced in an environmentally friendly way. Six sentences have been removed from the article. Choose from the sentences **A–G** the one which fits each gap (**37–42**). There is one extra sentence which you do not need to use.

Mark your answers **on the separate answer sheet**.

Selling ice cream – made by pedalling a bicycle!

It may seem too simple, or too comical, but Ed Belden did just that when he started a bike-powered ice cream shop in Los Angeles, in the US, a city more often known for its car culture. Belden's shop, Peddler's Creamery, is the first of its kind in Los Angeles. The store opened on the same day as a quarterly bike event called Ciclavia that transforms many of the city's streets into car-free spaces. The Ciclavia route went by Belden's storefront and he sold out of all nine flavors by the day's end.

Belden had first started selling bike-powered ice cream from a specially adapted tricycle at events around Los Angeles. **37** ____ Belden created special flavours, such as Mexican chocolate, salted caramel, and mint chocolate cookie. For every four miles, or about 20 minutes of cycling, he could make 23 liters of ice cream.

Belden soon decided he wanted his own shop, a place where people could come to him. He believed a bike-powered ice cream shop would perfectly suit many people's commitment to trying to do something to protect the environment in Los Angeles. **38** ____ Indeed, events like Ciclavia are becoming more popular and the city is establishing miles of new bike lanes.

Belden saw central Los Angeles as the perfect site for his new venture. **39** ____ It represents the revitalisation that is happening in city centres across the US as many Americans seek more environmentally friendly lifestyles.

At first, Belden wanted to open a shop in a historic building. He eventually chose a new apartment building that contains both reasonably priced housing and artists' studios. **40** ____ He considered it a good fit for

his own vision of sustainability. Belden can be spotted at the shop in the evenings after a full day of work at the National Forest Foundation, another green business. The shop is a labour of love for him. It is supported by the generosity of investors (friends, family, people who invest in environmental businesses) and his own savings.

The evening is also the liveliest time to visit the shop. That's when residents come in for a scoop after dinner. Random onlookers also poke their heads in after seeing the bike contraption in the window. Once a lone salesman pedalling his bike, Belden now has six employees. Employees and customers alike take turns at the wheel. **41** ____

For Belden, this isn't just a novelty food fad, but a calling. He obviously believes in using the renewable resource of human-powered energy. But he also believes in sourcing organic ingredients and using compostable cups and spoons. **42** ____ Even if people were drawn in by the wheels, they return for the simple pleasure of a smooth, slightly sweet scoop of tasty ice cream.

A That's because this area is unusual compared to the rest of the city, as many residents don't own cars.

B That didn't mean they'd accept anything that didn't actually taste delicious.

C Pedalling its wheels turned the stainless steel ice cream maker attached to the back of the bike.

D However, you must be prepared to bike for 20 minutes straight to maintain the quality and consistency of the ice cream.

E For Belden, this social mission was more important than architectural style.

F And of course, he insists on producing a quality product.

G This is increasingly evident in the way cars are having to share the road with cyclists.

You are going to read an article giving advice to teenagers about making films. For questions **43–52**, choose from the sections (**A–F**). The sections may be chosen more than once.

Mark your answers **on the separate answer sheet**.

In which section does the writer

warn that a failure to do something produces noticeably poor results?	**43**	
suggest an alternative to something that people may not be able to afford?	**44**	
mention that people may end up regretting a decision?	**45**	
advise people to think about what they are doing in a different way?	**46**	
encourage people to base their films on the things around them?	**47**	
recommend how filmmakers can get feedback on their work?	**48**	
say people should never stop developing their film-making abilities?	**49**	
say that making mistakes is necessary in order to improve?	**50**	
describe how to learn from what other people have done?	**51**	
say what can make up for a film's weaknesses?	**52**	

Tips for young filmmakers

A

Lots of teenagers are making films these days. Here's some advice if you're thinking of doing so too. First of all, work with what you've got. Don't write that epic crowd scene unless you know there's a festival happening next week that you can steal as a backdrop. Play to your strengths. There's probably something unique that you or your family have access to that you can use in your movie. If your dad has a tractor, write a movie about that. If he doesn't, *don't*.

B

A lot of the mistakes that young filmmakers make could be avoided if teenagers actually just paid attention to their favourite films. Pick a movie you love and watch it with the sound down; look closely at the camera angles, the editing and the lighting. Watch short films on the Internet and see how an effective story can be told in five minutes. You won't be able to match the production values of these films—and you don't need to, anyway—but often the craft of good filmmaking doesn't cost any money. You just have to actually *watch films*.

C

Every film you make should teach you something you didn't know before, and achieve something you didn't know you were capable of. This doesn't mean you have to go out every time and do something that you have no idea how to do. You should draw on the skills and techniques you've already learned—but if you're not building on them, if you're not pushing yourself further in some way, you're playing it safe. It will show and you may eventually regret staying in your comfort zone in this way.

D

Showing your film to an audience is one of the most important ways of figuring out what you're doing right or wrong as a filmmaker—but that isn't the same as saying that you always have to try to please the audience, or make a film that you think "they" will like. A lot of the time just seeing your film with other people in the room will help you see it more objectively. And if you're still thinking your film has to be 20 minutes long, just imagine how long that 20 minutes is going to feel when 300 people are sitting beside you watching it…

E

Audiences will forgive a lot of technical flaws in your film if your story is compelling, your actors are engaging or your jokes are funny—but there's still a point where the technical mistakes start to get in the way. That point is usually when they're no longer able to clearly see, hear or follow what's going on. So get to know your equipment, and practise with it. Learn the basics of shot composition. Do your best to record quality sound and, if that's too expensive, make a silent movie—there's too much talking in most movies anyway.

F

The limitations of teenage filmmaking can often be discouraging. How on earth are you supposed to make a great film when all you've got is this rubbish camera and your silly friends? Well, the first step is to change your attitude. In fact, you should be celebrating the fact that that's all you've got: that means all your solutions to the problems you encounter are going to have to be *creative* ones. And whatever you do, don't give up. If you haven't failed at filmmaking yet, then you probably weren't being ambitious enough. If you have, congratulations; you're on your way to becoming a great filmmaker.

You **must** answer this question. Write your answer in **140–190** words in an appropriate style **on the separate answer sheet**.

1   In your English class you have been talking about technology. Now your English teacher has asked you to write an essay for homework.

Write your essay using **all** the notes and giving reasons for your point of view.

It's always better to chat with friends and family face to face rather than online.

Do you agree?

Notes

Write about:

1. what time of day it is

2. what the conversation is about

3. .... (your own idea)

Write an answer to **one** of the questions 2–5 in this part. Write your answer in **140–190** words in an appropriate style **on the separate answer sheet**. Put the question number in the box at the top of the answer sheet.

---

2 You have seen this announcement on an English-language website for young people.

> We are looking for stories for our website. Your story must **begin** with this sentence:
>
> *Laura realised the girl's bag was still on the café chair.*
>
> Your story must include:
>
> • a bus
>
> • a surprise

Write your **story**.

3 You have received this letter from a classmate.

> Hi everybody,
>
> As you know, our English teacher, Ms Daniels, is leaving. How about organising a party to say goodbye to her? I'm sure our teachers will help! Have you got any ideas about what we can do at the party and how we can prepare for it? Also, what sort of present could we give her?
>
> Thanks for your help,
>
> Chris

Write your **letter**.

4 You see this announcement in an English-language magazine.

> *Articles wanted!* **Sport and exercise**
>
> Do you like sport? Why / Why not?
>
> What do you think is the best way of getting enough exercise?
>
> Are there any sports you like to watch rather than play?
>
> The best articles will be published in our magazine.

Write your **article**.

5 Answer the following question based on the set text.

You have been talking about the set text in class. Now your teacher wants you to write an essay answering the following question.

Do you think the story ended well for the main characters in the set text? Why / Why not? Do you think it was a good ending for the book?

Write your **essay**.

05 You will hear people talking in eight different situations. For questions **1–8**, choose the best answer (**A, B** or **C**).

1   You hear a brother and sister talking about their aunt.
    What do they agree about?

    A   She makes time to chat to them.

    B   She gives them helpful advice.

    C   She shares their taste in music.

2   You hear a teenager talking about a sports centre.
    What does she think of it?
    A   It is not big enough.
    B   It needs modernising.
    C   It is usually too noisy.

3   You hear a brother and sister talking about a meal their father cooked.
    What does the girl say about it?
    A   She would like to be able to cook as well as their father.
    B   She wishes their father would cook more varied meals.
    C   She will make an effort to help their father cook in future.

4   You hear a mother talking to her teenage son about a walk he is going on.
    What is she doing?
    A   warning him against taking a particular route
    B   reminding him to take appropriate clothes with him
    C   advising him to check the weather forecast

5   You hear two friends talking about their art class.
    Why is the boy feeling anxious?
    A   He is not sure the teacher will like his painting.
    B   He has not managed to complete his homework.
    C   He cannot find a picture he has been working on.

6   You hear a woman talking on the radio about a TV programme.
    What kind of programme is it?
    A   a nature documentary
    B   a comedy programme
    C   a reality TV show

7   You hear a brother and sister talking about a holiday.
    What did the girl think of it?
    A   She liked the campsite they stayed in.
    B   It was more fun than she had expected.
    C   The journey there was rather boring.

8   You hear someone talking about a concert he has just played in.
    How does he feel now?
    A   relieved not to have made any mistakes
    B   excited about his next performance
    C   glad the audience was so large

06 You will hear a teenager called Tim Jones talking to students at a secondary school about a shop he helped set up when he was 15. For questions **9–18**, complete the sentences with a word or short phrase.

Setting up shop

Tim started to work in a shop owned by his **(9)** ....

Tim's **(10)** .... teacher gave him the idea for what to sell.

Tim's school friends helped him to make a **(11)** .... for the shop.

Tim advertised the shop by giving out **(12)** .... in the street.

One of Tim's first customers talked about the shop in a **(13)** .... interview about shopping in Tim's town.

Tim was amazed when a famous **(14)** .... player came into the shop.

Tim realised he could sell his **(15)** .... in the shop as well as pottery.

Tim was asked to design a **(16)** .... for the local jazz band.

Tim's parents think he should become a **(17)** .... in the future.

Tim likes to play **(18)** .... with his friends when he's not busy working.

07 You will hear five short extracts in which teenagers talk about clothes. For questions **19–23**, choose from the list (**A–H**) what each speaker says about what is important to them about the clothes they wear. Use the letters only once. There are three extra letters which you do not need to use.

A   I want to express my personality.

B   I want to wear clothes that match.   Speaker 1   [   ] **19**

C   I want to wear comfortable clothes.   Speaker 2   [   ] **20**

D   I want to spend as little as possible.   Speaker 3   [   ] **21**

E   I want to please my family.   Speaker 4   [   ] **22**

F   I want to wear a certain type of material.

G   I want to be fashionable.   Speaker 5   [   ] **23**

H   I want to look like my friends.

(2 08) You will hear a radio interview with a teenager called Tom Dean, who writes a cookery blog for teenagers. For questions **24–30**, choose the best answer (**A, B** or **C**).

24   Tom's interest in cooking began when
   A   he attended cookery lessons at his school.
   B   he helped his mother in the kitchen as a small child.
   C   he watched some programmes about it on television.

25   What does Tom say about his diet?
   A   He used to avoid food that was good for him.
   B   He eats more healthily nowadays.
   C   He wishes he could choose what he wants to eat.

26   What do Tom's brother and sister think about the food he makes?
   A   Some of Tom's dishes take too long to prepare.
   B   Tom should make some of his meals more tasty.
   C   They are surprised that other people like his recipes.

27   Tom says his family help him by
   A   doing the washing up.
   B   writing down his ideas.
   C   checking he has the right ingredients.

28   Why did Tom decide to write a cookery blog?
   A   He wanted something to do in his free time.
   B   He thought it was the best way of sharing his recipes.
   C   He realised there was nothing similar available online.

29   What has writing the blog taught Tom?
   A   how to write in an appropriate style
   B   that it is hard to keep on inventing new recipes
   C   why people all over the world like reading about food

30   Tom says he hopes to
   A   work as a chef.
   B   write a recipe book.
   C   open his own cookery school.

Part 1 2 minutes [3 minutes for groups of three]

First we'd like to know something about you.

Holidays

- What do you like to do during the holidays? (Why?)
- Who do you usually spend your holidays with? What do you do together?
- Do you ever go away on holiday? (Where do you go?)
- What's the best / most exciting holiday you have ever had?
- Tell us about somewhere special you'd like to visit on holiday.

Part 2 4 minutes [6 minutes for groups of three]

Interlocutor In this part of the test, I'm going to give each of you two photographs. I'd like you to talk about your photographs on your own for about a minute, and also to answer a question about your partner's photographs.

(*Candidate A*), it's your turn first. Here are your photographs on page C16 of the Speaking appendix. They show **people doing things with their friends**. I'd like you to compare the photographs, and say **why you think the friends have decided to do these things together**.

All right?

Candidate A
🕐 *1 minute* ....

Interlocutor Thank you.

(*Candidate B*), **which group of people would you prefer to be in? (Why?)**

Candidate B
🕐 *Approximately 30 seconds* ....

Interlocutor Thank you.

Now, (*Candidate B*), here are your photographs on page C17 of the Speaking appendix. They show **people exercising in different ways**.

I'd like you to compare the photographs, and say **why you think the people have chosen to exercise in these ways**.

All right?

Candidate B
🕐 *1 minute* ....

Interlocutor Thank you.

(*Candidate A*), **which way of exercising do you think needs the most skill? (Why?)**

Candidate A
🕐 *Approximately 30 seconds* ....

Interlocutor Thank you.

Part 3 4 minutes [5 minutes for groups of three]

Interlocutor Now, I'd like you to talk about something together for about two minutes.

I'd like you to imagine that a school wants students to learn more about the environment. Here are some ideas the school could use and a question for you to discuss. First you have some time to look at the task on page C18 of the Speaking appendix.

Now, talk to each other about **how these ideas might help students to learn more about the environment.**

Candidates

🕐 *2 minutes (3 minutes for groups of three)*

Interlocutor Thank you. Now you have about a minute to decide **which two ideas would be the most successful.**

Candidates

🕐 *1 minute (for pairs and groups of three)*

Interlocutor Thank you.

Part 4 4 minutes [6 minutes for groups of three]

Interlocutor

- What do you think people can do in the future to reduce pollution in your neighbourhood?

- Is it important to look after the environment? (Why? / Why not?)

- How can students take care of the environment?

- Do you think that older people are more interested in protecting the environment than teenagers? (Why? / Why not?)

- Should the government make recycling compulsory for everybody? (Why? / Why not?)

- Have you and your friends done anything to help the environment recently? (What was it?)

> **What do you think?**
> **Do you agree?**
> **And you?**

Thank you. That is the end of the test.

For questions **1–8**, read the text below and decide which answer (**A**, **B**, **C** or **D**) best fits each gap. There is an example at the beginning (**0**).

Mark your answers **on the separate answer sheet**.

Example:

0   **A**   hold   **B**   stand   **C**   stay   **D**   exist

0	A	B	C	D
	⬜	⬜	⬛	⬜

How frogs survive the cold

Not many creatures can **(0)** .... alive in the freezing cold of the far north. However, there are a number of creatures which **(1)** .... to survive in places where the temperatures can fall as **(2)** .... as minus 28 degrees.

One of the most **(3)** .... of these creatures is the Alaskan wood frog. When it gets **(4)** .... cold in the winter months, up to two thirds of the water in the frog's body actually freezes. But once the days begin to **(5)** .... slightly warmer in spring, the frogs thaw out again.

Scientists have long been trying to discover the process that makes this rebirth **(6)** .... and now they have discovered how it is done. The frogs produce a chemical in their body that resembles the antifreeze that people use to **(7)** .... their cars from freezing. This chemical in the frog's body **(8)** .... in a very similar way in order to protect its most important organs.

1   **A**   succeed   **B**   manage   **C**   enable   **D**   achieve

2   **A**   deep   **B**   hard   **C**   low   **D**   far

3   **A**   noticeable   **B**   remarkable   **C**   observable   **D**   credible

4   **A**   harshly   **B**   utterly   **C**   absolutely   **D**   bitterly

5   **A**   turn   **B**   come   **C**   move   **D**   set

6   **A**   available   **B**   probable   **C**   capable   **D**   possible

7   **A**   prevent   **B**   halt   **C**   avoid   **D**   block

8   **A**   goes   **B**   takes   **C**   works   **D**   does

For questions **9–16**, read the text below and think of the word which best fits each gap. Use only one word in each gap. There is an example at the beginning (**0**).

Write your answers **IN CAPITAL LETTERS** on the separate answer sheet.

Example: | **0** | T | O | | | | | | | | | | | | | | | | | |

World Pea Shooting Championships

Did you know that something naughty schoolchildren used to do is now a competitive sport? In the annual Cambridgeshire World Pea Shooting Championships, competitors have **(0)** .... blow a dried pea through a small tube called a blowpipe. They aim at a round target 3.5m away. The contest was first organised in 1971 by a teacher called John Tyson **(9)** .... had taken several blowpipes away **(10)** .... his pupils when they had used them at school. Now competitors come from all over the world to take **(11)** .... in the championships.

The pea is always supplied by the organisers to make **(12)** .... nobody cheats, but the tubes can be made of any material provided they are 30 cm long. Traditionally the tubes have **(13)** .... made of wood or plastic, but some people use other materials **(14)** .... carbon fibre. Even **(15)** .... some adults bring complicated equipment like lasers to focus on the target, they are regularly beaten by kids years younger than **(16)** .... using simple plastic tubes.

For questions **17–24**, read the text below. Use the word given in capitals at the end of some of the lines to form a word that fits in the gap **in the same line**. There is an example at the beginning (**0**).

Write your answers **IN CAPITAL LETTERS on the separate answer sheet**.

Example: | 0 | M O N A R C H Y

Jersey

Jersey is one of a group of islands, known as the Channel Islands, lying not
far from the coast of France. Politically it is a **(0)** .... ruled by   **MONARCH**
the king or queen of Britain but it is not part of the United Kingdom or of the
European Union. However, it does have a special **(17)** .... with   **RELATION**
both. The UK, for example, is responsible for the **(18)** .... of   **DEFEND**
Jersey. However, the island has its own parliament which is able to deal
(19) .... with other aspects of the country's administration.   **DEPEND**

From an **(20)** .... point of view the country is considered part of   **ECONOMY**
the European Community which gives it **(21)** .... trading rights.   **ADVANTAGE**
For instance, the free **(22)** .... of goods between countries in this   **MOVE**
Community is permitted.

Jersey is a beautiful island which enjoys great **(23)** .... with   **POPULAR**
tourists. The fact that it is a relatively **(24)** .... destination is one   **EXPENSE**
of the things that attracts them.

For questions **25–30**, complete the second sentence so that it has a similar meaning to the first sentence, using the word given. **Do not change the word given.** You must use between **two** and **five** words, including the word given. Here is an example (**0**).

Example:

0   Karen didn't really want to go to the party.

     FORWARD

     Karen wasn't really .... to the party.

The gap can be filled by the words 'looking forward to going', so you write:

Example: | **0** | LOOKING FORWARD TO GOING |

---

25   Katy's parents allowed her to go swimming on her own.
     LET
     Katy's parents .... herself.

26   Paul now regrets spending so much time skateboarding.
     WISHES
     Paul now .... time skateboarding.

27   It's possible that Sally took your jacket home.
     MAY
     Sally .... your jacket home.

28   Most people think that the climate is changing.
     GENERALLY
     The climate .... changing.

29   The film probably won't last more than two hours.
     UNLIKELY
     The film .... on for more than two hours.

30   Dina has a talent for looking after young children.
     CARE
     Dina is very good .... young children.

You are going to read an extract from an account of a journey that a group of Norwegian explorers made across the Pacific Ocean on a raft (a very simple boat) called the Kon-Tiki. For questions **31–36**, choose the answer (**A**, **B**, **C** or **D**) which you think fits best according to the text.

Mark your answers **on the separate answer sheet**.

Once in a while you find yourself in an odd situation. You get into it by degrees and in the most natural way but, when you are right in the midst of it, you are suddenly astonished and ask yourself how in the world it all came about.

If, for example, you put to sea on a wooden raft with a parrot and five companions, it is inevitable that sooner or later you will wake up one morning out at sea, perhaps a little better rested than ordinarily, and begin to think about it.

On one such morning, I sat writing in a dew-drenched logbook: – *May 17. Norwegian Independence Day. Heavy sea. Fair wind. I am cook today and found seven flying fish on deck, one squid on the cabin roof and one unknown fish in Torstein's sleeping bag. . . .*

Here the pencil stopped, and the same thought interjected itself: This is really a strange seventeenth of May – indeed, taken all round, a most peculiar existence. How did it all begin?

If I turned left, I had an unimpeded view of a vast blue sea with hissing waves, rolling by close at hand in an endless pursuit of an ever retreating horizon. If I turned right, I saw the inside of a shadowy cabin in which a bearded individual was lying on his back reading, with his bare toes carefully dug into the latticework in the low bamboo roof of the crazy little cabin that was our common home. Outside the cabin three other fellows were working in the roasting sun on the bamboo deck, looking as if they had never done anything else than float wooden rafts westward across the Pacific. Erik came crawling in through the opening with his instruments and a pile of papers.

'98° 46' west by 8° 2' south – a good day's run since yesterday, chaps!'

He took my pencil and drew a tiny circle on a chart which hung on the bamboo wall – a tiny circle at the end of a row of nineteen circles that curved across from the coast of Peru. Herman, Knut and Torstein too came eagerly crowding in to see the new little circle that placed us a good 40 sea miles nearer the South Sea islands than the last in the chain.

line 41

'Do you see, boys?' said Herman proudly. 'That means we're 850 miles from the coast of Peru.'

'And we've got another 3,500 to go to get to the nearest islands,' Knut added cautiously.

So now we all knew exactly where we were, and I could go on speculating. The parrot did not care; he only wanted to tug at the log. And the sea was just as round, just as sky-encircled, blue upon blue.

Perhaps it had all begun ten years earlier, on a little island in the Marquesas group in the middle of the Pacific. Maybe we would land on the same island now, unless the northeast wind sent us farther south in the direction of Tahiti and the Tuamotu group. The island was called Fatu Hiva; there was no land between it and us where we lay drifting, but nevertheless it was thousands of sea miles away. I could see the little island clearly in my mind's eye, with its jagged, rust-red mountains, the green jungle which flowed down their slopes toward the sea, and the slender palms that waved along the shore. I remembered so well how we sat there on the lonely beach and looked out over this same endless sea, evening after evening. I was accompanied by my wife then, not by bearded pirates as now. We were collecting all kinds of live creatures, and images and other relics of a dead culture.

31 How does the writer suggest he is feeling in the first paragraph?

A regretful
B puzzled
C amused
D shocked

32 What does 'it' refer to at the end of the second paragraph?

A the morning at sea
B the writer's previous night's rest
C the explanation for being in this situation
D the reason for the parrot being on the raft

33 Why does the writer stop writing the logbook?

A He realises the date which sparks off a train of thought.
B The noise of the sea takes his mind off the task.
C He knows it is time to begin preparing dinner.
D He is distracted by the people around him.

34 What does the word 'chain' refer to in line 41?

A a ring of islands in the Pacific
B the group of people on the raft
C a line of marks indicating the raft's progress
D a row of charts along the bamboo wall of the cabin

35 What does the extract say about the location of Fatu Hiva?

A There are no other islands separating it from the raft.
B It is in the middle of the Marquesas group of islands.
C The men on the raft hope it is where they will land.
D It is thousands of sea miles from the Tahiti islands.

36 Why had the writer and his wife previously spent time on a Pacific island?

A They went to the island to take photographs for a book.
B They were painting pictures of the island.
C They enjoyed a holiday on the island's beaches.
D They were gathering information about the island.

You are going to read a magazine article about a teenager who has completed an unusual swim. Six sentences have been removed from the article. Choose from the sentences **A-G** the one which fits each gap (**37–42**). There is one extra sentence which you do not need to use.

Mark your answers **on the separate answer sheet**.

The Isle of Wight is a large island – about 380 square kilometres – off the south coast of Britain. You need to be an extraordinarily strong swimmer to swim round the island as it means covering a distance of over 110 kilometres. Yet this feat has just been completed by a nineteen-year-old woman called Nell O'Connor.

Nell became one of the few people to have ever swum solo, non-stop, around the Isle of Wight – a notable feat for a couple of reasons. **37**

The swimmer was welcomed by a large crowd as she touched Ryde Pier, the point where she set off last Friday at 10.31am. The ferry that leaves the island for the mainland every hour had even delayed its departure to let passengers watch her arrival. Hundreds of people were waiting on deck as well as on shore. **38** She was officially congratulated by Brian Merriman on behalf of the European Swimming Association. He is no stranger to long-distance swimming himself as he has swum across the English Channel on several occasions.

Before setting off Nell had said that she was well aware that she was attempting a very challenging task, particularly because she could not avoid occasionally having to swim against the tide. **39** She saw

sunset and sunrise and had to race against the clock to reach critical points to beat the time. Indeed, she frequently felt as if she was spending hours swimming on the spot.

40 A decision then to head inshore allowed her less tide to swim against and within an hour she was making forward progress again.

Speaking to reporters after the swim, Nell said that knowing people were thinking of her and willing her on definitely helped when the going got really tough. Her reason for doing the swim also spurred her on. **41**

The swim was carried out under the generally accepted rules of the sport wearing just a standard swimming costume, goggles and a swimming cap. It was the culmination of the three-year Seven Island Swim Challenge which Nell had set herself. She had already successfully completed circumnavigations of five other islands. **42** This happened because strong winds combined with bitterly cold water to force her to give up on her attempt to swim round Foula, one of the Shetland Islands, in the far north of the British Isles.

A She was doing the challenge to raise money for a number of charities.

B And she was right to expect it to be tough.

C As is the rule on such swims, Nell was accompanied by a team on a range of craft.

D Not only was she one of the youngest people ever to complete the swim, but she also did it in only 26 hours, 37 minutes and 45 seconds, arriving more than three hours ahead of schedule.

E But she had to abandon her next challenge after doing 32 kilometres of a 48-kilometre swim on August 13 this year.

F They all applauded her achievement and, after being helped out of the water, she shouted a big thank you to everyone.

G One of the toughest points of the swim was as she approached St Catherine's Point, when the current pushed her back more than a kilometre.

You are going to read some reviews of theme parks. For questions **43–52** choose from reviews (**A–E**). The reviews may be chosen more than once.

Mark your answers **on the separate answer sheet**.

Which of the theme parks

is praised for being situated in a fitting place?	43	
has developed from something that was part of a major event?	44	
has made good use of a former industrial site?	45	
is noteworthy for the opportunities it offers for sport?	46	
was built in a style to match its theme?	47	
frequently hosts impressive musical performances?	48	
has potentially inconvenient opening times?	49	
has an exciting ride that holds a record for its size?	50	
has an attraction that is operated in a traditional way?	51	
is most likely to appeal to one age group?	52	

A Southern Fun Park

Southern Fun Park is a brilliant theme park on the south coast and is situated close to the popular resort of Telton. Perhaps its one drawback is that, unlike the larger parks on the north coast, it operates seasonally. Included in its attraction line-up are a single small rollercoaster, a selection of off-the-shelf thrill rides, and a variety of water slides. The park first opened to the public in 1979, when it was known as Crossman's Fun Park. It was constructed on what was once a limestone quarry, with the area being effectively re-landscaped to include a number of lakes. A total of 420,000 tonnes of sand were used to create its attractive new look.

B Air World

The aircraft-themed Air World is one of the world's largest indoor theme parks, and is located inside a sprawling, 180,000 square metre structure. The building is impressive in that it's designed to resemble the side profile of the body of a jumbo jet, and features models of three historic planes on its roof. The park is home to a variety of breathtaking thrill rides and family attractions, including the world's fastest rollercoaster, Concorde Cascade. Air World opened in November, 2013, and has an appropriate location close to the country's first-ever airstrip. It offers a range of restaurant facilities to suit all pockets and has quickly become a popular destination for a day out.

C Sunlands

The second-largest theme park in the entire country, Sunlands, is now a member of the largest international chain of theme parks. Located on the edge of the capital, it hosts an array of thrilling rollercoasters and flat rides. The park's headline attractions are Titan (once the tallest coaster in the country), Pluto (the world's tallest dual-track wooden coaster) and Dracula (an inverted coaster). Look out, though, for the older but no less enjoyable rides such as the Merry Rider and the Monorail transportation system. Sunlands

opened in June 1962 as the midway area of the capital's extravagant 'Centenary Exhibition', and was intended to be its lasting legacy. At that time it featured a number of family-friendly rides with a particular appeal for younger children.

D Adventure Town

One of the most popular theme parks in this country and throughout the world, Adventure Town combines classic amusement park attractions with beautiful landscaping and a huge variety of restaurants. Open all year round, the park's most famous attraction is Rolling Rainbow, one of few wooden coasters remaining that still requires a brakeman to control its speed. Modern offerings include the sixty-metre-tall Mystery Tower drop tower and the borderline-insane Niagara, which sees guests plummeting towards the ground in plane-themed gondolas. Live entertainment is a major part of Adventure Town's appeal, with acts of almost every type appearing regularly. Having first opened in 1884, Adventure Town is one of the ten oldest amusement parks in the world.

E Starry World

Starry World is an attractively unusual space-themed attraction aimed primarily at the under-tens. It has a small but not uninteresting selection of rides and is also popular because it is home to an action centre offering archery, laser shooting and golf. The Terrifying Tornado is the largest rollercoaster in the west of the country, hitting a not unimpressive top speed of 88 kilometres per hour. Bredon Farm, which hosts the park, used to be a dairy farm until its owners decided to transform it into a tourist attraction. Initially it focused purely on farm exhibits, but gradually evolved into something closer to a traditional theme park. The park plans to start hosting musical events next summer.

You **must** answer this question. Write your answer in **140–190** words in an appropriate style **on the separate answer sheet**.

1   In your English class you have been talking about the environment. Now your English teacher has asked you to write an essay for homework.

Write your essay using **all** the notes and giving reasons for your point of view.

Schools should teach students about the importance of protecting the environment by setting a good example. Do you agree?

Notes

Write about:

1. recycling

2. saving energy

3. .... (your own idea)

Write an answer to **one** of the questions 2–5 in this part. Write your answer in **140–190** words in an appropriate style **on the separate answer sheet**. Put the question number in the box at the top of the answer sheet.

---

2   You see this announcement on a website.

> ## Story Competition
>
> Could you write a story for our teenage readers? The story must **begin** with this sentence:
>
> *Feeling very excited, Gina picked up her bag and got on the train.*
>
> Your story must include:
> - some flowers
> - a stranger
>
> The best stories will win a prize and will be published on our website.

Write your **story**.

3   This is part of a letter you have received from your Australian friend, Sam.

> Could you help me with some homework, please? We have to find out about the music young people like in different countries. What kinds of music are most popular with you and your friends? When and how do they listen to it? Do you play music yourself as well as listen to it?

Write your **letter**.

4   You see this announcement in an English-language magazine for young people.

> *Some TV programmes aim to inform rather than just to entertain. Write a review of a TV documentary you have watched recently. Why did you decide to watch it? Would you recommend it to your friends or not? Why?*

Write your **review**.

5   Answer the following question based on the set text.

Your English class has had a discussion about the set text. Now your teacher has given you this essay for homework:

Explain why you think the title of the text is or is not a good one.

Write your **essay**.

01 You will hear people talking in eight different situations. For questions **1–8**, choose the best answer (**A, B** or **C**).

1   You hear a news item about some teenage scientists.
The girl's discovery could
A   lead to a beneficial use of waste materials.
B   help to encourage more students to study science.
C   reduce the country's dependence on oil.

2   You hear an interviewer introducing a recorded interview with Darren Grey, a young writer.
What did the interviewer find surprising?
A   Darren's adult writing style
B   Darren's other leisure interests
C   Darren's way of speaking

3   You hear a radio interview on a programme for teenagers with a biology teacher.
What does she think the students enjoy about her lessons?
A   her sense of humour
B   the way she uses the Internet
C   doing projects outdoors

4   You hear two friends talking about a concert they have been to.
What most impressed the girl about the singer?
A   the range of her voice
B   her ability to express feeling
C   her interaction with the audience

5   You hear a mother talking to her son about a rugby match.
What problem did her son have?

A   He had difficulty getting to the stadium on time.
B   He forgot to take something he needed with him.
C   He got some basic information about the match wrong.

6   You hear a teacher talking to her class about some coursework.
What would she like the class to focus on?
A   doing a statistical analysis
B   making a detailed comparison
C   reading some information critically

7   You hear two friends talking about their holidays.
On holiday the girl enjoyed
A   swimming in the evening.
B   visiting a place she had seen in a film.
C   eating something she had never tried before.

8   You hear a news item about a wildlife campaign.
What is the aim of the campaign?
A   to learn more about the habits of the butterfly
B   to help conserve various types of butterfly
C   to discover whether butterfly numbers are decreasing

(3 02) You will hear a student called Giorgio telling a class about his project on the spice called cinnamon. For questions **9–18**, complete the sentences with a word or short phrase.

Cinnamon

Cinnamon has been used as a spice for at least **(9)** .... years.

The Roman historian Pliny wrote about cinnamon being imported to Rome in boats that were powered only by

(10) ....

In Roman times a third of a kilo of cinnamon cost the equivalent of wages for

(11) .... of work.

In Roman times cinnamon was added to dishes containing **(12)** ....

In the Middle Ages many people in the West thought that cinnamon came from the

(13) ....

Cinnamon is still used in medicines that treat **(14)** ....

Cinnamon oil is thought to keep **(15)** .... away.

Today **(16)** .... is one of the main countries importing cinnamon.

Giorgio was surprised to learn that people use cinnamon in the preparation of

(17) .... dishes.

Giorgio's favourite use of cinnamon is in **(18)** ....

(3) 03) You will hear five teenagers talking about a special celebration they remember. For questions **19–23**, choose from the list (**A–H**) the opinion each speaker expresses. Use the letters only once. There are three extra letters which you do not need to use.

A   The best thing was being with so many members of my family.

B   Some music I heard then made a strong impression on me.   Speaker 1   [ ] 19

C   I enjoyed helping with the preparations.

Speaker 2   [ ] 20

D   It turned out to be more enjoyable than I had expected.

Speaker 3   [ ] 21

E   An unplanned occurrence changed our plans.

Speaker 4   [ ] 22

F   I kept something special as a memory of the occasion.

G   I regret forgetting to do something.   Speaker 5   [ ] 23

H   I met someone who became very important in my life

3 04 You will hear an interview with a young film actor called Diana Bainbridge who has just starred in a science fiction film. For questions **24–30**, choose the best answer (**A**, **B** or **C**).

24 Diana first became interested in acting because of
   A   a relative's involvement in the profession.
   B   a teacher's enthusiasm and encouragement.
   C   a drama school's convenient location.

25 What led to Diana getting her first major cinema role?
   A   She was recommended by someone who saw her acting.
   B   She saw an announcement about auditions in an acting magazine.
   C   She volunteered as an extra for a crowd scene.

26 What surprised Diana when she was making her first film?
   A   how much time she spent waiting to film her scenes
   B   how helpful and friendly the famous stars were
   C   how hard she found it to ignore the technical equipment

27 What does Diana find difficult about being a film star?
   A   not having as much privacy as she would like
   B   reading critical reviews of her work
   C   not knowing what her next role will be

28 Diana enjoyed her most recent role because
   A   the film was made in several wonderful places.
   B   it gave her the opportunity to learn a new skill.
   C   she appreciated the company of her co-stars.

29 Diana says that in the future she is particularly keen to
   A   play a comic role.
   B   produce a film.
   C   win an award.

30 What does Diana plan to do next?
   A   spend some time relaxing
   B   take a role in a theatre production
   C   teach some schoolchildren about acting

Part 1	2 minutes [3 minutes for groups of 3]

Interlocutor First we'd like to know something about you. Where are you from?

Travel

- Do you prefer travelling by train or by air? (Why?)
- What's your journey to school like every day?
- Who do you most enjoy travelling with?
- What's the most memorable journey you've ever taken? (Why do you remember it so well?)
- Tell us where you'd like to go for your dream holiday.

Part 2	4 minutes [6 minutes for groups of 3]

Interlocutor In this part of the test, I'm going to give each of you two photographs. I'd like you to talk about your photographs on your own for about a minute, and also to answer a question about your partner's photographs.

(*Candidate A*), it's your turn first. Here are your photographs on page C19 of the Speaking appendix. They show **people doing outdoor activities at different times of the year**.

I'd like you to compare the photographs, and say **what you think the people are enjoying about doing these activities**.

All right?

Candidate A
🕐 *1 minute* ....

Interlocutor Thank you.

(*Candidate B*), **which of these activities would you prefer to be part of? (Why?)**

Candidate B
🕐 *Approximately 30 seconds* ....

Interlocutor Thank you.

Now, (*Candidate B*), here are your photographs on page C20 of the Speaking appendix. They show **students studying in different ways**.

I'd like you to compare the photographs, and say **why you think the students are studying in these ways**.

All right?

Candidate B
🕐 *1 minute* ....

Interlocutor Thank you.

(*Candidate A*), **which of these two ways of learning is more useful? (Why?)**

Candidate A
🕐 *Approximately 30 seconds* ....

Interlocutor Thank you.

Part 3   4 minutes [5 minutes for groups of 3]

Interlocutor Now, I'd like you to talk about something together for about two minutes.
I'd like you to imagine that a school would like to organise an end-of-year event for students and parents. Here are some of the ideas for the event and a question for you to discuss. First you have some time to look at the task on page C21 of the Speaking appendix.
Now, talk to each other about **why these ideas would be good for both parents and students.**
Candidates
🕐 *2 minutes (3 minutes for groups of three)*
Interlocutor Thank you. Now you have about a minute to decide on **an end-of-year event that would be enjoyable for both the parents and the students.**
Candidates
🕐 *1 minute (for pairs and groups of three)*
Interlocutor Thank you.

Part 4   4 minutes [6 minutes for groups of 3]

Interlocutor

- What's the most enjoyable school event you've ever been to? (Why was it so good?)

- How important do you think it is for schools to organise after-school activities?

- Do you think it's better for after-school events to be for just one age group or for all ages of student? (Why do you think that?)

- When do you think is the best time of year for schools to organise after-school events? (Why?)

- Some people say schools shouldn't organise extra events for their students, they should just teach lessons. Do you agree?

- Should parents know about everything that happens in lessons at school? (Why? / Why not?)

Thank you. That is the end of the test.

> **What do you think?**
> **Do you agree?**
> **And you?**

For questions **1–8**, read the text below and decide which answer (**A, B, C or D**) best fits each gap. There is an example at the beginning (**0**).

Mark your answers **on the separate answer sheet**.

Example:

| **0** | **A** | engaged | **B** | absorbed | **C** | occupied | **D** | employed |

```
0 | A   B   C   D
  | ▭   ▭   ▬   ▭
```

Young people help society

Young people tend to spend most of their out-of-school hours **(0)** .... with homework and other school commitments. These keep them so busy that they have no time to **(1)** .... for other major projects. But there are some remarkable exceptions to this **(2)** ....

Some use any free time they have to **(3)** .... themselves to environmental issues. Ava Lang, for example, is only 14 but at weekends she goes round restaurants to persuade the owners to **(4)** .... her with their used cooking oil. She then arranges for this to be **(5)** .... into biodiesel.

Another youngster who does a considerable **(6)** .... to help others is Tim Fried. He races go-karts as a **(7)** .... of raising money for charitable causes. In this way he manages to **(8)** .... his love of sport with some socially useful work.

1	**A**	spend	**B**	waste	**C**	pass	**D**	spare
2	**A**	case	**B**	rule	**C**	set	**D**	test
3	**A**	dedicate	**B**	contribute	**C**	reserve	**D**	involve
4	**A**	provide	**B**	offer	**C**	donate	**D**	give
5	**A**	substituted	**B**	adapted	**C**	converted	**D**	exchanged
6	**A**	degree	**B**	extent	**C**	deal	**D**	amount
7	**A**	chance	**B**	kind	**C**	means	**D**	possibility
8	**A**	adjust	**B**	combine	**C**	join	**D**	merge

For questions **9–16**, read the text below and think of the word which best fits each gap. Use only one word in each gap. There is an example at the beginning (**0**).

Write your answers **IN CAPITAL LETTERS on the separate answer sheet**.

Example: | 0 | T | H | E | R | E | | | | | | | | | | | | | | |

Website for tigers

If you are interested in the environment, **(0)** .... is an excellent website called Tigernation. The website was set **(9)** .... to help with the conservation of tigers. It focuses its work particularly on India, a country **(10)** .... many thousands of tigers once lived. There are now thought to **(11)** .... fewer than 2,000 remaining there.

Did you know that a tiger's stripes are like a person's finger prints **(12)** .... the sense that every individual is unique? This makes **(13)** .... possible for the website to track the tigers as it recognises them by the pattern of their stripes. If someone is lucky **(14)** .... to catch sight of a tiger, then they take a picture and upload it to the website. The website is gradually collecting a large quantity of photos, **(15)** .... enables researchers to identify how the animals move from one place to **(16)** .... The hope is that an improved understanding of how tigers live will help us to ensure their survival.

For questions **17–24**, read the text below. Use the word given in capitals at the end of some of the lines to form a word that fits in the gap in the same line. There is an example at the beginning (**0**).

Write your answers **IN CAPITAL LETTERS on the separate answer sheet**.

Example: | 0 | B | A | L | A | N | C | I | N | G | | | | | | | | |

The first bicycle

The first vehicles with two wheels used for transporting people and requiring

riders to develop (**0**) .... skills appeared in Germany in the   **BALANCE**

early 19th century. The design was registered in 1818 and it was the first

(**17**) .... successful vehicle which, although it did not have   **COMMERCE**

pedals and was not called a bicycle, has a clear (**18**) .... to the   **RESEMBLE**

vehicle we know as a bicycle. It was popular for several decades but the

(**19**) .... of accidents resulting from its use led to its eventual   **FREQUENT**

(**20**) .... in some European cities.   **PROHIBIT**

There is some (**21**) .... as to who exactly invented the pedal-   **AGREE**

powered bicycle, but its (**22**) .... began in France in the 1860s.   **PRODUCE**

Designs gradually improved its speed and (**23**) .... then, as road   **SAFE**

surfaces also got better, its use became widespread.

We usually think of the bicycle as just a means of transport but its role in the

emancipation of women should not be (**24**) .... , as it allowed   **ESTIMATE**

them a freedom of movement that they had not previously enjoyed.

For questions **25–30**, complete the second sentence so that it has a similar meaning to the first sentence, using the word given. Do not change the word given. You must use between **two** and **five** words, including the word given. Here is an example (**0**).

Example:

0   Karen didn't really want to go to the party.

FORWARD

Karen wasn't really .... to the party.

The gap can be filled by the words 'looking forward to going', so you write:

Example: | **0** | LOOKING FORWARD TO GOING |

---

25   I can't talk for long as my parents think I'm doing my homework.
SUPPOSED
I can't talk for long as I .... my homework.

26   Mum didn't expect the tickets to be so expensive.
LESS
Mum thought the tickets .... they did.

27   The path down the mountain was so slippery that it was hard for us to stay on our feet.
DIFFICULTY
The path down the mountain was so slippery that .... on our feet.

28   James is the best goalkeeper at the school.
THAN
James is a .... else at our school.

29   Sam is too young to learn to drive.
ENOUGH
Sam isn't .... driving lessons.

30   The teacher said we didn't need to spend too long on the exercise.
WORTH
The teacher told us .... too long on the exercise.

You are going to read a teen magazine article about teenagers and their use of the latest technology. For questions **31–36**, choose the answer (**A, B, C** or **D**) which you think fits best according to the text.

TECHNOLOGY AND US!

by Rowena James

Like me, you've probably read newspaper articles in which adults are talking about the bad effects that technology such as computers and mobiles are having on teenagers like us! In fact, it sometimes seems as if our digital lives are under constant scrutiny from the older generation. According to some adults, our online socialising is creating a culture where everything is very trivial, and we're in danger of losing our social skills completely. Of course, we can probably all think of friends that spend virtually all their time online. But I think we'd also agree those people are in the minority, and that the majority of us have learnt to use technology in a responsible and useful way.

Anyway, our parents would probably admit that any advances in technology, such as the radio or the record player, have always caused concern among parents, because they worry about the harmful effects on young people, and want to protect them. But if the same technology had been available when they were young, they would have used it just as we do now, to socialise and establish independence from *their* parents. Of course, there have been extremely rapid developments since our parents were young – but then every generation says that when they look back, I guess.

One of the main things that teachers worry about is that our over-use of technology is having a bad effect on our education, particularly in our literacy. Teachers say teens are using language that's too casual, like we use in texts, even when we're writing formally, and that the influence of texting is producing far more mistakes in our writing than young people made in the past. However, some researchers say these thoughts are based on what they're calling 'misguided nostalgia'. When they looked back at student composition papers, even a hundred years ago, they found they contained just as many errors as students' work today.

As I said, though, we can all think of someone we know who spends half their lives in front of a computer. But those people might still be gaining benefits from that time. Take my friend Luke, for example. In his early teens he was very keen on one particular TV series, and began to follow a fan page online, which he started spending all his free time on. It wasn't long before he got more involved, and was soon editing other teenage fans' contributions, which he became skilled at. That led to an interest in publishing as a career.

Teachers have also realised the huge potential of technology in their classes, no matter what field they're in. Computer teachers at my school now encourage us to use up-to-the-minute software to get us to explore and develop our own talents – with great results. One guy in my class who wasn't interested in school at all, suddenly discovered he was really good at producing elaborate sketches of buildings around the city. He's now considering training to be an architect – a real turnaround for someone who once hated coming to school.

Of course, much as I hate to admit it, there are downsides to advances such as the Internet. One of them is distraction – flicking onto a favourite website in the middle of doing a homework assignment. You'd have to be pretty skilled to achieve good results by trying to do several things at once in that way. There's also a tendency for teenagers not to question whether the sources of information they get online are actually reliable, and just to take what they find there at face value. And I hardly dare mention the effects on sleep patterns – that's one area where my parents have to step in and set boundaries, otherwise I'd be up all night. But as we mature, I reckon we'll get better at learning to moderate that sort of thing ourselves – just as we'll need to in all other aspects of our lives.

line 33 (margin note)

31 In the first paragraph, what is Rowena's purpose in writing about adults and their views on teens' use of technology?

    A   to say which of their views she thinks are justified

    B   to suggest reasons why older people may hold such opinions

    C   to demonstrate how much exaggeration she thinks they contain

    D   to explore how different she is from the majority of teenagers

32 In the second paragraph, Rowena suggests that new technology

    A   makes young people's lives easier than their parents' lives were.

    B   has always tended to cause concern among older generations.

    C   allows young people more independence than their parents had.

    D   has developed much faster than for previous generations.

33 Which mistaken belief do researchers mean when they refer to 'misguided nostalgia' in line 33?

    A   using the present as a guide to understanding the past

    B   trusting that the present is a great improvement on the past

    C   being unable to see any difference between the present and the past

    D   thinking everything was much better in the past than it is in the present

34 Rowena gives the example of her friend Luke to demonstrate

    A   the advantages of becoming absorbed in online activity.

    B   the opportunities offered by online sites to become more creative.

    C   the benefits of publishing one's own writing online.

    D   the possibilities of finding paid work online.

35 What is implied about the computer teachers at Rowena's school in the fifth paragraph?

    A   They are unwilling to give up on students who find it hard to fit in.

    B   They are quick to spot undeveloped talents in their students.

    C   They are keen to use technology to help students discover themselves.

    D   They are leading the field in computer-assisted learning.

36 In the final paragraph, what does Rowena say is a disadvantage of new technology?

    A   It has created a generation of teenagers that is always multi-tasking.

    B   It can tempt teenagers away from what they should be focusing on.

    C   It makes teenagers realise their parents are still continuing to monitor them.

    D   It discourages teenagers from using a range of information sources.

You are going to read a magazine article about the discovery of some dinosaur bones. Six sentences have been removed from the article. Choose from the sentences **A–G** the one which fits each gap (**37–42**). There is one extra sentence which you do not need to use.

Mark your answers **on the separate answer sheet**.

New dinosaur discovery

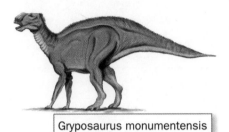

Gryposaurus monumentensis

The dinosaur species known as Gryposaurus monumentensis lived seventy-five million years ago but people only learnt of its existence at the beginning of the twenty-first century. Its name means 'hook-beaked lizard of the monument', with 'monument' referring to the place in the US state of Utah where this dinosaur's bones were found by a team of archaeologists.

37 . It had an enormous bill resembling that of the duck-billed platypus, a curious egg-laying mammal native to Australia. The dinosaur, which existed on a diet of leaves, would have found this extremely useful when it wanted to pull something to eat off a nearby plant.

However, the archaeologists who discovered the dinosaur's bones were even more amazed by what they found inside the skull. **38** . There was also evidence of many extra ones waiting to drop into place as others wore out.

Taking all the replacements into account, it is estimated that the dinosaur managed to get through approximately 800 teeth during its lifetime. This indicates that Gryposaurus monumentensis chewed its way through a substantial quantity of leaves every day of its life. **39** . Tyrannosaurus rex, the enormous meat-eating dinosaur, for example, seems to have got by with considerably fewer.

The unusual number of teeth found in the skull suggest that the Gryposaurus monumentensis was a particularly large species of dinosaur. **40** . Other bones were discovered in Utah not far from the skull. These made it possible for scientists to calculate that the creature was at least 90 metres in length. The humerus (the bone of the upper arm), for example, is longer than an adult man's leg.

At the time when Gryposaurus monumentensis lived in what is now Utah, the area had little in common with its appearance today. **41** . Nowadays the region tends to receive relatively little rain and not much grows there.

Dinosaurs with duck bills have also been found a thousand kilometres further north in Canada but they appear to be rather different from those discovered in Utah. **42** . Some think that there may have been a mountain system making it impossible for them to move between Utah and Canada, while others believe that they simply had no need to leave an area with plenty of food. However, others are not convinced by either theory. Certainly a great deal more remains to be learnt about Gryposaurus.

Duck-billed platypus

A It is known to have been wet and swampy there then and the land was covered by plants.

B The creature was seen to possess at least 300 teeth, making it easy for it to grind up the leaves that it ate.

C And there is evidence to show that this was indeed the case.

D This is in striking contrast to the habitats where other dinosaur bones have been found.

E Scientists are puzzled as to why they do not bear more resemblance to each other.

F The outside of the skull (the bone of the head) that the Utah archaeologists discovered was unusual.

G Otherwise it would never have worn out quite so many of them.

You are going to read a magazine article about a young Japanese snowboarder taking part in a major competition called 'X Games' in Aspen in the USA. For questions **43–52**, choose from the sections of the article (**A–D**). The sections may be chosen more than once.

Mark your answers **on the separate answer sheet**.

Which section of the article

describes some negative attitudes towards Hirano's lifestyle?	**43** ☐
comments on Hirano's lack of fear?	**44** ☐
shows how easy Hirano finds it to ignore noise?	**45** ☐
outlines Hirano's early experience of the sport?	**46** ☐
mentions some advice Hirano has been given?	**47** ☐
describes how snowboarders relax between competitions?	**48** ☐
compares how Hirano is thought of in different places?	**49** ☐
shows how ambitious Hirano is?	**50** ☐
mentions that Hirano is unaware of his reputation?	**51** ☐
explains Hirano's growing popularity?	**52** ☐

Ayumu Hirano, Young Snowboarding Star

A   The room was hopping. Seemingly everywhere you looked, X Games athletes were eating, laughing and enjoying a few minutes out of the spotlight. Some played video games. Others received a massage. And the rest were glued to the Women's Snowboard final on one of the oversized flat screen televisions in the room. Except for one person, that is. On this night in the X Games athlete lounge, the youngest competitor at this week's X Games Aspen, 14-year-old Japanese snowboarder Ayumu Hirano, was oblivious to everything going on around him. Tucked into the corner of a couch, he sat slumped on his side, his head resting on a white pillow while his ski cap was pulled over his eyes. The kid was sound asleep. Even when the room erupted after Elena Hight landed the first double rodeo in the Women's final, Hirano didn't budge.

B   On Sunday night, Hirano will hopefully be able to stay awake long enough to join six other competitors who will try to keep the current champion from winning his record sixth consecutive gold medal. In Thursday night's elimination, the 1.5-metre eighth grader became a fan favorite thanks to his trademark big air jump. His top score of 78.66 placed him sixth. He is quite clear about his goals for Sunday night's finals. "I want to be on that podium," he said through a translator.

Not much is known about Hirano, who has followed in the footsteps of fellow Japanese snowboarder Kazuhiro Kokubo, who also emerged onto the scene in his early teens. Now 24, Kokubo has served as a mentor to Hirano, who spends about 60 per cent of his year in Japan and 40 per cent training in the United States. Kokubo's tips come on and off the hill, covering everything from how to be a good person to how to land a particular trick.

C   This week, Hirano has been joined by his parents, who are visiting the United States for the first time. Hirano was introduced to action sports through his father, Hidenori, who owns a surf shop and a skate park in a small city on the coast of Japan. When a family friend gave his older brother a snowboard, Ayumu followed along. At the time, he was just 4 years old. Hirano doesn't remember that day. His earliest snowboarding memory is competing in a junior competition when he was 6.

Luckily for Hirano, he has little idea what the U.S. press is saying about him. "He doesn't even realize it," Hirano's manager, Carl Harris, said. "It's probably better that way. There isn't a lot of pressure. He's just the coolest kid in the competition. He goes out there and is like, 'Whatever. I'm just here to ride.' When asked this week what scares him, Hirano struggled to answer, pondering the question for several minutes before finally confessing "Nothing comes to mind."

D   Hirano's parents have some concerns about the fact their son has missed so much school to chase his snowboarding dreams. Hirano attends classes whenever he is in Japan, but that is only 60 per cent of the year. Friends have questioned why Hirano's parents were letting their son miss such an important part of his life. "Not everyone has the same chance that he has," said Hirano's father, Hidenori. "Because he is doing so well and trying so hard we don't want to take it away from him. Although sometimes people can get duped if they don't have a good education, I feel, if he can try this hard at snowboarding, nothing can stop him."

While Hirano's popularity is growing in the United States, back in Japan he's just another kid. "He's a nobody back home," his dad said. "Just another middle schooler who misses a lot of class." But come Sunday night, that nobody will find himself under the bright lights in the final event of X Games Aspen. If he can keep awake.

You **must** answer this question. Write your answer in **140–190** words in an appropriate style **on the separate answer sheet**.

1   In your English class you have been talking about language learning. Now your English teacher has asked you to write an essay for homework.

Write your essay using **all** the notes and giving reasons for your point of view.

Learning a foreign language is very useful for young people today.

Notes

Write about:

1. travel

2. work and studies

3. .... (your own idea)

Write an answer to **one** of the questions **2–5** in this part. Write your answer in **140–190** words in an appropriate style **on the separate answer sheet.** Put the question number in the box at the top of the answer sheet.

---

2   You see this announcement in an English-language magazine for young people.

> *Articles wanted!*
>
> We are preparing a special issue about travel and would like readers to send us articles about a special journey they have made. Where did you go? Who did you travel with? What made the journey particularly interesting for you?

Write your **article**.

3   This is part of an email you have received from an American friend.

> ○○○
>
> I'd like to learn more about your country by watching a film from there. Can you tell me about a film that you'd recommend? In what ways would it help me learn about your country? And how typical is it of films from your country?

Write your **email**.

4   The school where you study English has asked students to write short stories for an English language competition. The short story must **begin** with the words:

> *When Chris woke up, he expected the day to be like any other one.*
>
> Your story must include:
>
> • a famous person
>
> • an invitation

Write your **story**.

5   Answer the following question based on the set text.

Your English class has had a discussion about the set text. Now your teacher has asked you to write a review of the set text. Your review should focus on explaining why the text would or would not be a good one to take on holiday with you.

Write your **review**.

(3 05) You will hear people talking in eight different situations. For questions **1–8**, choose the best answer (**A, B** or **C**).

1 You hear two friends talking about going to a classic car show.
   What do they agree about it?

   A There was more to see than they expected.
   B They spent more than they had intended.
   C Some of the exhibits were more interesting than others.

2 You hear a teacher talking about a visitor coming to school.
   Before the visitor comes, the teacher wants the class to

   A find some information about the visitor.
   B create a display for their visitor in their classroom.
   C make something to present to the visitor.

3 You hear two friends talking about doing up a room.
   What does the boy want to do?

   A get some new furniture for his room
   B exchange rooms with his sister
   C redecorate his room himself

4 You hear two friends talking about a film they would like to see.
   What do they know about it?

   A It is based on a true story.
   B The actors are unknown.
   C It has some comic moments.

5 You hear a radio report about a zoo.
   What is the zoo planning to do?

   A extend its opening hours
   B put some information online
   C organise an event for schools

6 You hear two friends talking about doing presentations in class.
   How did the boy feel about his presentation?

   A relieved his teacher liked it
   B pleased by his classmates' response
   C confident he has learnt from the experience

7 You hear a father talking to his daughter about plans for her birthday.
   The girl says she would like to spend her birthday

   A paying a visit to someone special to her.
   B going to a town where she has never previously been.
   C doing what she did on her last birthday.

8 You hear two friends talking about a cake they have made.
   What do they agree about?

   A They would do something differently if they made the cake again.
   B The boy made a useful suggestion when they were making the cake.
   C It was one of the most delicious cakes they have ever tasted.

06 You will hear a man called Nigel telling some students about his experiences in Antarctica.

For questions **9–18**, complete the sentences with a word or short phrase.

Working in Antarctica

Nigel first became interested in Antarctica after enjoying a **(9)** .... about it when he was ten.

The year that the first person arrived in Antarctica was probably **(10)** ....

The subject Nigel studied at university was **(11)** ....

Nigel first went to Antarctica to do research on **(12)** ....

Nigel arrived in Antarctica by **(13)** ....

Nigel did a lot of work in Antarctica with a scientist from **(14)** ....

The main problem in Antarctica for Nigel was the **(15)** .... there.

In their free time Nigel and his colleagues in Antarctica spent a lot of time

(16) ....

When he got back home Nigel missed the **(17)** .... in Antarctica.

Nigel has written a novel called **(18)** .... based on his time in Antarctica.

07 You will hear five teenagers talking about school trips to different museums. For questions **19–23**, choose from the list (**A–H**) the opinion each speaker expresses. Use the letters only once. There are three extra letters which you do not need to use.

A   It was more enjoyable than a previous school trip.

B   We spent too much time preparing for the trip.

Speaker 1 ☐ **19**

C   It was far better than going round the museum on my own.

Speaker 2 ☐ **20**

D   A member of staff organised some original activities for us.

Speaker 3 ☐ **21**

E   It was a good idea to concentrate on just one part of the museum.

Speaker 4 ☐ **22**

F   There will be another trip to the same place in a few weeks' time.

Speaker 5 ☐ **23**

G   The best part of the trip was a DVD we watched there.

H   Something that I had hoped to see there was not on display.

08 You will hear an interview with a young man called Mark Collins who spends his spare time playing in a band that is gradually becoming well-known in his local area. For questions **24–30**, choose the best answer (**A, B** or **C**).

24   How did Mark and his friends choose the name for their band?
   A   They based it on their own names.
   B   They took it from a place that was special to them.
   C   They picked it by chance from something they overheard.

25   How has Mark's band changed since it first started?
   A   It features a different lead singer.
   B   It uses a wider range of instruments.
   C   It has more members than it used to.

26   What does Mark say about the music his band plays?
   A   They mainly do numbers they have written themselves.
   B   They like to experiment with different styles of music.
   C   They attach importance to the words of their songs.

27   Mark says he admires the singer Flora Hernandez because
   A   she has helped many young musicians.
   B   she has overcome many difficulties.
   C   she performs in a very original way.

28   What does Mark say about the performances his band does?
   A   They often play in small venues.
   B   They rarely refuse an invitation to play.
   C   They frequently travel long distances to play.

29   Mark says that when his band did a foreign tour
   A   they found it less enjoyable than they expected.
   B   they learnt what their particular strengths were.
   C   they failed to make any profit from their performances.

30   Mark thinks that in the future his band
   A   will focus on playing at summer festivals.
   B   will mainly perform at local clubs.
   C   will work hard at becoming well known.

    2 minutes [3 minutes for groups of 3]

Interlocutor	First we'd like to know something about you. Where are you from?
Weekends	

- What sports do you like to do at the weekends? (Why?)
- Who do you usually spend your weekends with? (What do you do together?)
- How much time do you spend studying at the weekend? (Do you think that's enough?)
- Tell us what you did last weekend.
- Do you do different things at the weekends at different times of the year?

    4 minutes [6 minutes for groups of 3]

Interlocutor In this part of the test, I'm going to give each of you two photographs. I'd like you to talk about your photographs on your own for about a minute, and also to answer a question about your partner's photographs.

(*Candidate A*), it's your turn first. Here are your photographs on page C22 of the Speaking appendix. **They show people painting in different situations.**

I'd like you to compare the photographs, and say **why you think the people are painting in these situations.**

All right?

Candidate A
🕐 *1 minute* ....

Interlocutor Thank you.

(*Candidate B*), **which kind of painting would you prefer to do? (Why?)**

Candidate B
🕐 *Approximately 30 seconds* ....

Interlocutor Thank you.

Now, (*Candidate B*), here are your photographs on page C23 of the Speaking appendix. They show **people with animals in different situations.**

I'd like you to compare the photographs, and say **what the people are enjoying about being with animals in these situations.** All right?

Candidate B
🕐 *1 minute* ....

Interlocutor Thank you.

(*Candidate A*), **which of these two situations would you prefer to be in? (Why?)**

Candidate A
🕐 *Approximately 30 seconds* ....

Interlocutor Thank you.

Part 3　4 minutes [5 minutes for groups of 3]

Interlocutor　Now, I'd like you to talk about something together for about two minutes.

I'd like you to imagine that your school wants to encourage students to read more and has asked for ideas about how to do this. Here are some ideas and a question for you to discuss. First you have some time to look at the task on page C24 of the Speaking appendix.

Now, talk to each other about **how each of these ideas might encourage students to read more.**

Candidates

🕐 *2 minutes (3 minutes for groups of three)*

Interlocutor　Thank you. Now you have about a minute to decide **which two ideas would be the most interesting to choose.**

Candidates

🕐 *1 minute (for pairs and groups of three)*

Interlocutor　Thank you.

Part 4　4 minutes [6 minutes for groups of 3]

Interlocutor

- Do you think reading is a less important skill than it used to be?
- Is it better to read a printed book or read a book on an electronic device? (Why?)
- How do you decide which books or magazines you're going to read?
- What books would you recommend to other people of your age?
- Which do you prefer – reading a book or watching a film? Why?
- When and where are you most likely to spend time reading?

Thank you. That is the end of the test.

What do you think?
Do you agree?
And you?

Test 1 Audioscript

LISTENING PART 1

 **Training**

Girl: My friends gave me a great T-shirt for my birthday! I've never come across anything like it in the shops, so they must've spent ages choosing it. But then that's typical of them. They're really thoughtful friends, always thinking what you'd *really* like. They even asked me, before my birthday, whether I liked T-shirts with dogs on them. I remember thinking, 'Why on earth would I want a picture of a dog on my T-shirt?' But then my family had just got a dog, so it was a kind thought! I think I said then that I only really liked simple designs, so they obviously remembered that! The only thing is, it could be a bit looser around the arms, and I doubt if I'll be able to exchange it for another one. But it's special so I'll still wear it!'

 Exam practice

One

You hear a girl talking about a running race she is going to compete in soon.

It's the big running race on Saturday, and I know loads of local people are coming along to watch – and cheer! I'm feeling really nervous about it, which is a bit unexpected, but then a lot depends on the result this time. If I win, I can go on to compete in the national championships! That's putting a lot of pressure on me. I just know the other competitors will have spent months preparing for it, and I can't really claim that, if I'm honest. So I suppose if I don't get the result I'm hoping for, which is likely, I've only got myself to blame....

 Two

You hear the beginning of a radio programme for teenagers.

Mark: Here with me today is scientist Louise Jason, who's going to tell us what's coming up in today's programme. Louise.

Louise: Thanks, Mark. Yes, our regular listeners will remember the fascinating discussions we've had on this programme regarding the future of the planet. We've covered just about everything, haven't we, from the effects of global warming to the way we release far too many toxic gases into the atmosphere. And we've been particularly interested in the effects of all this on wildlife worldwide, and that's our focus this morning – how the next generation should deal with all these problems and avoid the loss of any more rare species if they can ...

 Three

You overhear a boy phoning a friend.

Alfie: Hi Jake? It's Alfie. I'm just ringing about our school geography quiz next week – hope you've been practising! As you know, there's a great prize for the winners and our team's got a really good chance of getting it but Tom Sutton's just rung me to say he's got to drop out because he's not well – and he was really good! Anyway, we need another team member, so how about Fergus? Shall I ask him instead? Oh, and my dad says we can pick you up in the car on the way there if you haven't got any transport. Let me know ...

 Four

You hear two friends talking about a school photography exhibition.

Girl: Hi Sam! I'm just off to the school photography exhibition. And I'm guessing there's lots of your stuff on the walls – you're a great photographer!

Sam: Oh, my teacher asked me to put some up, but nothing's ready – the most recent ones still need some work ... the ones I showed you?

Girl: Well, they looked brilliant to me, I know you wanted to work on the colours a bit on your laptop ... But I bet none of the photos in the exhibition are as good as those. You should give it a go – it's not too late.

Sam: Well ... I'll come with you and have a look – then I'll see what I think!

 Five

You hear two friends talking about a shopping trip they've just been on.

Boy: Phew! I'm exhausted after all that walking around the shops. I need a nice cool drink!

Girl: Yeah, there were far more than I'd expected, with just about everything you could ever want.

Boy: Mm, except the T-shirt you were looking for. We must have gone into every single shop ...

Girl: Oh, never mind, I'm sure I'll find one eventually. And at least I didn't go and buy that dress I saw. It was lovely, but I couldn't really afford it, so I would've regretted it if I'd got it. Anyway, now I've got something left to go shopping with next week.

Boy: Yeah – well, maybe your friend Maisie could go with you next time!

 Six

You hear a girl talking about her class trip to the theatre to see a play.

Girl: We had a trip to the theatre last week, which all my class went on, to see a play we'd been studying in class. We all knew what it was supposed to be like, and there are several scary bits in it, but even though I knew when they were coming, I still hid behind my school bag! The thing was, though, I didn't recognise some parts of the storyline, or even aspects of the characters, even though we'd all read it really carefully and acted out bits of it on stage at school. It's a difficult play, no doubt about that, but I'd somehow expected to feel more familiar with it ...

 Seven

You hear two friends talking about a canoeing lesson they have just had on the river.

Boy: Wow, that was amazing! I'm glad we gave canoeing a try, aren't you?

Girl: Absolutely! And I'm pleased I did all that weight training beforehand, otherwise my arms would've ached much more than they did.

Boy: I probably should have done that, then – my muscles were really sore! And the canoe tipped from side to side quite a bit – I was scared I was going to fall in amongst those rocks.

Girl: My brother warned me about that, but I was still anxious about going for a freezing swim on a few occasions! At least I managed to paddle the canoe in a straight line.

Boy: Yeah, I never did get that right – you were really impressive!

Girl: Thanks!

 Eight

You hear a teacher telling a class about a science project they are going to do.

Teacher: Now, this term we're going to be doing lots of work on our science project about discoveries in medicine. We'll be spending a lot of time in our school lab during our classes, of course, and I've got some experiments lined up for you to do there, but I've also got a trip planned to the Medical Institute in the city centre. Now, I know many of you think museums are boring, but I promise you this one is fascinating, so we'll all go there together. And for your homework you'll each have some research to do in the library here before we head off to the city centre. Right, let's get started ...

LISTENING PART 2

Training

 1c

Sally: During the summer months, my family and I tend to go to the beach a lot, because we all really like it. Dad's a busy doctor, so he usually just sleeps on the beach, and mum, who's an artist, sometimes goes in search of unusual things to use in her work – if she's got the energy! <u>My little sister's amazing, though – she just spends the whole time splashing about in the sea, with a huge smile on her face.</u> My older brother keeps an eye on her. Grandma mostly complains that it's too hot, but we all know she wouldn't really want to stay at home!

 2b

Sally: We sometimes do some water sports while we're at the beach, too. I go diving with my dad whenever he goes in the water. My little sister Sophie likes swimming in the shallow water, so I stay with her sometimes, when my brother wants to go surfing. And the water there is <u>perfect for sailing, so I go off and do that when it's windy enough – and not raining!</u> It's great!

 3b

Sally: We often go for walks along the beach together too, and my sister sometimes picks up things – an unusual piece of wood, say, or even some jewellery that someone has lost or forgotten. One day, she'd run ahead as she normally does, when she suddenly came running back because she'd spotted something. We all assumed it'd be a stone for her collection, but <u>it turned out to be a crab.</u> It was on a rock, so we took a photo for her to keep and then went off to collect sea shells in a bucket that had been left lying on the beach that my brother had picked up.

 Exam practice

You'll hear a girl called Flora telling her class about a recent trip to South Africa, where she saw some animals called meerkats.

Flora: My name's Flora, and I want to tell you about a fantastic trip I did with my parents and sister earlier this year. It really was the trip of a lifetime, as we went all the way to South Africa to visit relatives there. But we also got to see some of the sights, and the wildlife – including a colony of meerkats!

On the day we went to see them, we got up really early and drove off to meet our brilliant guide Gavin. He was incredibly knowledgeable about meerkats. For example, he told us that early explorers thought the meerkat was like a sort of desert monkey, although apparently some people say the meaning of the name is 'lake cat', even though it never goes anywhere near water! And in one region, the meerkat is still known as the 'sun angel' as it was thought to help warn farmers of possible dangers to their cattle.

Gavin also told us that meerkats can live in captivity for a long time, but for far less in the wild, in the desert areas where they tend to make their homes. This is due to things like changes in their habitat.

Once we'd arrived at the place where the meerkats lived, we were given hot drinks, and chairs to sit in while we waited. Gavin also gave us some blankets, which I hadn't really expected as we were in a desert area, but then it'd been cold in our car that morning, so we were glad of the extra warmth. We would have been freezing otherwise!

Because Gavin knew the area so well, we didn't have long to wait to see our first meerkats. He'd spent months in the area, observing the meerkats, and being close to them so that they got used to his presence and his scent, and most especially his voice, which might have frightened them away. As a result, he was able to talk to us easily without scaring the meerkats, although *we* stayed a bit further away. The meerkats stood looking around near their holes where they lived. They were really fun to watch, with their sweet faces and long thin tails, which Gavin said they use not only for balancing, but also for signalling to other meerkats if they want to warn them of danger. Gavin told us that when everything is OK, they stand on their back legs and make little peeping noises to the rest of their group. But as soon as they see anything out of the ordinary, they bark – which they did while we were there, when they saw an eagle flying over, and they all disappeared underground for a while. And apparently they can also whistle to each other, too.

We got a really good view of the animals through our binoculars. They have lovely fawn-coloured fur coats, but there's not much fur on their black tummies. That's because they need to absorb the warmth of the sun. They also have stripes across their back, which are unique. Gavin said that they allowed him to identify each meerkat quite easily.

Gavin also doesn't feed the meerkats, but encourages them to search for food in the ground. While we watched them, one found some plants to eat, and others found some spiders, which they shared as a tasty treat! Gavin told us he'd even seen them eat small birds, although they seemed to prefer things like insects.

Of course, we all wanted to take a meerkat home, but Gavin told us they don't make good pets because they're wild animals. So instead we had a look in the souvenir shop back in our hotel. There was an amazing range of DVDs and books about meerkats, but I finally chose two posters and my sister got a couple of cool T-shirts with meerkats on – one of which she gave to me! So we were very happy!

So does anyone want to ask me anything ...?

LISTENING PART 3

Training

 2a

Matthew: My family and I had planned to travel by train the length of the country for a holiday. It involved a four-hour train journey, plus a drive to the station first. My family usually does everything at the last minute, but this time at least we left home in plenty of time to avoid missing the train. I'd got lots of magazines to stop myself getting bored, as I knew the view from my seat by the window wouldn't be very inspiring – I'd seen it loads of times before, from the car. But what I hadn't expected was <u>to be presented with a tray by the attendant – sandwiches and drinks for the trip.</u> Great!

 3

Maria: I'd never really done such a long journey by train before – we'd always gone everywhere by plane. So I hadn't realised we'd be able to put all our bags near us, by our seats, which meant I was able to get out all the food I'd brought with me! I'd got a seat next to the window, although I clearly wasn't going to see very much as we were travelling at night so we all had to be quiet. <u>But I was getting more and more excited as we sat in the station waiting to leave. I just couldn't wait to get started!</u> And I wasn't disappointed.

 Exam practice

You'll hear five teenagers talking about their hobby, collecting different things. For questions 19–23, choose from the list (A–H) how each speaker feels about their hobby.

Speaker 1

I've collected figures from science fiction films for years. Mum says I used to spend hours playing with them, and we put up a shelf to make room for them all, even though there aren't that many of them. The figures started getting a bit expensive at one point, but what with presents and so on from relatives, I managed to keep going – and I spent all my money on them. Still, <u>I guess there comes a time for every collector like me when you wonder</u>

why you're doing it, and you get into something else. It's bound to happen I suppose. But they'll always have pride of place in my room!

Speaker 2

I've met lots of other people my age who have collections of something or other, but I'd really love to know how many other teenagers like me still collect stamps. My grandad gave me his collection when I became old enough to really appreciate it, and I've never looked back. I've spent hours over the years adding to what he gave me, and I suppose by now it might be worth a bit, although I've never really checked. It's just valuable to me personally because of the family connection. But no-one's really been as keen to see it as I hoped they'd be. I've taken it into school and some teachers had a look, but that's been about it.

Speaker 3

I've still got a glass case in my bedroom where all my dolls are displayed. They're each dressed in the national costumes of different countries, so family and friends always knew what to buy me when they went on holiday! Even now, I sometimes get them out and rearrange them a bit in the way I used to – I don't think I'll ever stop doing that. And friends who come into my room are just amazed at how many I've got which is great. I'll always tell them all about the dolls – and the history of one or two of the most valuable ones. It makes me appreciate the whole collection more, somehow.

Speaker 4

I think for me the magic went out of collecting for a while when the coins I collect became so easy to get online. The thrill of going into a little shop with my grandfather, never knowing what we'd find, was amazing and that was lost when I started to buy them on websites. But since then, my interest has revived – my older sister's husband was fascinated by what I've managed to build up, and one day he showed me some blogs written by lots of other people who are coin collectors too. I had no idea it was still so popular among teenagers! I might even contribute to the blog!

Speaker 5

For years my older sister and I have been interested in collecting bits of jewellery. For me, it started when she used to take me into second-hand shops and we'd find rings and bracelets that were beautiful – and really cheap. Now it seems lots of those pieces are vintage, so they've become fashionable again – and they're actually worth quite a bit now, too, which is amazing! But we'd never sell them, and we'll keep on adding to them while we can still afford it. It's a bit of an obsession now – and anyway, it's lovely that so many people notice when we wear some of it. They always seem to want to know how we got it.

LISTENING PART 4

Training

 2

Jack: My friend's parents had just bought a luxury boat to go wakeboarding with. Wakeboading's a bit like waterskiing, but on a sort of surfboard! My friend couldn't stop talking about how amazing it was, so I thought I had to give it a go, even though I'm useless at waterskiing. So I wasn't that hopeful of success to be honest. But then it was a beautiful morning – the birds were flying around lazily overhead and, anyway, I love being in the water when it's a hot day, so what had I got to lose?

 3a

Jack: Anyway, we arrived at the lake, got our wakeboarding kit on, and before long it was my turn. I crouched down in the water on the wakeboard, as I was supposed to, holding tightly onto the rope while the boat driver waited for me to give him the signal that I was ready. But almost as soon as I did, he opened up the engine and

roared off, and the pressure on my legs to keep the wakeboard in front of me was suddenly immense! I hadn't been prepared for that, so what do you know? I fell into the water to the sound of laughter from my spectators, which I joined in with … and, apparently, my friend's father had managed to get some good shots of it all!

 4

Jack: I was determined not to be discouraged, though, so I went back a second time and got into position again.

This time I was ready. I saw the rope become tight in the water as the boat drove off and I clung on – and there was no way I was letting go! I'd been told the technique was to stand only when I was fully out of the water – so I tried that and it worked like a dream! I shifted my weight onto my back foot – and there I was, standing up! People were waving on the bank, but I still didn't feel quite confident enough to wave back. Still, I'd done it and I was thrilled – although that feeling didn't last long when I discovered that both my friend and his dad had stood up on their first attempt … But never mind!

🎧 1 21 Exam practice

You'll hear an interview with a boy called Jamie Davidson, who has just tried rock climbing for the first time.

Interviewer: Today I'm with 15-year-old Jamie Davidson, who's just taken up rock climbing! Jamie, tell us all about your first climb. You went to a climbing centre, didn't you?

Jamie: That's right. I'd wanted to go rock climbing for years, but my family weren't keen. Then the youth group I belong to organised a trip to the centre – and that's how I found myself setting off on a weekend beginners' course! It turned out that the centre was set at the foot of some very high and scary-looking rocks! And there was a sailing school a few miles away too, although the sea always looked a bit rough where we were.

Interviewer: So how did it feel when you first put on all your climbing equipment?

Jamie: Er, a bit strange, really. There was loads of stuff, and we had to make sure everything we were given fitted perfectly. For example, it was important that the shoes we wore would grip the rocks properly, and wouldn't slip. We also had lots of different ropes and hooks to attach us to the rock face, which our guide told us all about, and we had to put it all on in the right order. I didn't really begin to feel like a proper climber until I'd got it all on. Then I finally felt ready to tackle whatever lay ahead! And off we went.

Interviewer: So tell us something about your guide.

Jamie: Well, he was called Max, and he was only 23. He'd done his first climb at the age of 15 – like me! He told us that we should always climb with a smile on our faces to show everyone what a great time we were having. I wasn't convinced, but once we'd started I began to see what he meant. He also got us to check the whole length of our ropes which I could see was important. He told us that the good climbers do that on every climb, in case the ropes had developed a weakness in them.

Interviewer: So how easy was it once you started to climb?

Jamie: Well, Max led us up the rocks at quite a speed – he obviously didn't have any problem finding things to hold on to, but I certainly did sadly, and I really just wished I could keep up with him! A few drops of rain had started falling, too, although I didn't really notice. I was too busy struggling to hold on to the rocks, and the tips of my fingers were really hurting – but I was determined not to let any of that stop me. I was going to get to the top!

Interviewer: And then Max told you to try letting go of the rock, didn't he? How did you feel?

Jamie: Oh, that was the hardest moment! He said he wanted to train us to trust our equipment, so that we wouldn't feel scared, and I was fairly happy everything was secure. There was a moment, though, when I couldn't help wondering … when I saw the ropes tightening under my weight! But most of the people in my group were having a go without any problems, so that made me feel better!

Interviewer: And eventually you and your group got to see the view from the top, didn't you?

Jamie: Yes, we did! It felt like a bit of a reward for the climb as, although you couldn't exactly see for miles because of the mist, there were loads of birds just flying around above our heads and over the tree tops. The whole scene was just like I'd seen in the posters at the climbing centre, and it brought back memories of looking out right from the top of a castle we visited once on holiday. That was amazing, too!

Interviewer: So what did you do when you got to the top?

Jamie: Well, we had a kind of group picnic for lunch, where everyone shared all the different food they'd brought – which was lucky, as mine was still back at the climbing centre, so I felt rather bad, but no-one minded. The sun was quite hot, but we were able to take off some of the thick clothing we were wearing. It was all very relaxing after a tiring climb. And I'll definitely go climbing again – except next time I'll take a slightly better camera than I had this trip!

Interviewer: Right! Well, thanks very much for talking to us, Jamie.

SPEAKING PART 1

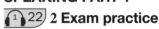 **2 Exam practice**

1 Where are you from?

2 What are your favourite subjects at school?

3 Have you got any brothers or sisters?

4 What do you spend most of your time doing at home?

5 How did you spend your last school holiday?

6 What sort of job would you like to do in the future?

SPEAKING PART 2

Training

 5/6

Interlocutor: Jana, it's your turn first. Here are your photographs. They show people spending their free time in different ways. I'd like you to compare the photographs and say why you think the people have chosen to do these activities.

Jana: Well, both pictures show people enjoying themselves. The first photo is of people at a picnic. They are sitting on some grass, talking and eating, whereas in the second picture, the people are taking part in a race. They seem very focused on what they are doing, and all of them look determined to win. In the first photo the people appear to be in some kind of park, because I can see trees in the background, while in the second photo they look as if they are at a sports centre or somewhere like that, because they are running on an athletics track.

In the picture at the top, I would say that the people have chosen to have a picnic because it's a relaxing and enjoyable way to spend time with friends. They can share good food and it gives them the opportunity to chat and have a laugh together. In the second picture, in contrast, the people are far from relaxed. They are obviously having to make a big effort. They could have chosen to take part in the race because they want to prove they are the fastest, or because they want to test themselves and push themselves to win.

Interlocutor: Thank you, Jana. Now Fernando, which of these situations would you prefer to be in?

Fernando: I'd definitely rather be at the picnic, like the people in the first picture, because they are having fun and it isn't very stressful. That's a more enjoyable way to spend your leisure time, in my opinion. I also like trying different types of food, and these people may all have brought different types of food to share with their friends.

SPEAKING PART 3

Training

 5

Interlocutor: Now, I'd like you to talk about something together for about two minutes. Here are some reasons why teenagers might want to do sport and a question for you to discuss. Now, talk to each other about whether it is important for teenagers to do sport.

Jana: Right … Shall I start?

Fernando: OK.

Jana: Well personally, I think it's important for everyone to do sport, not just teenagers. I mean, everyone should try to be healthy and keep fit – otherwise, they might get ill, mightn't they?

Fernando: Mm, good point. And I believe it's good to do something different from schoolwork, too. After all, we spend a lot of time sitting concentrating and reading – things like that. Sport is a great way of relaxing, either during the school day, or after school or at the weekends. What do you think?

Jana: Erm yes … I know what you mean, but you can do other things, can't you? Like play a musical instrument, for example.

Fernando: Yes, that's true, but I still think some kind of physical activity, like football or running, can help you forget any worries you have about school.

Jana: That's true. And what do you think about this point? The one about being outside? In my opinion, that's pretty much essential for a healthy lifestyle, too, and so it's a good reason for doing sport.

Fernando: Well maybe, though lots of sports are played indoors too, like badminton and basketball, so it isn't necessarily why people do sport, is it?

Jana: Sure, but there are lots that are played outside, aren't there?

Fernando: Yes, you're right. And I think this point is important, too: sport's a great way of making friends, isn't it?

Jana: Yeah, it is. Obviously, people usually have similar interests to their friends, and if you play a team sport, then you'll probably meet people you have something in common with.

Fernando: Yeah, and because you have to train regularly, then you'll see each other at least once a week, and get to know your teammates very well.

Jana: And playing in matches together is really exciting, too, and you build up strong friendships when you have to support each other, for example when things are going badly.

Interlocutor: Thank you. Now you have about a minute to decide which two are *not* good reasons for teenagers to do sport.

Fernando: OK, well maybe for me, the least important reason for taking part in sport is being outside, because I think there are plenty of other times you can be outside that don't involve sport. So I don't think teenagers need to do sport for that reason. What do you think, Jana?

Jana: Yes, I think that's true. As you say, there are plenty of other times you can be outside, so that's not why doing sport is important. And what about the second reason? For me it's doing something different from schoolwork, but I'm not sure we agree about that, do we?

Fernando: I don't think we do agree on that one – I still think having a break from schoolwork is a good reason to do sport – a very good one, in fact.

Jana: Well, at least we've agreed on one, haven't we?

Interlocutor: Thank you.

SPEAKING PART 4

Training

 25 4

Interlocutor: Should people do more sport at school, Fernando?

Fernando: I reckon it isn't really necessary, because we have plenty of sport at school already. If people really want to do more, they don't need to do it in school time.

Interlocutor: And what do you think, Jana?

Jana: I tend to agree. I mean there's hardly enough time to do all the work we need to do, so I don't think we can spare any time for extra sport.

Interlocutor: Do you think sports stars are good role models for teenagers, Jana?

Jana: Not really. That's because nowadays, a lot of them seem to have cheated to get their medals, and that's not a good example, is it, Fernando?

Fernando: No, not at all. And it's hard to know what they're really like, anyway, because they're celebrities – you don't know what they're actually thinking.

Interlocutor: Do you think people talk about sport too much, Fernando?

Fernando: I don't think so. After all, it is a fascinating topic, isn't it? And there's always something new to talk about as there are so many matches and events you can watch live on TV.

Interlocutor: Thank you. That is the end of the test.

Jana / Fernando: Thank you.

Test 2 — Audioscript

LISTENING PART 1

Training

 26 1c

Boy: So are you coming with us to the sports centre on Saturday, Jasmine?

Girl: I am, yes, but some of our friends don't seem very enthusiastic about it. I thought we were supposed to be going to have fun!

Boy: Well, that's the general idea, and actually one or two people are really keen. They've heard there's a new skate park there and they want to try it out. The problem is, the skate parks we've been to so far have been awesome, and I'm just not sure this one'll match what we've seen elsewhere.

Girl: Well, if you're right, we can always go for a swim instead. The sports centre's got a great pool.

Boy: Mm – but I go there a lot, and I was hoping to do something different ... It *is* very hot at the moment, though ...

 27 2a

Girl: I'm off to an activity centre tomorrow – climbing trees with friends! You climb trees a lot with your mates, don't you?

Boy: Yeah, in the woods ... But I'm more careful than I used to be – that's the key, I reckon. I plan my route, and just stick to thicker branches that'll support my weight.

Girl: You can't think *too* much about that, though – it spoils the fun!

Boy: Well ... I do still tend to go up really far and then get stuck at the top.

Girl: Mm, I'll have to watch out for that, won't I?

Boy: Yeah – know your limits, my mum says.

Girl: But she also tells you to always do some warm-ups before you start.

Boy: Mm – but I never do!

 28 Exam practice

One

You hear a girl leaving a message for her brother.

Ella: Max, it's Ella. Sorry, I didn't mean to disturb you as I know you're out with your mates, but it completely slipped my mind to let mum know what time I'm back from the trip tomorrow, and her phone isn't working – she might have forgotten to charge it. So I wondered if you could remember to tell her when you get home. I'll need collecting from the station in the morning, which she may have forgotten. I know you've got your study project to finish off, so in return I can help you with that when I get back, if you like. That's fair, isn't it? Bye!

Two

You hear a girl telling her cousin about a music festival they are both going to.

Girl: Jack, I've managed to get some tickets for the music festival. You're still interested, aren't you?

Jack: Sure, and well done for buying the tickets. That can't have been easy, I guess, from what I've heard.

Girl: Well, loads of people want to go because there are so many groups booked to play this year – really big names.

Jack: Yeah? Well, that'll definitely make the journey worth doing, then. Brilliant! To be honest, I was a bit worried about how we'd get there as it's so far, but there are buses going right to the gates, apparently – specially for the festival!

Girl: Cool!

Three

You hear a teacher giving her students advice about writing application letters.

Teacher: Now, at some point in the future you'll probably need to write a letter of application, maybe for a college place. And of course you'll need to write as much as possible about yourself. But don't hold back the great things you can do ... your achievements at school. One thing that students often find difficult, though, is talking about what they're good at. None of us is really comfortable with doing that – in fact, it's often easier to focus on the negative things – but it's essential if you're in competition with other people. And don't forget *you're* responsible for how you talk about yourself. So ... let's start ...

Four

You hear two classmates talking about a stage performance they have just seen at their school.

Girl: Wow ... that was amazing – almost like watching professional actors, not people from our school.

Boy: I was focusing more on how fantastically all the orchestra worked together ... wish I could play like that ...

Girl: Well, there *were* a few wrong notes ...

Boy: Oh, really? Well, I'm not a musician like you! Anyway, what about those brilliant costumes they all wore – loads of work had gone into those.

Girl: I helped out with them – the teacher insisted we sewed on all those tiny buttons. They looked fab, so it was worth it – but it took ages.

Boy: I can imagine ... You know, we should audition to take part next time!

Girl: You're right!

Five
You hear the principal of a school talking about a teacher who is leaving.

Principal: Now, everyone, as you know, your teacher Mrs Arnold is leaving us at the end of term. She's made a significant contribution to the life of our school, particularly in events such as the swimming galas that she's always helped organise on Saturdays. And <u>her food technology classes</u> have always been popular – I know there've been lots of <u>wonderful things going home to parents, with some ingredients</u> coming from our school garden! That's really flourished, too, while she's been here to look after it. She's shown every class around it, and they're all better informed about plant life as a result. So let's all give a big thank you to Mrs Arnold …

Six
You hear a girl talking about a ski resort she recently went to.

Girl: ... So I went on holiday to a ski resort with my parents and older brother, where we met up with family friends who live there. I'm not a very proficient skier, so I felt really hopeless beside their four-year-old who was whizzing about all over the place. Hm! My instructor was great, though, so by the end I wasn't falling into the snow anymore! <u>I kept hoping that we'd come across some other teenagers, although the place didn't seem very popular with them, really – it was mostly for young families.</u> It was the end of the season, too, so it was quieter than usual, but at least the snow on the slopes made them fit for skiing.

Seven
You hear a brother and sister talking about new drinks at their local café.

Boy: Have you seen the new drinks on the menu here? They've got all these amazing flavours, and they'll even put drawings and designs on the top for you – a heart or your face – or whatever!

Girl: Yeah, they're OK – they might go down well with young people like us, I suppose. Let's just say, though, <u>I've tried a few different flavours and I'm not trying another ...</u>

Boy: Really? But not everyone's as particular as you! Anyway, the good thing is you can get a drink in here without having to spend loads of cash – unlike lots of places!

Girl: Mm, I guess so ...

Eight
You hear two schoolfriends talking about a book they have just read.

Boy: I really liked this book, did you? I mean, I've read tons of stuff about wildlife but I didn't know that much about wolves, and I've learnt loads about the way they live.

Girl: Yeah, I enjoyed it too. I actually checked on some things the writer said, though, 'cos I just thought some of the things they did sounded a bit *too* amazing … <u>but all the stuff about the landscape – I could just picture all of that.</u>

Boy: You'd probably have to be interested in wildlife to read it, though, wouldn't you?

Girl: Maybe ...

Boy: ... but <u>the descriptions of where they live made me feel as if I was there.</u> In fact, I've asked my dad if we can go next year.

Girl: Wow!

LISTENING PART 2
Training

 2b

Harry: I was determined that my brother and I should have a day out at the theme park that had just opened near where we were on holiday. Everyone had told us that the rides were awesome, and even though I'm not really very brave on fast rides, I was dying to see them. Anyway, when we turned up, the first thing I saw was a <u>massive roundabout.</u> It was going round at great speed, and my brother immediately wanted to go on it. But as there was a huge queue I managed to persuade him to come with me on a big wheel, where we got a great view of the whole theme park – including Mum and Dad on the swings!

 3a

Harry: After that ride, we both needed a refreshing drink, so we sat down at a café and Dad went off to find us something. My brother was hoping for some orange juice, although I really wanted <u>pineapple,</u> as they had lots of different ones available. But when Dad returned, he'd got two glasses of strawberry drink, which I guess he thought looked nice. It's really not my favourite, but never mind!

 4a

1 newspaper
2 exhibition
3 museum
4 library
5 journey
6 clothes
7 accommodation
8 environment
9 mountains
10 Wednesday

 ## Exam practice

You'll hear a girl called Karen talking to her class about an activity she did with her family.

Karen: My family and I have just had an amazing holiday – we went to Canada, so that we could go dog-sledding! If you've never seen a dog sled before, it's basically a big vehicle that has strips of wood under it instead of wheels. It can be pulled along across the snow, with you riding on it! Teams of dogs called huskies pull it along, and it's amazing fun! We arrived to find our accommodation was based in a small village, but there were <u>quite a few shops and restaurants, and other things like that because it was also a ski resort.</u> My brother and I were really pleased about that as we needed something to do in the evenings.

The <u>dog-sledding centre</u> was slightly outside the village, <u>in a valley,</u> which was really beautiful so <u>I got plenty of photos of it.</u> There was a steep slope with a forest on one side, and a high mountain on the other. On the day we went dog-sledding we arrived at the centre to find a group of other people already there, and nearly 50 dogs waiting for us, all harnessed to their sleds and ready to get started – in fact, they could hardly wait! We were a bit nervous of them to begin with as they looked quite fierce, and they were very loud, with their barking! But in fact <u>we soon discovered they were all very sociable – they really loved meeting and being around visitors.</u> We were allowed to go up to the different sleds and stroke the dogs. They were amazing to look at, with their curly tails, and many had bright blue eyes.

First our leader gave us a brief history talk, followed by a short introduction to the dogs we'd be using, and finally <u>a safety lesson, which I was very relieved to get,</u> as by this time I was wondering how I'd manage to drive eight excited dogs through the snow! You had to be at least 15 if you wanted to be the driver so my 11-year-old brother was a bit disappointed he couldn't drive, but he still loved being around the dogs. I felt a bit sorry for him but was pleased I was 16 and could get the chance to do it.

A few minutes later, we were ready to go, the dogs straining to get started even while the sleds were still tied down. My brother and I were in one, and mum and dad in another. All went well for a while, and it was great fun. First our sled was pulled by the dogs along a very snowy path, then we turned a corner, and they raced down a hill – but before we knew it we were crossing a frozen lake, which was scary! But luckily we made it to the other side! The dogs were running amazingly fast by then, and as we were going up a hill, my brother jumped off the sled and tried to run alongside them – but he just couldn't keep up! I soon discovered, as well, that while I was in control of the sled, it wasn't a good idea to stand up as it meant I'd probably fall off and once I'd let go, the dogs might just run off without us. But it was the most amazing fun, and you could see the dogs loved it too.

I'd expected we might see some wildlife while we were flying along. Of course, because of the harsh winter there, a lot of creatures, like reptiles, can't survive. But there are certainly bears in the area, which luckily we didn't come across! I was really hoping to see some wolves, though, but sadly there were no sightings. We did hear them one night back in the village. But the only creatures we actually spotted from the sled were deer, and a few mountain goats and sheep, which were very good at climbing!

Of course, it was really freezing cold during the trip. Everyone in the family had brought really warm clothes, but luckily we also managed to hire some winter boots, which were essential for walking on the frozen snow without slipping over – or getting very cold feet! The special snow trousers we had were useful, too.

Then, when the sled ride was over, we went off and saw the sights. We watched as some husky races were just coming to an end and took photos of the winners. Then we walked on and had a look round some ice sculptures, which we all agreed were totally amazing, and reminded me of the castles that my brother and I built one year on holiday in the sand!

Anyway, it was all fantastic! Now, any questions?

LISTENING PART 3

Training

 2a

Speaker 1

It was my friend's birthday party, which her parents had organised for her. It was quite a posh party, so I'd gone out and bought an expensive dress, which I was relieved to see was exactly the kind of thing everyone else was wearing! Anyway, we'd just got to the point where a few people were making speeches, and the family were giving out drinks, when I ran into a person I recognised, that I hadn't seen for years as she'd moved away. We've been best mates ever since!

 3a

Speaker 2

My friend and I were in a rush to get to the hotel where the party was – the traffic was awful. But finally we walked in just before everything got started, so no-one noticed. We sat down at the nearest table, got our breath back and looked around. Everyone was in fancy dress, including us, and the costumes were amazing, but it was difficult to recognise anyone because of how they were dressed. Anyway, it took a while before we realised that we didn't know anyone there at all – because our party was actually in another room next door. So we quickly got up and left, and crept into the event we were supposed to be at, which hadn't really begun yet. Luckily, everyone was too busy to notice in either room!

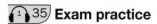 **Exam practice**

You'll hear five teenagers talking about helping to organise a surprise birthday party for a family member. For questions 19–23, choose from the list (A–H) the advice each speaker gives to ensure the party will be enjoyable for the family member.

Speaker 1

Surprise parties are always exciting, and if it's a good one, with great activities, people'll talk about it for ages afterwards. But before you start your planning, like considering venues, think carefully about what's involved and whether you're really up to it. For example, you may have to be less than honest to the party person about your arrangements or hide all your party things. Unfortunately, our mum found all our stuff, intended for her party – and threw it all away without even asking who it belonged to. But she didn't suspect, so we still went ahead – with new stuff! Not all her best friends could attend, sadly, but she had a great time anyway.

Speaker 2

My family wanted to give our Grandad a surprise party for his 70th birthday. We were well ahead with the planning, and even relatives and people that Grandad hadn't seen for years had agreed to come. Then one day Grandad suddenly announced how much he'd hate to be given a surprise party and would probably walk out if faced with one. Of course, if we'd checked beforehand, we would've discovered that, so I'd say that's probably a good idea – although that kind of misses the point, really! Anyway, we cancelled all the arrangements and organised a theatre trip for him instead, which he was thrilled with – and we never mentioned what had happened!

Speaker 3

My parents would say it's best to start planning a party really early. But the best ones I've been to were organised at the last minute, meaning there's less time for the birthday person to discover what's going on. The downside, of course, is there's also less time to find out whether they've made other plans, which is vital. Take my brother's 15th, for example. Despite our best efforts to tempt him down to the local swimming pool, where his closest friends had secretly laid on loads of activities, he declined as he'd arranged to watch a film at home with another friend. So they didn't go to the party – the party went to them ...

Speaker 4

I had a brilliant surprise party last year – all my friends were there, at our favourite cinema. So my parents wanted to plan a surprise for my older sister. But then at her party, her friends got a bit carried away and decided they'd give her a make-over – re-do her hair and make-up. From the look on her face, I'd say it wasn't really what she would've chosen, so I'd recommend avoiding doing anything you're not sure about – it could be a complete disaster! But she was good-natured enough to go along with it, and the party was immensely successful – people at school were still talking about it for months afterwards!

Speaker 5

Of course, the classic thing you're supposed to do for surprise parties is to pretend to the person that everyone's forgotten their birthday, but that always seems a bit cruel to me. So to avoid that for my sister's birthday, we wished her a happy birthday but then pretended we were holding a party for our Grandma – but at my sister's favourite restaurant. My sister did loads of planning for it in the months beforehand – only to find that the party was actually for her! The look on her face when she came in and saw all her closest friends was priceless – I'd say they're what really makes a party work.

LISTENING PART 4

Training

 2a

Interviewer: Now, you've won some photography competitions, Dan, but you didn't really like photography when you were younger, did you?

Dan: No, I was a bit slow in getting started, really! I did a few pictures with my older brother's camera, which my mum thought were great, and I didn't think they were too bad, either. But when my brother saw the results, he immediately started telling me what I'd done wrong! He hadn't done much photography himself, but I knew he was probably right, and just trying to help me improve, but it wasn't a good start, and I gave up for a while. But then a few months later my brother tried again to help me, and I was more ready to accept it then, as we'd started doing photography at school. Or probably I just wanted to know more and be better than my brother!

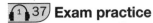 **Exam practice**

You'll hear an interview with a boy called Andrew Carpenter, whose hobby is making pots.

Interviewer: Hello, everyone. Today I'm with Andrew Carpenter, who's come to tell us about his hobby – pottery! Andrew, you haven't been making pottery for very long, have you? What made you want to start?

Andrew: Well, it was sort of by chance, really. My school has its own gallery and it held a ceramics exhibition, which our art teacher took us round, and then set us some work based on what we'd seen. At the time, I really wasn't that interested, to be honest, but then a few days later I was surfing the net and came across a video clip of one of the artists in the exhibition and the ideas he was trying to get across in his work. That made me want to have a go at making something similar.

Interviewer: So what pieces did you see that particularly inspired you?

Andrew: Well, it wasn't just the pieces. Lots of them were great to look at, but many were also made for a specific purpose – like a huge cup for several people to drink out of together. We were actually allowed to try it out and that's really unusual in a gallery! The cup didn't work too well, though, sadly! But there was a computer link showing what the artist was thinking when she made all her pots, and that was interesting.

Interviewer: And then your art teacher set up some lunchtime pottery classes, using a 'wheel', didn't she?

Andrew: Yes – and lots of us signed up. And for once, we could make as much mess as we liked without getting into trouble! Using the wheel is fun – you throw a lump of clay onto the middle as the wheel spins round. You shape the clay with your hand while it spins, and if you keep your hands steady, the wheel keeps the pot the same shape all the way round. There are other fun ways of making pots too, though. Anyway, my first pot wasn't great, but everyone at home thought differently, so it's on display in our kitchen! That's a bit embarrassing!

Interviewer: But then your friends soon dropped out of the class, didn't they? Why was that?

Andrew: Well, although using a wheel *looks* fun, it's also quite hard work. And a couple of friends found their pots just collapsed into a muddy mess as they were making them. That often happens at first, though, and they knew that might happen. They did have a good time doing it, too. But I suspect it was more that they had to give up their lunchtimes to go to the class, when they just wanted to play football, really!

Interviewer: But *you* made some great pots, didn't you?

Andrew: Yeah, and I learnt lots of different techniques, too. One was making a 'coiled' pot by coiling a length of clay round until it becomes a cylinder. You can end up with something fairly instant and quite good that way. I got really adventurous and even added a handle, which everyone else there thought was really cool, especially when it didn't fall off! Then I spent the next few weeks learning other techniques, and they worked well, too.

Interviewer: And you've also decorated some of your pots.

Andrew: Yeah, I put an image of myself on one pot. I'd done it as a joke, really, and I thought it was dreadful, but my parents insisted they could see it was me. I wasn't sure whether they were just being kind, though! But that pot was put in the school gallery, and when the artist I'd first admired came to the school, he spotted it immediately and gave it lots of praise. He's been really encouraging ever since.

Interviewer: But pottery's not very popular among people your age, is it? What would you say to other teenagers who want to give it a try?

Andrew: Just go for it! Get some clay and just play around with it, like you did when you were a kid. That's really important. You just never know what you might produce, and you'll soon find you're getting somewhere. But you may need to be patient if you want to get things to turn out exactly how you intended. Expect some failures along the way – but have fun and stick with it!

Interviewer: Andrew, thanks for talking to us!

SPEAKING PART 1

Training

 2/3

Interlocutor: Good afternoon. My name is Jane Morrell and this is my colleague Simon Longford.

Jana: Good afternoon.

Fernando: Good afternoon.

Interlocutor: And your names are?

Jana: Jana Svarova.

Fernando: Fernando Garcia.

Interlocutor: Can I have your mark sheets, please? Thank you. Where are you from, Jana?

Jana: I'm from the Ukraine.

Interlocutor: And you, Fernando?

Fernando: From Buenos Aires, in Argentina.

Interlocutor: First we'd like to know something about you. What do you like about your school, Jana?

Jana: Well, the classrooms are large and bright, because it's a very modern building. I also like the teachers!

Interlocutor: And what are your favourite subjects, Fernando?

Fernando: I suppose I really love subjects like art and music best, but I also enjoy other things, such as maths, as well as science subjects like chemistry, for example.

Interlocutor: How far do you live from your school, Jana?

Jana: I'm sorry, I didn't quite catch that.

Interlocutor: How far do you live from your school?

Jana: Oh, very close by – it's only 10 minutes from my home on foot, so I can walk.

Interlocutor: Have you been at this school for a long time, Fernando?

Fernando: No, not long. I just started here a year ago, when my parents moved to London.

Interlocutor:

1 Where did you go for your last holiday? (What did you do there?)

2 What are you going to do after school today?

3 Do you like watching sport on TV? (Is there a sport you've watched that you would like to try?)

4 What do you enjoy doing with your schoolfriends in breaks at school? (Why?)

5 Who is your favourite singer? (Why?)

SPEAKING PART 2

Training

 5

Interlocutor: I'd like you to compare the pictures, and say why you think the people might have chosen these activities. All right?

Girl: The people in the two pictures seem to be on holiday by the beach. It's sunny in both the pictures, and I think that maybe it's during the summer holidays. The girl in the second picture looks as if she's feeling very happy, and I think she must be smiling.

However, she's not the only person who seems to be enjoying herself in these two pictures. I have the impression that the boy is enjoying the book he's reading. I can't be sure, but he looks as if he's reading an interesting book.

I'm sure they've chosen these activities because they like them, so maybe the boy isn't really very interested in sport. The girl's doing something thrilling, whereas the boy's just relaxing, but they both appear to be happy with their choice of activity.

Interlocutor: Thank you. Daniel, which activity would you prefer?

Daniel: In my opinion, it would be more enjoyable to read on the beach, because I don't like sport very much. I usually prefer not to move around too much when the weather's really hot, because I find that a bit tiring.

Interlocutor: Thank you.

SPEAKING PART 3

Training

 1b/2

Interlocutor: Now, I'd like you to talk about something together for about two minutes. I'd like you to discuss what young people can learn from older people. Here are some ideas for you to think about and a question for you to discuss. First you have some time to look at the task.

Now, talk to each other about whether it's always best to learn things from older people.

Jana: OK, Fernando, do you want to start?

Fernando: Sure. I think you can learn some things from older people, though I'm not sure whether they are always the best people to learn from. I mean, grandparents can teach their grandchildren a few things, I suppose. What do you think about this point, Jana? All our teachers are older than us, obviously. But at home, if we want to find out more about history, for example, older family members can help us. And sometimes they may even have experienced some of the things we're learning about in our lessons.

Jana: That's true. And even if they didn't they might know something about it that we haven't been taught. What about this idea here? I don't think older people can advise us on what we should wear, do you? Their ideas on fashion are usually a bit out of date – when it comes to teenagers, anyway.

Fernando: I know what you mean, but sometimes they can help younger people by telling them how smart they need to be – like

wearing a suit for a wedding – things like that. This suggestion looks good, doesn't it? I don't think anyone my age could teach me to make a good dinner!

Jana: Well yes, but you can find that sort of thing out from books and the Internet, too, if you really want to. I don't think it's something you'd necessarily learn from older people.

Fernando: Maybe you're right. What about this idea, then, the one about behaviour?

Jana: Well I suppose they might be able to help with that, in certain situations. Do you agree?

Fernando: Yes, but they don't always know about younger people and what we think is the right way to do things.

 3/4

Interlocutor: Thank you. Now you have about a minute to decide which two things would be most useful to learn from older people.

Fernando: OK, let's try and decide, then. Which one do you think would be most useful, Jana?

Jana: I suppose it might be school subjects. I mean, older teachers, or older people at home, you know, are more likely to help us effectively than people our own age, in my opinion.

Fernando: That's true, they really are the best people to teach us. Though I do get help with my homework from people my own age, too.

Jana: And how about the second thing? I think they can sometimes give good advice on how to behave – but not always, I know!

Fernando: Yes, but they often expect young people to do things exactly the way they used to, don't they? And the world has changed, so they're not always right, even if they think they are!

Jana: I know what you mean, but we should still listen to what they say, shouldn't we? If all teenagers just did whatever they wanted to, that wouldn't be good, either.

Fernando: Hm, maybe ...

Interlocutor: Thank you.

SPEAKING PART 4

Training

 2

Interlocutor: Do you think young people spend enough time talking to older people, Fernando?

Fernando: Well, I'd say we do, at least the people I know do. Our parents talk to us a lot, and many people have grandparents they can chat to. It's good because if you only talk to people your own age, you only see one point of view, really.

Interlocutor: Can young and old people enjoy activities together, Jana?

Jana: In my opinion, they can enjoy lots of things together. I don't think it's true that young people are all sporty and wanting to move around all the time, or that old people just want to sit quietly and watch TV, for example. I know older families who all go cycling together, and it's relaxing to go round to my grandmother's house after school and sit and watch TV with her! There are other activities where age doesn't matter, like playing music together, for example. Lots of music groups in my town have people of all ages in them.

Interlocutor: Is it a good idea for several generations in a family to live together, Fernando?

Fernando: I haven't really thought about that before, because I just live with my parents and my sister. I don't think my grandmother would like to live with us, because we're such a noisy family, and she likes peace and quiet. I imagine a lot of old people might feel the same.

Interlocutor: What do you think, Jana?

Jana: I know what Fernando means, but I actually think it can work really well. My friend's grandparents live with her and her parents, and they seem to get on very well. And my friend always has someone to help her with her homework, even if her parents are busy.

Interlocutor: Thank you. That is the end of the test.

Test 3   Audioscript

LISTENING PART 1

One
You hear two friends talking about a science website.

Girl: Have you tried that new science website the teacher told us about?

Boy: Yeah, what did you think? I wasn't too sure about some of the graphics, but otherwise I think it looks OK.

Girl: I know what you mean about the graphics, but I still think there's plenty on there that'll be good for homework and stuff.

Boy: Can't disagree with you there. But some of the information wasn't that easy to find, was it? I mean if you don't know exactly what you're looking for, then it isn't all that clear on the home page, is it?

Girl: You're right – it could have been better designed, and a bit more user-friendly.

Two
You hear a teenager talking to her mother on the phone.

Girl: Hi mum, you know that dress I told you about last week? Well I've just been into the shop again and it's still there. They've got a few things in the sale at the moment, but the dress isn't one of them, unfortunately. I know you'll probably say it's too expensive, but it would really suit you. And maybe I could borrow it sometimes, too! Anyway, all I'm asking is for you to have a look – I'm sure that if you see it, you won't be able to resist trying it on. I'd get it myself, but I haven't got any money at the moment.

Three
You hear two classmates discussing a history project.

Girl: We'd better get started on that history project, hadn't we? It's due in in a couple of weeks.

Boy: You're right, it is – I wish they'd told us about it sooner. And it isn't exactly thrilling, is it? I mean all that stuff we have to look up about conditions in factories and things.

Girl: I think it's OK. Anyway, we don't have much choice, do we?

Boy: No, that's true – and even though I don't want to do history at university, we are developing research skills, I suppose, and we'll need those, whatever we go on to do.

Girl: You sound just like the teacher when you say things like that!

Four
You hear part of a radio programme.

Presenter: It really is amazing how music can move a crowd of people – of course it's sometimes hard to put your finger on why one song makes such an impact, but another doesn't. And some singers can really communicate with an audience – that's one of the things that makes John so successful, I guess. You just had to be there, really. After that night, John's career really took off – for the next couple of years, virtually every single he released became a hit. But there were other bands there, and other singers, and on that special evening, which I'm here to tell you about, something magical happened.

Five
You hear a brother and sister talking about a party they organised.

Boy: That went well, didn't it?

Girl: I think it did, actually. It's a good thing not everyone turned up, or we'd have run out of food even sooner than we did.

Boy: Something to bear in mind next time – if there ever is a next time, of course!

Girl: I don't see why not – I know it wasn't exactly a triumph in terms of organisation, but everybody seemed to enjoy themselves, and that's what matters, isn't it?

Boy: Absolutely. It's a pity it had to end, really!

Girl: Oh, I'm glad we can relax a bit now. I mean you can't really enjoy your own parties, can you?

Boy: Well I just did!

Six
You hear a teacher talking to some students on a geography trip.

Teacher: Now I can see some of you are ready to write all this down, which is great, but there's really no need, because I'll give you all a handout when we get back to school. What I want you to do is concentrate, and above all, be careful, because it's very windy out there today. We're going to have a look at the rock formations I showed you pictures of yesterday. To get there, we have to go through the woods rather than use the cliff path, because that's being repaired at the moment. I'll tell you a bit more about what we're going to see before we set off.

Seven
You hear a teenage tennis player talking about her new coach.

Girl: I like my new coach – he hasn't just come in and asked me to do everything differently, like some of them do. In fact he's encouraged me to carry on much as I have been. I do sometimes wonder if he realises how tough it is for me to train so many hours a day as well as keep up with my school work. All he ever talks about is tennis. I know it's his job, but he should sometimes see things a bit more from my point of view. Since he's been coaching me, though, I've begun to feel I can actually win matches, you know, and that's amazing.

Eight
You hear a brother and sister talking about a long car journey they are going to go on.

Boy: I'm really looking forward to our holiday this year.

Girl: Are you ready for the drive tomorrow?

Boy: Well I've got a football magazine to read, and you know I like looking at the scenery, too – what about you?

Girl: I think I'll sleep most of the way – I'm really tired at the moment.

Boy: It's good Mum and Dad want to leave before breakfast, then we'll get there in time for dinner. You know how they can take ages to get ready. I'm glad we're taking the quiet coast road, anyway. Remember the bus we took last year and how it never left the motorway, which was totally boring!

Girl: Yeah, it was!

LISTENING PART 2

You'll hear a teenager called Harvey Mellor talking to younger students at his school about a school play he was involved in.

Harvey: Hi, my name's Harvey Mellor, and I'm going to talk to you about the last school play we put on, a comedy called *Key Player*. I hope that some of you will feel inspired by what I tell you today, and get involved in the next one – it's really a great thing to do!

This time last year, if you'd asked me about the school play, I'd just have given you a blank look, because I don't do drama, and the school hadn't put a play on for a few years. It wasn't until my history teacher mentioned it to me that I even knew about it, because I'd been off sick the day our English teacher talked about it to the class and most of my friends weren't very interested.

Anyway, I went along to a meeting about it a few days later, and I felt so excited about it all that I ended up offering to do more than just act in it: there were a lot of things they needed people to do, like make and paint the stage sets, get hold of things like furniture... So I agreed to help with the costumes too.

We also needed things like posters to advertise the production, and the teachers wanted my class to do the programme, and we had a lot of fun designing that. In fact I've got some here I can show you.

The teachers decided who would play which part, and I was relieved to be playing a minor role as a waiter rather than be in the lead as the musician – it put me under a lot less pressure, but I could still enjoy the thrill of being part of the cast.

Most of the rehearsals took place in the school hall, though the actual performances were in the school gym because, as you know, it's a bit more spacious. And when it was hot, we rehearsed in the garden too, which was fun.

I did need some help from my family, because I sometimes found it hard to remember what I was supposed to say, and when I was supposed to say it – so I needed someone to go over my lines with me but my mum and dad were too busy. So my sister offered to read through my scenes with me – my brother wasn't very helpful – he just laughed whenever he heard us!

We'd decided to provide food for the audience during the interval, so the day before the first performance – we actually performed the play three nights running – we were all madly preparing food, as well as getting everything else ready. Some people made fruit salad, and I baked several cakes, and the teachers made lots of sandwiches, too.

It was all such a rush, in fact, that on the day of the first performance, about ten minutes before we were due to start, I still hadn't got changed into my costume. And then I realised that something was missing: I had to wear black trousers and a black T-shirt, and shoes of the same colour, but I'd left those at home and only had my trainers – which were white! Luckily I don't live very far away, so my mum just had time to go back home and get them for me.

And it went brilliantly – the audience were great – loads of parents were there, and over the three days all the teachers came, but I hadn't expected so many children to come too. They really seemed to enjoy it and laughed in all the right places.

It was a great experience, and you should definitely consider getting involved in any future school productions. It's inspired me to try to get into the theatre business in the future – I think I'd have few career prospects as an actor, but I'd love to do something behind the scenes, maybe even be a director one day.

Now, do any of you have any questions?

LISTENING PART 3

You'll hear five short extracts in which teenagers talk about their best friends. For questions 19–23, choose from the list (A–H) what each speaker says about how they met their best friend.

Speaker 1

I met my best friend at another friend's house. There were loads of people there, and lots of people I knew from primary school. I saw this girl sitting on her own, and I felt a bit sorry for her – so I went over and chatted to her. She was there for my friend's birthday, but didn't know anyone else. We discovered that we liked the same films, sports stars, everything. We had so much in common – we'd

even been to the same concert the day before! Before we knew it we were spending all our free time together. It's a pity we're not at the same school, though.

Speaker 2

I met my best friend through a school project I was doing about the Olympic games. A school friend of mine said I should meet him, because his grandfather had been an Olympic athlete and won a silver medal. So she took me round to his house and he showed us the medal and let me take photographs of it for my project. Then we started chatting about other stuff, and it turned out we liked the same bands and things. I started hanging out with him and his mates, then we started playing in a football team together on Saturdays – now I'd definitely say he's my best friend.

Speaker 3

My best friend and I met in a massive queue outside the ticket office at the city hall. I was really excited because my favourite band were coming to play there the following month, and I'd managed to save up for a ticket to see them. I'd got the bus there early, but even so there were loads of people ahead of me. Then this girl right in front of me, who was wearing a T-shirt with the band's name on it, well she turned round and started telling me how worried she was she might not get to see them – and that's how our friendship started!

Speaker 4

I met my best friend on my first day at secondary school. I was feeling a bit like I had when I'd started primary school: I didn't know where anything was, and there was no-one I knew in my class. In the morning we were told things like which group we'd be in for our first piece of project work, and how much homework we'd be getting. All fairly boring, I thought, until after lunch, when we went outside and they organised some races. I'm pretty fast, but I was beaten by a boy who came up to me afterwards and introduced himself. After that, we were soon firm friends.

Speaker 5

My best friend is amazingly kind and thoughtful. That's why I got to know her, in fact. She'd just joined our hockey team at school, and we'd chatted a bit but not much. After training I always catch the bus home, but one day I missed it, so I was wondering what to do, because the bus only comes once an hour. Then I saw her waving at me. She was waiting for her mum, and she said her mum would be happy to give me a lift home too. I called my mum, who said that was fine – and that was the beginning of a beautiful friendship!

LISTENING PART 4

You'll hear a school Internet radio interview with a teenager called Stella Smith, who has recently had her first surf lesson.

Interviewer: In our school Internet radio studio today, we have 14-year-old Stella Smith, who's come in to tell us about her first surfing experience.

Stella: Hi!

Interviewer: So first of all, Stella, had you always dreamed of becoming a surfer?

Stella: Well, it wasn't really something I'd ever thought of doing, and we actually live a long way from the sea. But just before my family went to the seaside for a holiday, I was looking at all the activities and things teenagers can do there, and a friend posted a video online of her first attempt at surfing. I thought, yeah, I'd like to do that too!

Interviewer: And did you feel nervous before your lesson?

Stella: I thought I would be the night before, but I was OK, actually. It's not as if we were going to do anything risky in our first lesson, and I just felt curious really about what it would be like. I was a bit concerned about maybe waking up too late to get there on time, but that didn't happen.

Interviewer: So what happened when you got down to the beach?

Stella: Well there were about ten other kids there, all around my age – I'd thought I might be the oldest person there, so that was cool. Of course I assumed they were a group of friends, because of the way some of them were chatting together, but in fact they were just a nice, relaxed bunch of people. Some of them were fairly sporty types, but not all of them.

Interviewer: And what was your instructor like?

Stella: Keith? He spent ages explaining everything to us at the beginning, and we didn't get off the sand and into the sea until we'd all mastered the moves we'd need to get started – like lying flat on the board to paddle, then jumping up to kneel and then standing when we caught a wave. If you don't have all that clear in your head before you're in the water, then you'll find it hard to do very much. And he was very patient – though he did tell off a couple of the boys who were messing about – that was fair enough, I think.

Interviewer: And how did you get on in the water?

Stella: We had these big foam boards, which are easier for beginners to learn on than the fibre glass ones the experienced surfers use. Some people still found it hard to stand up on them and balance, though. I didn't find it too bad, actually. It made me think I should try skateboarding when I got home, and see how I got on with that! It's probably all the gymnastics I do – it seems to help with most things in fact – when I tried yoga once, I found that quite easy too.

Interviewer: Great! So what happened at the end of the lesson? Did they give you a certificate or something?

Stella: You get one after you've achieved a bit more, I think! But I did improve during our stay, because my dad bought me what they call a 'lesson card' – you pay for five lessons, and then you get a sixth one free. Lots of local shops hire out surfboards and stuff, but you need to be quite confident to do that. My dad had come down to the beach and taken some pictures of me standing up on the board, and I also got one from the surf school photographer – I'd expected to pay for that, but we didn't have to – it's great to have a souvenir of my first lesson!

Interviewer: When I first went surfing, I was absolutely exhausted for the rest of the day. Were you?

Stella: I was at first, and thought that in the evening, I'd just go to bed quite early instead of going to a friend's party I'd been invited to. But after my parents made me a huge lunch, I felt fine again, so I went out as originally planned.

Interviewer: Well thanks, Stella, for telling us about your first surfing experience!

Stella: Thanks!

Test 4   Audioscript

LISTENING PART 1

One
You hear a brother and sister talking about their aunt.

Boy: I really like it when we stay with Aunt Carol for the weekend, don't you?

Girl: Yeah, she's great! Some of those songs she was playing us yesterday were a bit boring, though, don't you think?

Boy: Oh, I loved them! Especially those folk songs. Anyway, the kind of music she likes doesn't really matter, does it? She's always

been a good person to ask if you have any kind of problem, hasn't she? She always has a good idea to help you solve it.

Girl: That's been my experience too. And she's always happy to talk things through properly.

Boy: Well, she's often in a rush, I find.

Girl: Yeah, I suppose...

Two
You hear a teenager talking about a sports centre.

Girl: I always go to Parkways Sports Centre. It's the best sports centre in the area, I think, although it's by no means perfect. I go with all my friends once a week, and there's a great atmosphere because there are always so many other people there – it wouldn't be the same somehow if it were quieter. I know they could do a bit more to bring it up to date. They could make better use of all the space in the changing rooms, for example. The café is great, though – there's plenty of room for everyone and they don't mind if you don't actually order anything.

Three
You hear a brother and sister talking about a meal their father cooked.

Boy: That was good, wasn't it?

Girl: Yeah, but it usually is, isn't it? We're pretty lucky really – I mean we were talking about it at school, and some of my friends eat the same thing every day – or that's what they say, anyway. At least you can't say that about dad, can you?

Boy: No, definitely not!

Girl: I learn a lot when he lets me help him, as well. You should have a go too sometime.

Boy: Well, you know I'm rubbish at cooking – I even burn popcorn!

Girl: That's no excuse! Anyway, if I'm ever that good, I'll be pretty pleased.

Boy: Yeah, and I should try harder.

Four
You hear a mother talking to her teenage son about a walk he is going on.

Mother: Whatever you do, make sure you charge your phone battery before you go – remember what happened last year and we had to come and look for you? I know you're going the same way as you did that time, avoiding the cliffs, and that's great. But you must find out whether or not it's going to rain while you're out there – have a look on that website I told you about, it's very good. I know you always dress warmly, so you won't forget your hat or gloves or anything like that – but you'd better see if your coat's dried out since yesterday.

Five
You hear two friends talking about their art class.

Girl: Hi, um, you look a bit worried – what's up?

Boy: I'm in a bit of a mess – you know that thing I was doing last week?

Girl: Oh, yeah, the picture of the horse?

Boy: No, I've handed that in now. The teacher said I needed to do a bit of extra work on it, and I'll need some more paint if I'm going to do that – but that's not the problem.

Girl: Oh?

Boy: You know that drawing of the tree I was in the middle of?

Girl: Yeah?

Boy: Well I've no idea where it is!

Girl: Oh no! What are you going to do?

Boy: There isn't much I can do, really.

Six

You hear a woman talking on the radio about a TV programme.

Woman: I can't recommend it highly enough – the camera work is brilliant. Of course they spent ages filming it and the programme makers have picked the best parts, leaving out anything they think might bore the audience. Even if you've seen similar things before, I can't imagine anyone not laughing when <u>the young are learning to fly.</u> They just look so funny as they try to copy the adults but can't quite manage it. They all succeed in the end, but you do get very involved and there are moments when you worry they might not. That's what keeps the audience hooked, of course. Whatever you do, don't miss it!

Seven

You hear a brother and sister talking about a holiday.

Boy: Cool holiday this year, yeah?

Girl: Yeah. Apart from the rubbish campsite.

Boy: Well we didn't spend much time there, did we? The beach was wonderful – and just have a look at these pictures of us on the train on the way.

Girl: <u>I'd thought that would be a bit dull, but the time passed very quickly, really. In fact the whole two weeks just flashed by – who'd have thought? I certainly wouldn't.</u>

Boy: There was plenty to do, so we can't complain – I hope we go there next year, don't you?

Girl: I'm not sure about that – it'd be nice to go somewhere different I think.

Eight

You hear someone talking about a concert he has just played in.

Mother: How did the school concert go, then?

Boy: Not bad really – at least I think it was OK. I mean, I hit quite a few wrong notes, but nobody seemed to notice, and I suppose that's the thing, isn't it: being able to carry on anyway. <u>And there were all those people there, which was amazing</u> and not at all what I'd expected. Of course I have to do it all again tomorrow, and I'm not looking forward to it much. There may be hardly anyone there at all – I'd hate that. But at least I've got the first one over with now – that's the main thing.

LISTENING PART 2

You'll hear a teenager called Tim Jones talking to students at a secondary school about a shop he helped set up when he was 15.

Tim: Hello, thank you for inviting me to speak to your school today about the business I helped to set up three years ago, when I was fifteen years old.

It all started when my aunt and uncle retired. He'd worked for years as a mechanic, and was happy to relax at home. <u>She, on the other hand, was worried she might get bored and had decided to use her savings to set up a small shop in our town.</u> I asked, 'Can I help?' and my parents told me that was impossible – I was still at school! I eventually persuaded them to let me, and promised that I wouldn't let it interfere with my school work.

So then we had to decide what exactly we'd sell. I'd always loved art at school, so we decided to choose something connected with arts or crafts of some kind. My maths teacher said she'd give me some extra help if I needed it for the business, but <u>it was my English teacher who suggested we should try selling pottery.</u> She knew some people who made beautiful mugs, as well as bowls and vases – things like that.

We found a tiny shop that wasn't too expensive to rent, and some friends and I put up a sign I'd painted on the wall outside. <u>We also created a really good logo for the shop on the computer.</u>

On the day we first opened, we were going to give out leaflets, then we thought that people usually just throw those away and they're expensive to print. So instead, <u>I stood outside the shop and handed out flowers!</u> It was such an unusual thing to do that loads of people stopped and chatted, and many of them came into the shop then too, which was cool.

The morning after we opened, my mum heard someone who'd come in and bought something talking about it in an interview about shopping in our town! I was getting ready for school and <u>my mum called me into the kitchen to listen. She always has the radio on in the mornings</u> and won't let me watch TV.

A few weeks later, we seemed to be becoming quite popular, and one afternoon after school when I was helping in the shop, who should come in but someone well-known! And by that I don't mean a local football player or anything like that – only famous in our little town – but <u>the chess grand master,</u> Marlan McPherson! I was so surprised I could hardly speak!

It soon became clear that pottery wasn't the only thing we could sell. Someone asked if we could display the silver jewellery they made in the shop, and <u>I saw that it might be worth trying to sell some of my drawings as well.</u> I'd done quite a lot of paintings too, but didn't think they were good enough – I was right about that!

Then the person in charge of the local jazz band came into the shop one day and admired a poster I'd designed for the shop. <u>He wondered if I'd be interested in designing a sweatshirt for the musicians to wear when they were playing.</u>

So that's how I started out – I'm now studying art and design at the local college, and still helping with the shop every afternoon. <u>My parents think</u> that being a designer might not be a very secure career to choose, and <u>would prefer me to consider being a businessman</u> instead, but I'm going to try and get into the fashion industry eventually.

And although the shop does take up a lot of my time, <u>I still manage to have fun with my friends. I love to relax with them and have a game of basketball,</u> and I'm planning to start playing tennis soon – it's something I've always wanted to do. And if any of you want to know more about helping to run a shop when you're still a teenager, I'm here to answer all your questions!

LISTENING PART 3

You'll hear five short extracts in which teenagers talk about clothes. For questions 19–23, choose from the list (A–H) what each speaker says about what is important to them about the clothes they wear.

Speaker 1

My friends all wear different types of clothes, and to be honest I don't think any of us care very much about what we wear in terms of appearance. As far as I'm concerned, <u>what matters is what things are made of – I try to wear organic cotton</u> if I can, but it's expensive so I just have a few things and wash them a lot! I could dress more cheaply, but that isn't the point. I'm hardly the most fashionably dressed person you'll ever see, and that's fine by me. Nor would I say you can tell much about my character from what I wear, really.

Speaker 2

I'm a twin, and as we were growing up, my parents dressed my sister and myself in matching clothes all the time. I know it made them happy, and we didn't mind at the time, but now we try to look as different as possible! My sister's always quite fashionably dressed, though I'm not – I suppose <u>I use clothes to try to tell the world what I'm like.</u> I have a blog where I post photos of myself in clothes that I've designed. I spend most of the money I'm given on clothes, and I do try to look good – without being too obsessed with my own appearance.

Speaker 3

I'm like most of my friends, really. It's not that we dress the same, or anything like that – it's just that we tend to put on what we're given to wear, without bothering about fashion or looking cool. My big brother's very different, and my mum sometimes gets annoyed with him about his clothes – she doesn't think he dresses smartly enough. I'd rather not argue with anyone, and I don't think clothes are particularly important, anyway. I don't actually know why some people spend so much on what's basically bits of cotton – maybe I'll see it differently when I'm older, but somehow I don't think so.

Speaker 4

My parents don't understand it, but they don't really mind. I wouldn't say it's a fashion thing at all, but my friends and I do tend to wear similar clothes – I suppose it makes us feel like part of a special group. It's not as if we have similar personalities, so I suppose we just feel comfortable like that – nobody stands out.

We don't do it to save money, but it does mean we're not always trying to keep up with the latest trends. And another thing I like is that we don't compete with each other, either, at least not in terms of what clothes we're wearing.

Speaker 5

I work in a sportswear shop every Saturday afternoon, and so I know quite a lot about different materials used in sports clothes. We sell things like football shirts that are light but keep you warm: clothes that are waterproof but allow your skin to breathe. I'm not very sporty myself, but obviously I have to wear that sort of thing when I'm in the shop. The rest of the time I'm in jeans and a T-shirt, nothing trendy or smart, though my friends and I do care about what we look like. I don't want to waste money on clothes though – I'm more into computer games!

LISTENING PART 4

You'll hear a radio interview with a teenager called Tom Dean, who writes a cookery blog for teenagers.

Interviewer: Tom Dean, who writes a cookery blog for teenagers, has come into our studio today to talk to me. Hi Tom!

Tom: Hi!

Interviewer: Now, first of all, when did you start getting interested in cooking?

Tom: People think I must have spent hours helping my mum in the kitchen when I was little. In fact I spent most of the time playing with my brother and sister and watching TV – and cookery programmes certainly weren't what we were into at that age! Recently though, we started doing cookery at school and the teacher inspired us all. And I was no exception.

Interviewer: Has your love of cooking changed the way you eat?

Tom: I suppose it has, in a way. I mean, we've always eaten well at home – my parents have always made sure we ate things that were healthy. But now I'm doing so much cooking, I'm very aware of what's in everything, and vegetables do feature more often these days in our dishes. My parents will usually buy the food I'd like to cook, as long as it doesn't cost too much!

Interviewer: And do your brother and sister enjoy what you cook?

Tom: Generally, they do. My sister's quite young, so some of what I make is rather spicy for her, and my brother complains about that too, sometimes. They can get a bit impatient, too, at times, when I'm making something complicated and they're having to wait for their dinner. When they realised that people were reading my recipes on the Internet and trying them out, they were very proud.

Interviewer: But do your family help you when you're cooking?

Tom: Well, we have a family rule that if you cook, you also clear up

after yourself – that means washing up, wiping surfaces, everything. They will look and see if I have the food I need for a recipe – that means I can just start cooking once I've done my homework after school. I make notes as I'm going along if I'm doing something new, and it would be nice if they'd help with that, but they don't like sitting around and I can understand that!

Interviewer: Why did you start to write a blog about your cookery?

Tom: I'd read loads of blogs by other people on the Internet – I hadn't expected there to be so many by teenagers like me. So at first I didn't see the point of writing one myself, especially as I have so little time to spare after school every day. Then it struck me that if I wanted people apart from my family and friends to try out what I was doing, nothing else would be as effective. It means I get loads of feedback too – both positive and negative!

Interviewer: And what would you say you've learned through writing your blog, Tom?

Tom: Loads of different things, really. It's amazing how interested everyone seems to be in the subject of food and cooking, wherever they're from. I find it easy to express myself in writing, fortunately, so that side of things is straightforward. When I started, I was full of ideas for all sorts of dishes, but there are times when I just can't think of anything, and I still have to write my blog – or at least I feel I owe it to my readers! I hadn't expected that to be such a challenge.

Interviewer: And finally, Tom, what are your plans for the future?

Tom: I think I'd love to carry on writing – books may be the way some cooks make their names, but in my case, I'll remain a blogger, I think. I'd also like to try to put more of this into practice, in a restaurant kitchen ideally. That would be my dream. There are colleges where you can learn all the techniques you need, and then I'd love to just get on with it myself – be the boss, you know!

Interviewer: Well I'm sure you'll succeed, Tom. Good luck with it all.

Tom: Thanks!

Test 5   Audioscript

LISTENING PART 1

One

You hear a news item about some teenage scientists.

Presenter: Young Egyptian scientists have been in the news several times lately – a teenage boy hit the headlines last week with some amazing ideas for the next generation of space vehicles, and now another teenager has come up with a brainwave about recycling. A sixteen-year-old girl has found that an inexpensive chemical could be used to create $78 million worth of biofuel each year. Egypt's plastic consumption is estimated to total one million tons per year, so her proposal could transform the country's economy, allowing it to make money from recycled plastic. Egyptian schools are obviously doing something right when it comes to teaching boys and girls about science.

Two

You hear an interviewer introducing a recorded interview with Darren Grey, a young writer.

Interviewer: Last week Darren Grey was nominated for the New Writer of the Year Award. Darren is only seventeen but his debut novel – *The Franklin Years* – received much critical acclaim. This is despite the fact that reviewers initially had no idea that its author was so young.

In many ways Darren is the typical teenage boy with a passion for rock music and skateboarding. But as soon as he opens his mouth you realise he is unusually articulate for his years. I certainly didn't imagine he'd be such a joy to interview when I went to meet him this morning at the skate park where he goes before school every day.

Three
You hear a radio interview on a programme for teenagers with a biology teacher.

Interviewer: Sarah, you recently gave up a career as a comedian to go into teaching. Do you find your experience as a comedian helps in the classroom?

Sarah: Well, I don't tell a lot of jokes to my students or anything like that. But I guess it's helped me have a sense of how I'm going down with an audience. I then modify my approach accordingly.

Interviewer: For example?

Sarah: Well, I was doing lots of project work in the open air with classes but I realised that they weren't as keen on that as me. So now they do more of their work online. They prefer that and so presumably learn more too.

Four
You hear two friends talking about a concert they have been to.

Boy: That was a brilliant concert, wasn't it! Miguette is such an amazing performer. She always really wows the audience.

Girl: Yes, and her voice is so powerful. You'd never expect someone so tiny to sing such deep notes.

Boy: I know. As well as being able to hit such high ones too! She is extraordinary.

Girl: That's right. And she uses her face and her body to put across the emotion in the songs she sings too. She does that so well and that's what makes her really special I think.

Boy: Mm. I know what you mean. Not many singers do that, do they!

Five
You hear a mother talking to her son about a rugby match.

Mother: Did you get there in time for the match, James?

Boy: Well, I just missed one bus but another one came along fairly quickly. I texted Ben to say I might not get there to meet him at quarter past two as we'd arranged. He texted back to say he was running late too. He'd left the tickets at home and had had to go back for them!

Mother: Oh dear! So what happened?

Boy: In the end, amazingly, we both got there by just after two-fifteen in reasonable time for a two-thirty kick-off but then we discovered the game was actually due to start at three, so we had masses of time!

Six
You hear a teacher talking to her class about some coursework.

Teacher: Now, let me give you some information about the geography coursework you have to do over the next two weeks. You're going to be doing it in groups of four and each group'll need to decide how you're going to split up the work between you. I'm going to give each group the names of two countries and you have to look at them from a geographical point of view, analysing their relative advantages and disadvantages as far as location, physical features and natural resources are concerned. You'll need to go into some depth and then come to a conclusion about which of your countries is more favoured, geographically speaking.

Seven
You hear two friends talking about their holidays.

Boy: How was your holiday, Meg?

Girl: Great, thanks. The food was amazing – I had the best ice cream I've ever tasted. And we were just 500 metres from the beach so we went swimming three or four times a day.

Boy: Was the water warm?

Girl: Like a bath. Even when the sun had gone down. It was brilliant to be out there in the water in the moonlight.

Boy: Did you do any sightseeing?

Girl: Sure. We went somewhere or other every day. There was one old city where they've made films about a detective based there. I haven't seen any of them yet but Mum's going to try and get them on DVD.

Eight
You hear a news item about a wildlife campaign.

Presenter: Today the National Butterfly Campaign was launched and it is hoped that listeners will support a number of events over the coming months. There is considerable concern that a number of species of butterfly have disappeared from this country. This is in large part due to the destruction of butterfly habitats as more and more land is given over to housing development. In an attempt to counter this, the campaign's objective is to get as many people as possible to transform their gardens into butterfly-friendly zones. You can do this by making informed decisions about what to plant and by thinking carefully about your gardening habits.

LISTENING PART 2

 3 02

You'll hear a student called Giorgio telling a class about his project on the spice called cinnamon.

Giorgio: Hi, there. I'm going to tell you about the project I've done. As you know, we all had to choose an ingredient used in cooking, and I've gone for cinnamon. It's a spice made from the bark of a tree. It grows in warm climates – its main producer is Sri Lanka – and it has a very distinctive and attractive smell.

Actually, cinnamon has been used as a spice for a very long time. Archaeologists know that it was imported into Egypt as early as 2000 BCE, so it's been popular for four thousand years or more. It appears in Greek and Roman literature from the seventh century BCE so its use was clearly spreading from Egypt to other countries in the Mediterranean.

To give you an example, it was mentioned in writings by the Roman historian Pliny. He explained how it was transported in boats up the Red Sea. The wind simply blew the boats along without the sailors having to use oars – they didn't even need sails.

During this period cinnamon was clearly extremely valuable. It was considered to be a present worthy of a king or a god. In fact Pliny writes that one Roman pound of cinnamon – the equivalent of one third of a kilo – cost 300 dinari, which was roughly the amount that someone would earn after labouring for ten months. So it was very much a luxury item. Now, the average person would earn enough to buy that amount of cinnamon in, perhaps, two days.

During this early period cinnamon may have been predominantly valued as a perfume. But it was also used in food preparation. We know for example that it was a typical ingredient in recipes involving oysters. We often use it these days in cakes and other sweet things but it's not clear whether the Romans added cinnamon to these too.

In the Middle Ages in western Europe cinnamon was valued but most people didn't know what it actually was. Many people thought, for instance, that it was found in the sea. They didn't realise that, in fact, it comes from trees. I've mentioned how cinnamon was used for perfume and in cooking. And that wasn't all. It was also thought to have medicinal properties. People used to believe that it could cure snake bites, for example. Even today it's used in medicines that aim to alleviate indigestion. Many people claim that it can do this effectively.

Another long-held belief is that <u>mosquitoes hate the smell of cinnamon and cinnamon oil is used in various products that aim to prevent them from coming near people.</u> Whether it's really effective has still to be proved, but there are some studies which suggest that it may well be. So it's definitely worth trying.

Most of the world's cinnamon comes from Sri Lanka – and that's where we usually import it from – but the spice in its various forms is also produced in large quantities in Madagascar, China, India and Vietnam. <u>Mexico uses a great deal of cinnamon in the production of chocolate, and in fact it imports more cinnamon than any other country.</u>

When I was doing the project, I was amazed to find out how much cinnamon is used in all sorts of recipes. I knew of course that it's a common ingredient in sweet dishes <u>but I'd never realised it could be included in meat recipes too.</u> I actually tried using it in a lamb dish and it did taste pretty good though I say it myself!

I chose to find out about cinnamon because I love its smell and its flavour. My mum uses it a lot when she makes fruit cakes and they're delicious, but <u>my favourite dish with cinnamon in it is apple pie.</u> I just love that. It can be delicious in bread too.

So, now let me ... [fade]

LISTENING PART 3

You'll hear five teenagers talking about a special celebration they remember. For questions 19–23, choose from the list (A–H) the opinion each speaker expresses.

Speaker 1

We always have a big family celebration at New Year. It's usually fun but the time I remember most was the year I turned twelve. I'd had to spend all day helping my mum prepare food for the meal – lots of different salads and a huge cake. I was a bit fed up about that as while we were cooking mum insisted on listening to the sort of music she likes rather than to anything modern. Anyway, it was OK once guests started arriving. <u>One of my cousins brought along a new friend of hers and she and I now spend most of our free time together.</u> I'd never have imagined that then though – she annoyed me by not liking the cake I'd made.

Speaker 2

The celebration that stands out most in my memory was my great-grandfather's 90th birthday. The whole family got together and there were aunts and uncles and other relatives from five different continents. <u>We'd invited his favourite singer to come along and perform for him before dinner. Unfortunately, though, her train was very delayed and she didn't arrive till late in the evening. But we had an informal sing-song instead</u> and I'm sure he really enjoyed that. And she did sing for him too and gave him a signed copy of her latest album as a memento of his special day. Ah, it was a fantastic occasion and certainly one that I'll never forget!

Speaker 3

We had a big celebration at school last Saturday. It was to mark 150 years since the school was founded. There were all sorts of events planned, finishing with a concert in the evening. <u>We'd been getting ready for it for ages and in some ways that was the best bit of it all.</u> We found out loads about the history of the school and about what had happened to previous pupils. One or two have actually become quite famous or important people. My class was responsible for the concert and there was an awful lot we had to remember to do. Inevitably one or two things got forgotten but nothing too crucial, fortunately.

Speaker 4

Our town has a special celebration on the 6th of February every year. It's an important date in the town's history, but I'm ashamed to say that I forget exactly what happened and why it's so important. Anyway it's always a fun day. <u>Last year I went along with lots of my cousins who I don't see very often and that's what made it particularly special.</u> There was a parade in the evening with people dressed up in all sorts of weird and wonderful costumes and loads of good music and stalls selling typical foods of our region. It was a really good day.

Speaker 5

I've got a twin brother and last year we became teenagers, so my parents planned a big party to celebrate and everything went just as smoothly as they'd hoped. Lots of family and friends came along. We'd been looking forward to it so much that I was afraid it'd turn out to be a bit of a let-down, but it wasn't at all. An awesome local band played and we all danced. <u>One of them left his pen behind and I've hung on to it. Whenever I use it, I think about the great time we had.</u> I guess we'll have to wait till we're 18 for another celebration like that!

LISTENING PART 4

You'll hear an interview with a young film actor called Diana Bainbridge who has just starred in a science fiction film.

Interviewer: So with me on *Film Today* I have Diana Bainbridge, the star of the new movie, *Galaxy 3000*. Diana, can you tell our listeners how you first got into acting?

Diana: Well, actually I discovered very recently that my great-grandmother was on the stage as a young woman so maybe it's in the genes! <u>But the fact is that I grew up more or less next door to a stage school that used to put on lots of shows which I went along to as a young kid and that's what got me hooked.</u> I didn't end up as a pupil there myself but I did have a great drama teacher and she certainly helped to fuel my enthusiasm.

Interviewer: So how did you get your first main film role?

Diana: That happened when I was fourteen. I was doing lots of amateur drama and was beginning to wonder if I'd have any chance of making a career out of it. So I subscribed to *Stage*, the main magazine for actors and wannabe actors. I applied for all sorts of roles through notices I saw there. I got a few walk-on, non-speaking parts, which was fun. But then <u>what happened was that someone who was working for a casting company came to see one of our club's productions and he thought I'd be just right for the role of the main girl in *Space Tour*, the film he was working on at the time.</u> The rest is history, as they say.

Interviewer: So how did you find the experience? Was it what you expected?

Diana: In many ways, yes. I'd read articles which went on about how film actors spend far more time hanging around the set killing time until they're needed, than they do in front of the camera. So that didn't come as a surprise. <u>What struck me was the way the top stars mixed with unknowns like me. They were so welcoming and taught me so much.</u> I thought I'd find it difficult not to be distracted by all the cameras and lights when I was on set but fortunately that wasn't the case.

Interviewer: Is there anything you find difficult about being a film star?

Diana: I do feel very lucky. Of course, journalists take a bit more interest in my private life than I'd really like – though I must admit that doesn't bother me too much. Some reviewers can be very unpleasant but I don't let it get to me. <u>What keeps me awake some nights is the fact that I've no idea when or even if I'll ever be offered another part. That's very unsettling.</u>

Interviewer: You've just finished *Galaxy 3000*. How was that?

Diana: It was great. I was working with some brilliant people. <u>And I had the opportunity to go to some amazing desert and jungle</u>

locations. That was absolutely the best thing for me. I felt so privileged. I had to learn to ride a horse for one scene, and that was pretty cool too.

Interviewer: So what ambition would you most like to achieve in the future?

Diana: Hm, that's difficult. I suppose like most actors I'd love to get an Oscar but, if I don't, then I'm certainly in very good company. I've had mainly quite serious drama roles and I sometimes wonder about having a go at comedy – I'm not sure that'd be my thing, though. Eventually I'd love to try my hand at making a movie. There's a book I simply adore and I've already got the film version planned in my head.

Interviewer: So last week you finished shooting *Galaxy 3000*, what are you planning to do now?

Diana: Well, I'd love to just chill out on a beach with my friends but that's not going to happen, I'm afraid. I've actually arranged to do some courses on theatre skills for kids at a summer camp. Then in the autumn I've been invited to perform in a play and I'll be on stage for the first time since I was at school! So lots of good things ahead, I hope.

Interviewer: Thank you, Diana.

Test 6   Audioscript

LISTENING PART 1

 05

One
You hear two friends talking about going to a classic car show.

Girl: It was expensive today but it was fun, wasn't it, Mike?

Mike: Yes, I loved seeing all those old cars, especially the sports ones. And at least getting our tickets in advance meant it didn't cost as much as if we'd bought them on the door.

Girl: Yes, and it meant we didn't have to queue which was good. There was so much to get round and it'd have been annoying to waste time standing in line.

Mike: True. Though I wouldn't have minded missing the old farm vehicles section. That wasn't really my sort of thing.

Girl: Oh I quite liked that. It was better than the section on the development of the engine. I could have given that a miss. The rest was all pretty good though, I thought.

Two
You hear a teacher talking about a visitor coming to school.

Teacher: OK, class. So have you remembered that next week John Coates is coming to speak to us? Mr Coates has been to the school before and everyone always enjoys his talks very much. He was our country's ambassador in Spain for a number of years and he's going to give us an informal presentation about his life in the diplomatic service in general and in Spain in particular. Before he comes I'd like you all to get hold of some information about Spain and make posters that I'll put up. I'll give each pair a topic to research and then you can decide how best to show the material you find. OK?

Three
You hear two friends talking about doing up a room.

Girl: So, Leo, how are things now your sister's gone off to college?

Boy: I managed to persuade her to swap rooms with me now she's not going to be at home in term-time – it's great to have a bigger one but it does look rather girly. Though the furniture's not too bad – it's got a lovely big desk.

Girl: So are you going to make any changes then?

Boy: Well, I wondered about asking mum if I could get rid of one of the cupboards. But I might just try papering the room – there's some tartan paper I've seen which I really like. Then if I put up my own posters and stuff, it'll soon feel totally like a new room, I think.

Four
You hear two friends talking about a film they would like to see.

Girl: Have you seen that new film *Antonella* yet?

Boy: No, I haven't. But I'm definitely going to go soon. It sounds really good even though I've never heard of any of the actors in it.

Girl: Haven't you? I've seen the woman who plays Antonella in a couple of things. She's brilliant.

Boy: My brother went to see it last night. He said the plot is extraordinary and even though it hangs on a set of amazing coincidences it's all actually about something that really happened.

Girl: That's what I heard. My cousin saw it and she said she got through a whole box of tissues.

Boy: Yes, I don't think there are many laughs in it.

Five
You hear a radio report about a zoo.

Presenter: Marston Zoo has just announced plans to raise its profile with animal lovers. As people who live in the south-east will know, the zoo has a wonderful collection of chimpanzees. These are very popular with school parties – as well as other visitors of course – so much so that the zoo has stayed open seven instead of six days a week since the beginning of the year. The zoo is going to put a webcam in the chimps' enclosure so that viewers will be able to log in at any time of the day or night to observe what is going on there. Similar schemes have proved successful at other zoos around the world and have proved an excellent way of reaching people – for example schoolchildren in remote areas – who would not otherwise be able to see these animals and how they behave.

Six
You hear two friends talking about doing presentations in class.

Girl: I thought your presentation was fantastic, Dan. You looked so confident.

Boy: Thanks, Meena. I didn't feel it. And I can't tell you how pleased I am that it's all over now. I don't really like doing that sort of thing, though I must admit it felt good that they all seemed interested in what I had to say, and some students even asked me a few questions – I hope I got all my facts right for them.

Girl: Yeah – you could tell everyone was really interested.

Boy: Now I've just got to see whether my teacher was satisfied with it. But I won't find that out till everyone's done their presentation so it might be quite a wait.

Girl: Oh, I'm sure you'll do brilliantly, Dan.

Seven
You hear a father talking to his daughter about plans for her birthday.

Father: Have you decided how you'd like to celebrate your birthday this year, Louisa?

Louisa: I'm not sure, Dad. I really enjoyed last year when we went to that wonderful bowling place in the town centre and I wondered about just going for that again. But actually I think I'd rather do something different. Ideally something I've never tried before.

Father: So what do you fancy?

Louisa: Oh, I'll let you decide. Make it a surprise. But in fact the main thing is that we go and see Grandpa as Mum says he's got to stay in hospital for another week. I know it takes a while to get to the town where he is but we could stay and do something else there after that.

Father: OK. Mum and I'll give it some thought then.

Eight

You hear two friends talking about a cake they have made.

Girl: That cake we baked yesterday was delicious, wasn't it, Tom?

Tom: It certainly was. We must make it again some time – perhaps with a bit more chocolate.

Girl: Oh there was quite enough for me. I was glad you came up with the idea of adding walnuts to it, though. That made it really special, I think.

Tom: I was pleased with that idea too. It suddenly came to me when I remembered a cake my aunt sometimes used to make. She used to bake the most delicious cakes in the world.

Girl: Even better than ours?!

Tom: I'm afraid so!

LISTENING PART 2

You'll hear a man called Nigel telling some students about his experiences in Antarctica.

Nigel: Good afternoon, everyone. My name's Nigel Grosvenor. Your teacher invited me here to tell you about my experiences in Antarctica as I gather you've been studying the area this term. I hope you're enjoying your studies. It's certainly a part of the world that's held great fascination for me ever since I was your age. Younger, in fact. I was only ten when I saw a film about the continent and that really awakened my curiosity. After that I read every book related to Antarctica that I could get my hands on.

I was particularly fascinated by one I read about its history. It was amazing to me that no one had seen the continent until 1820 when a Russian expedition came within 32 kilometres of the land mass and saw ice fields there. However, the first time anyone set foot on the continent is generally acknowledged to have been in 1895, although there has been an unconfirmed claim that an American sealer landed there in 1821. Anyway, from a very young age I dreamt of going to Antarctica myself.

As a teenager, I continued reading about the history and geography of the polar regions. However, I also loved biology and was unsure what to study at university. Eventually I made up my mind and went for ecology. That turned out to be a good decision for me as it led to the opportunity to visit the place I'd been dreaming of for so long.

After graduation I got a job on a research project looking at various problems relating to wildlife and changing habitats. I was sent to Antarctica to carry out an investigation of penguins. I went with a colleague who was focusing on climate change and we were able to help each other by sharing our findings.

There are a lot of different international research stations on Antarctica. We were based at one called the Mawson Station. In the past, people of course had no choice but to go to Antarctica by sea, but most scientists get there by air these days. I flew to New Zealand but wanted to arrive in the traditional way from there, even though it'd take me ten more days. I'm so glad I did. The views as we approached were out of this world!

The scientists based in Antarctica come from many different countries. Lots from New Zealand, of course, and Argentina as they're the closest countries to the continent, but also from further afield like Canada – more or less everywhere. There was someone from China, in particular, who was working on the same area as me and we were able to collaborate very productively in our work. I became quite friendly with someone from Norway but we didn't actually work together.

When they learn that I've worked in Antarctica people always ask me how awful the cold was. The temperatures were very low, of course, but we were all prepared for that and it was less of an issue than you might expect. Being outside in the snow is no problem in the right clothing. And I quickly learnt to cope with the ice. In fact, it was the wind that I found quite difficult at times. It could be unbelievably strong and there was nowhere much to find shelter.

Life there wasn't all work of course. I'd expected I'd spend most of my free time reading and had downloaded lots of books, but in fact we spent most of our evenings playing chess. We all got very good at it and became extremely competitive. Occasionally we'd switch to playing cards but that was much less popular.

It was surprisingly hard at first to readjust to life here when I came back home after six months there. I thought I'd miss the people I was working with but we're in touch so much that I can't say I do. The scenery there was spectacular but it's pretty good here too. However, I often wish the light here was as clear as it is there. It was wonderfully bright and unpolluted – totally amazing!

While I was there I wrote a blog. It's called *Iceman* and it's still online. You can read it if you're interested in finding out more about my life there. I've also just completed a detective story set in Antarctica. I wrote it for your age group and its title is *Snowstorm* – it should be available next year, I think. Anyway, have you …

LISTENING PART 3

You'll hear five teenagers talking about school trips to different museums. For questions 19–23, choose from the list (A–H) the opinion each speaker expresses.

Speaker 1

Our class went on a trip to the Science Museum last week. We go there quite regularly actually. This time I'd been studying engines and the museum's got a huge hall devoted to them. When we first arrived they showed us a DVD about the history of engines and then we had to fill in a worksheet. There are lots of other things to see at that museum but we didn't have time for anything else. The teacher said we'll be heading back there before too long as there's a special exhibition about space exploration on there soon. I'm really looking forward to that.

Speaker 2

I'd never been to the National Museum before I went with school last month as part of our history work on the eighteenth century. It was great and I'd love to go back there on my own at some point. I'd like to look at a famous sculpture of a ballet dancer that belongs to the museum – I was disappointed to find it was on loan to a museum in France when we went there. We spent ages in school preparing for the trip – we watched a great DVD and read quite a lot about all the exhibits in the museum – and that really helped us to make the most of the trip.

Speaker 3

Our art teacher loves taking us on trips to galleries and museums. They're usually pretty good. On our last trip we went to a gallery specialising in African art. We got to try lots of hands-on stuff which was fun. One of the people who run the gallery used to work as a teacher and she's got lots of really imaginative ideas for things that classes can do there – we did a brilliant treasure hunt game. Usually we do much more preparation before going on a trip than we did this time. But it didn't matter. Sometimes I think it's better to go round a museum on your own rather than with a group, but even so I enjoyed this particular trip.

Speaker 4

I almost always enjoy our school trips and the one we did last Monday was no exception. We went to a place called the Museum of Childhood and it was really interesting. A member of the museum staff took us round and told us lots of really fascinating things about the various exhibits and we watched quite an interesting DVD about how kids used to live. It's a small museum so we were able to see more or less everything properly – much better than going to a bigger place like the National Museum. That's where we went last time and it was frustrating 'cos we had to choose between seeing everything quickly or looking at a few things in a more thorough way.

Speaker 5

I usually prefer to go round a museum alone or with just one friend. When you go with your class, you have to stay together and sometimes the staff make you stay too long round just one display and sometimes they don't give you enough time. And this time when we went to the History Museum we had to stay in just one hall, the one with lots of stuff in it about the nineteenth century. I can't say it was my favourite school trip. They showed us an interesting DVD when we arrived but it all went downhill after that. And the teacher says we might be going back again soon!

LISTENING PART 4

 08

You'll hear an interview with a young man called Mark Collins who spends his spare time playing in a band that is gradually becoming well-known in his local area.

Interviewer: In our local Dalton studio today, I have a young man – Mark Collins – a student who spends most of his free time playing in a band. Mark, your band is called *Seaton Park* and you're gradually becoming quite well known particularly in this area. First, can you tell me how you chose the name for your band?

Mark: Yes, well most people imagine it's the name of a place we've got happy memories of or something like that. But it was a bit more complicated than that. At first we wanted to do something with our names. I'm Mark, of course, and one of my bandmates is called Phil Goode so we considered calling ourselves *Goode Marks* but then we weren't too sure about that idea. Then one day we were sitting around saying we just had to find something. The radio was on in the background and there was a news item on about something really important that had happened in a place called Seaton Park – I can't remember what now – but we all kind of simultaneously thought we could go with that!

Interviewer: That was five years ago, wasn't it? Has your band changed much since then?

Mark: In some ways, yes. We started out with four of us – two guitarists, a drummer and a singer, though the vocalist's a man now rather than a woman, so I guess that gives us a rather different sound. We went through a stage of having someone on the keyboard as well and that went down quite well. But then she moved away and we thought we'd go back to how we were rather than try to replace her.

Interviewer: For listeners who don't know your music, how would you describe what you play?

Mark: We sort of mix rock and folk, I guess. We write a fair few of our songs ourselves but we also do a lot of covers and some traditional stuff, too. So it's quite varied but what all our numbers have in common is that their lyrics are always meaningful. We want to say something to the listeners and not just through the melody or the rhythm.

Interviewer: Is there any other singer or band that you particularly admire?

Mark: Ah, there are lots. But I guess if I had to settle for one, I'd choose Flora Hernandez. I love both her beautiful sound and her approach. It's the way she's been able to produce such stunning work despite her humble origins and her complete lack of musical education. Most performers have had far less to put up with than she has but still haven't achieved as much. She's a fantastic role model for young performers, I think.

Interviewer: Mm, tell us a bit more about your band now. Where could listeners go to hear you play?

Mark: We do quite a few performances around this area and occasionally beyond. We even did a few concerts abroad last year. We haven't played in any of the famous big venues, though we've played to some quite large audiences as well as doing the odd night on the smaller club scene. To be honest, up to now we've gone more or less anywhere we've been asked, though I think we may be a bit more selective in future. It's beginning to get more complicated to fit things round the rest of our lives.

Interviewer: Tell us some more about your foreign tour. Was that a good learning experience?

Mark: It certainly was on all sorts of levels. We had a fantastic time. The thing was though, that we ended up out of pocket, what with flights, hotels and meals, hiring a van, agents' fees and so on and so forth. It was an amazing experience – we're now much more aware of what we can and what we can't do musically but I don't think we'll be repeating it for a while.

Interviewer: So what plans do you have for the future?

Mark: I guess we used to dream of making the big time and becoming really famous. We're gradually giving up on that now but we still love playing and I hope that'll never stop. We did several summer festivals this year and that was great fun. I suspect we might concentrate on those rather than playing lots of smaller local clubs on odd evenings throughout the year.

Interviewer: Thank you, Mark Collins.

Teacher's Notes & Keys

Test 1
Reading and Use of English
Part 1

Task type:
Multiple-choice cloze containing eight gaps.
There are four multiple-choice options for each gap.

Training

Students often make mistakes with prepositions, and the keys to Part 1 can depend on knowing which prepositions go with certain phrases.

1 These verbs could be put up on the board or written on individual slips of paper so that students can match the verbs with the prepositions. Once answers have been checked on the board, get students to make sentences using the verbs and prepositions in the exercise.

result *in*   participate *in*   co-operate *with*   approve *of*   rely *on*
succeed *in*   apologise *for*   insist *on*   consist *of*   concentrate *on*
believe *in*

Extension

You could make a wall display with the verbs and prepositions that the students can add to over time to help them remember the phrases.

2 Ask students to complete the exercise individually and then compare in pairs. Can they do the exercise without looking back at the verbs? Remind students that they will often have to change the form of the verbs to fit the gaps, as the text is in the past tense, e.g. *succeed → succeeded.*

1 succeeded **2** approve **3** consisted / consists **4** resulted
5 believed **6** relying **7** concentrating **8** insisted

3 Students complete the exercise in pairs and then check together as a class.

do	your homework your best you good better the washing up some exercise an exam
make	a difference friends sure a noise a mess sense
have	a good time fun a break a shower a party an exam friends some exercise
take	your time a break a photo an exam a shower some exercise

Extension

Students work in pairs again, this time to describe one of the phrases, without actually saying it. The partner has to guess the phrase. For example: Description: *If you go to a party and see your friends, dance and feel happy, what are you doing?* Answer: *having a good time.*

4 This extends Exercise 3. This kind of collocation is very important Reading and Use of English Part 1. You could display these phrases in the classroom for students to add to.

1 catch **2** spend / save **3** miss **4** go **5** pass / miss **6** play
7 cross **8** move **9** change **10** run

5 Ask students to try to do the exercise without looking back at the verbs. Can they remember which ones to use? Alternatively, write just the verbs on the board.

1 save	go	**5** take	doing
2 crossed	missed	**6** did	passed
3 play		**7** do	had/took
4 moved	make	**8** made	make

6/7 Students always have problems remembering phrasal verbs and need to learn them in context to make them more memorable. They should record any new phrasal verbs they come across.

put off   pick up   break down   come across   fall through
get out of   look into   pull over   run away   stand by

1 ran away **2** picked up **3** pull over **4** get out of **5** broke down
6 put off

Lead-in:

Put some verbs on the board that appear in the unit and ask students if they can remember the prepositions that follow, e.g. *co-operate, rely, believe, deal, apologise.* Then ask them to pay particular attention to the prepositions in the sentences.

8 Once their answers have been checked, get them to use the verbs and adjectives by asking questions, e.g:

What should you *take into consideration* when applying for a new job?

How difficult it is for you to *concentrate on* what you're doing?

Do you always *agree with* your friends about everything? What do you *disagree about*?

1 I would agree ~~to~~ **with** the opinion that keeping animals in zoos is cruel.
2 When I am reading and the television is on, it bothers me because I am concentrating ~~in~~ **on** reading my book.
3 If you decide to come ~~in~~ **to** my country, I would advise you to visit the capital.
4 I am always fascinated ~~of~~ **by** your garden.
5 This shows that it should be taken ~~to~~ **into** consideration.
6 We could finish ~~by~~ **with** some Spanish lessons.

9 This exercise focuses on the differences in meaning between words which look quite similar – which students have to distinguish in Part 1. Ask students to look at the four words before they start each exercise. Can they say what the differences are between them? Is there a difference in meaning? Or is the difference in how they are used?

a support	**i** confusion
b benefit	**j** fault
c assist	**k** error
d cooperate	**l** accident
e definitely	**m** resulted
f totally	**n** succeeded
g absolutely	**o** managed
h Surely	**p** achieved

Exam practice

One useful strategy for tackling Part 1 is to read through the text and try to think of a word that might fit the gap, without referring to the four options. This helps students to get a sense of the whole text, and the context surrounding each gap.

> 1 D   2 D   3 B   4 A   5 B   6 C   7 B   8 A

Part 2

> **Task type:**
> An open cloze test containing eight gaps.

Training

1   Write the words in the box on the board, and elicit examples from students of how to use them. Then get students to complete the exercise.

> 1 when   2 who   3 where   4 why   5 which   6 whose

2   Students complete the text individually and then compare their answers in pairs. Ask them to discuss any differences between their answers. Can they decide which answer is correct, and why? Then check answers together as a class.

> 1 who   2 where   3 when   4 where   5 why   6 who   7 whose
> 8 when   9 which (this could be replaced by *that* or omitted – *the amount of stuff that we take away* …)

Extension

Can students retell the text in their own words? See if they can roughly remember how the words on the board were used.

3/4 Linking expressions are often tested in Part 2, so it's important that students build up their knowledge of them – and how to spell them, as they will lose marks otherwise. Regular spelling checks at the beginning of each lesson can help.

> 1 Despite the fact that   2 whereas   3 owing to   4 instead of
> 5 in order to   6 as long as

> 1 yet   2 so as to   3 until   4 in view of   5 In addition   6 unless

5   Ask students to read through the whole text first to get an idea of what it is about, and then to briefly talk about the content with a partner. Ask some comprehension-checking questions – *What is a blobfish? What does its name suggest about its appearance? What problems is it having? What are conservationists trying to do?'*. Then get students to complete the exercise in pairs and check as a class.

> 1 whose   2 view   3 In   4 due / owing   5 unless   6 which
> 7 Despite   8 instead

6   Briefly review how articles are used in English, particularly that the indefinite *a / an* is often used the first time something is referred to, but this changes to the definite *the* when the same thing is referred to again. Once answers have been checked, get students to retell the story in pairs in their own words with their books closed.

> 1 a   2 the   3 a   4 the   5 any / many   6 a   7 few   8 the
> 9 more / some   10 most / some   11 none   12 an   13 few
> 14 both   15 one   16 the   17 Every

7   Quickly revise with the students when we use *who*, *when*, *which*, *where*, and *that* and when these words can be omitted.

Once students have completed the exercise, extend the exercise by asking them to supply their own endings to these sentences:

The biggest cinema in our town is the Regal, where ….

My favourite teacher is Mrs Smith, who ….

One special day in the year is New Year's Day, when ….

I want to wear my new T-shirt which …..

> 1 which   2 when   3 which   4 that   5 who   6 which

Exam practice

As with Part 1, get students to quickly read through the text to get an idea of what it is about. This makes it easier to identify the kind of word that might fit in the gaps, as it encourages students to read more widely than just the immediate context. Once students have finished, ask them to compare their answers in pairs, and discuss any differences.

> 9 spite   10 making   11 owing / due   12 the   13 not   14 few
> 15 instead   16 which / that

Part 3

> **Task type:**
> Word formation in a text containing eight gaps.
> Each gap corresponds to a word.
> The stem of the missing word is given beside the text and must be changed to form the missing word.

Training

Part 3 tests how familiar students are with the different categories of word that can come from one base word – i.e. verbs, nouns, adjectives and adverbs. Ideally, whenever students come across a new word, they should consider the different forms of that word, and how they are made, e.g. by adding prefixes and suffixes.

1a   There are a lot of suffixes here, so this could form part of an ongoing class project to build up familiarity with words taking different suffixes. The twelve words given here are examples, but there are many more that students could find. The table can be extended, so that students can keep adding new words each lesson.

> 1 childish   childhood
> 2 arrival
> 3 comfortable
> 4 agreement   agreeable
> 5 explorer   exploration
> 6 acceptable   acceptance   accepting
> 7 involvement
> 8 attractive   attraction
> 9 consciousness   consciously
> 10 friendly   friendship   friendliness
> 11 hopeful   hopeless   hopefully   hopelessly   hopefulness
> hopelessness
> 12 threaten   threatening   threateningly

1b/2   Remind students that it is not just a question of adding the suffix onto the word – there may be other changes to make, as in *survive* – the *e* has to be removed before the *-al* suffix can be added to make *survival*.

noun	verb	adjective	adverb
impression	impress	impressive	impressively
child / childhood		childish	childishly
arrival	arrive		
comfort	comfort	comfortable	comfortably
agreement	agree	agreeable	agreeably
explorer / exploration	explore		
acceptance	accept	acceptable	
involvement	involve	involving / involved	
attraction	attract	attractive	attractively
consciousness		conscious	consciously
friend / friendship		friendly	
hope	hope	hopeful / hopeless	hopefully / hopelessly
threat	threaten	threatening	

> 1 successful 2 membership 3 survival 4 memorable
> 5 admiration 6 appearance 7 active 8 widen

3/4 Put the prefixes on the board and elicit some examples from
students before they begin the exercises. Then get students to
complete the exercises in pairs.

> 1 impossible 2 irregular 3 inexperienced 4 illegal 5 impolite
> 6 incorrect 7 impatient 8 irresponsible

> 1 dissatisfaction 2 unsatisfactory 3 misunderstanding
> 4 unpopular 5 dishonesty 6 disapprove 7 uncertain
> 8 unhappiness 9 misbehave 10 disorganised

5 This exercise highlights the kind of changes students might
need to make when forming new words. Can they make
examples using each word in the pair to show the difference?
E.g. *Jack was very lucky. Luckily he didn't tread on the banana
skin and slip over.*

> 1 luckily 2 mysterious 3 activity 4 continuous 5 survivor
> 6 responsibility 7 financial 8 sensible 9 maintenance
> 10 criticism

6a/b This gets students to think about how many possibilities they
can make from one base word, by adding prefixes and suffixes,
and to think what *kind* of word they are making. This is very
important when they come to decide on words to fill the gaps in
Part 3.

> 2 e 3 c 4 a 5 b

> ***Suggested answers***
> competition competitive competitively competitor
> encourage discourage courageous courageously encouraging
> discouraging
> actor active actively activity action
> friendship friendly friendliness unfriendly

Exam practice

Encourage students to read quickly through the text before they
begin, to see what it is about. Ask them to cover the base words
at the side of the text. Can they try and guess the words that are
missing? What words might fit? What kind of words will they be
(nouns, verbs, adjectives, adverbs)? Are positive or negative words
needed?

> 17 introduction 18 unbelievable 19 flight 20 activity
> 21 enthusiasm 22 dramatic 23 earliest 24 championships

Part 4

> **Task type:**
> Key word transformation of six separate items each with a lead-in
> sentence.

Training

1 This focuses on helping students to build up their knowledge
of the form that different verbs need to take when they follow
another verb. These can be very difficult for students to
remember, and apart from some general rules, such as the fact
that verbs of liking are often followed by the *-ing* form, students
generally just have to try to learn them. It's important to take
into account students' different learning styles – some will find
it easier to remember after reading examples and completing
exercises, whereas others will commit them to memory more
easily if they have heard examples. A combination of both
works best, so students need to be given plenty of opportunity
to both read and hear the examples in meaningful contexts.
Start by eliciting examples from students of verbs that they
think might fit into either category, or both. Write on the board
the headings that are used in the book and ask students to
contribute. When they have run out of ideas, give out the verbs
on cards/paper and ask them to sort them. If they're not sure,
encourage them to try out the verbs in different sentences and
think about what sounds right. They may have more of a feel
for these combinations than they think. If they are still not sure,
refer them to a grammar reference book such as *Grammar
and Vocabulary for First and First for Schools* (Cambridge
University Press) – but only for the examples they don't know,
as this can be time-consuming. Set a time limit, and then move
on to checking as a class. Note that *like* can also be followed by
to but with a slight change in meaning, e.g. *I like going to the
dentist every six months* (I enjoy my visits to the dentist); *I like
to go to the dentist every six months* (I think it is a good idea to
go to the dentist every six months – even if I don't enjoy going).

Verbs + -ing	Verbs + to + infinitive	Verbs + -ing + to + infinitive (no change in meaning)
like	intend	start
mind	refuse	continue
suggest	promise	prefer
finish	pretend	
consider	offer	
dislike		
	tend	
avoid	plan	
enjoy	decide	
deny	fail	
risk	afford	
	like	
practise		

Extension

Once answers have been checked, encourage students to use the verbs in their own examples. Elicit a few responses from around the room.

2 Ask students to look at the examples and check that they understand the differences between the two forms. Ask some concept-checking questions, for example: *If you were going on a long car journey, what might you have to stop to do on the way?* (e.g. *stop to have a meal.*) To prompt further examples, the teacher can act out some irritating behaviours, e.g. humming loudly, making a lot of noise, whistling, slamming the door. Ask students: *What will you ask me to stop doing?* (e.g. *Could you stop humming?*) You could then go to the closed door and mime that it's difficult to open. Ask students *What am I trying to do?* then ask them for suggestions on how to open the door. (e.g. *You could try pulling harder. Try calling the caretaker.*)

> 1 In a, Jack stopped his homework so that he could start watching TV.
> In b, Jack stopped watching TV so that he could do his homework.
> 2 In a, the teacher carried on talking.
> In b, the teacher stopped talking about the project, and then started talking about something else.
> 3 In a, the speaker is making a suggestion about what to try.
> In b, the speaker is reporting what they have attempted to do.
> 4 In a, this is something the speaker needs to do.
> In b, something needs to be done, but not necessarily by the speaker.
> 5 In a, the speaker means that s/he didn't forget to take the project to school.
> In b, the speaker is talking about a memory they have of something in the past.

3 Before doing the exercise, quickly revise with students the verbs that they've covered earlier in the unit, e.g. *intend, promise, consider, decide, enjoy, finish, like, mind.* Put verbs on the board and check whether students can make full sentences using these verbs. Check a few answers around the room, with students working in pairs. Then check answers to the exercise as a class.

> 1 to hearing   2 to meet   3 in applying   4 to suggest   5 to improve
> 6 to ask

4 Before tackling the exercise, do a quick refresher on how to form comparatives and their meanings. Ask them to compare,

for example, two films / books / bands that everyone knows. Can they make examples using *-er than, more ... than, not as ... as* – e.g. *In my opinion The Lord of the Rings is not as interesting as The Hobbit.* Remind them of different ways of stressing how big / small the differences are, e.g. *slightly ... than, not nearly ... as, much .... than.* Also, remind them of superlative forms, especially the irregular ones – *the best / worst,* etc. Ask them to complete the exercise individually and then compare answers with a partner.

> 1 far better   2 the worst   3 less interested   4 a lot more slowly
> 5 as expensive as   6 more difficult   7 the most   8 much older

5/6 Begin by writing the phrasal verbs on the board. Can students explain what they mean? They may find it easier to think up examples of contexts where the phrasal verbs might be used, e.g. *clear up* – the weather can *clear up* and *get better,* or something like a rash might *clear up* and *go away.* When this preparation has been done, get students to match the verbs with the meanings given and check answers. Complete Exercise 6 as a follow-up.

> 1 k   2 j   3 g   4 i   5 a   6 b   7 c   8 f   9 h   10 e

> 1 clears up   2 got round to   3 caught up with   4 fallen out
> 5 take care of

Extension

Include a regular 'phrasal verb' check in each lesson. Give students, say, five to learn, and give them a mini test the following lesson. Encourage students to record the phrasal verbs they are learning, together with an example of how to use it.

Exam practice

As a way in to tackling the sentences, write the first sentence on the board and then just the beginning of the second sentence and the missing word. Can students produce the answer without seeing the end of the second sentence? Then give them the end of the sentence and ask them to amend their answers if necessary. (Note that in the example given, there is an alternative correct answer: *looking forward.*)

> 25 was much better than
> 26 got round to tidying
> 27 to stop and / to fix
> 28 prefer watching football to
> 29 apologised to Sam for missing
> 30 can't come unless Mum gives / grants

Extension

Try including a couple of transformations in the lessons on a regular basis – at the end, for example. Include key examples such as passives, comparisons, conditionals and phrasal verbs. Display each example on the wall for reference.

Part 5

> **Task type:**
> A text followed by six four-option multiple-choice questions.

Training

1a/b Get students to skim quickly through the text about Anna to see what it is about, and then talk in pairs about what they can remember. After this get students to look at the questions in

Exercise b. Tell them that there is no absolute right answer to these questions. However, it is getting them to think about texts that they will come across in Part 5. They will be required to think about any characters they are reading about, who they are, and what their story is. Check that they understand the questions, e.g. words like *optimistic*.

> 1 Anna is clearly a young person who's a great music fan.
> 2 Anna was planning to go to a concert with her friends.
> 3 They were feeling excited because a rock guitarist was coming to their town.
> 4 They were slightly worried that their parents might not let them go to the concert unaccompanied.
> 5 They were optimistic about being given permission as it was a young people's afternoon concert.

2a/b Ask students to look carefully at the question and then find the part of the text where they think the answer lies. They then look through the four options to see which one is closest to the part of the text they have identified. If they are working in pairs, get them to compare their answer with another pair, then check as a class.

Students should underline: Our town wasn't particularly big or amazing, so we couldn't quite believe he'd included it in his concert tour. Answer: C

3 Ask students to read through the text first and then cover the text and see what they can recall. This helps them build up their reading speed and comprehension. Check any unfamiliar vocabulary with them. However, stress to them that they shouldn't worry about unknown words which they don't need to understand in order to answer the question.

> 1 They travelled by bus.
> 2 They were dressed up – wearing *carefully chosen outfits*.
> 3 It was wet – it had begun to rain suddenly.
> 4 Their clothes were slightly wet – they *didn't look quite as good as we'd hoped* but they were still cheerful .

4a/b This task gives students practice in identifying the meaning of a phrase that they may not necessarily have come across before. Ask them to find a word in the phrase that they recognise, i.e. *damp* and think about what it means. Once students think they have a feel for the meaning of the phrase, ask them to look carefully at the four options. They should also remember to look at the rest of the paragraph where the phrase occurs, as this will also give them clues.

The rain had made them damp, but it hadn't affected how they felt – they were *slightly wet, but with big smiles* on their faces.

4b The correct option is C.

> **A** is wrong. It implies that they felt bad even before the rain started, which isn't the case.
> **B** is wrong. They were unaffected by the rain. There is no suggestion that they were disappointed.
> **D** is wrong. They were so thrilled to be at the concert that they didn't need to try to look happy.

5 This section is aimed at helping students to *read between the lines* – to understand opinions and attitudes that are not directly stated. Students should work in pairs to identify where the writer is expressing positive or negative attitudes.

> **Positive words and expressions:**
> *... the longed-for moment came ...*
> *... (the music) certainly didn't disappoint ...*
> *... the skilful playing ...*
> *... the way he made the instrument sing so effortlessly ...*
> *It was amazing ...*
> **Negative words and expressions:**
> *... he looked absolutely nothing like all the pictures ...*
> *... we barely recognised him ...*
> *... determined not to be put off ...*

6 Students should look carefully at the focus of the question – the writer's feelings about the musician – and then underline the part that reveals her feelings. Ask students to work in pairs and also ask them to say why the other options are wrong, and then discuss answers as a class.

> **A** Students should underline: He ... made the instrument sing so effortlessly, in just the way I'd always hoped to – but had always failed miserably.
> **B** is wrong. The musician looked nothing like they expected, but there is no suggestion that the writer or her friends were amused by this.
> **C** is wrong. We don't know how long he played, but they don't seem to have been disappointed.
> **D** is wrong. We know he played all his old hits but we don't know whether he also included some of his recent work, or how the writer felt about it.

Extension

Ask students to talk in pairs about a live music concert they have been to, or seen on TV. Then ask them to write about it for homework. Elicit vocabulary that might be useful: *musician, guitarist, solo singer, drummer, keyboard player, backing group, stage, audience, performance, atmosphere.*

Exam practice

Give students a limited amount of time to read through the whole text – say two minutes. Then ask a few comprehension-checking questions: *Who is the text about? What is he planning to do with his friends? So where is he going first? Why?* Help with any items of vocabulary that arise, but don't look at every word, as students have to learn to make sense of the text, possibly without understanding everything. Then get students to work through the questions. They can compare answers at the end. Discuss any differences of opinion. Remind students to refer to the *Advice* section for extra help.

> **31** B   **32** A   **33** D   **34** C   **35** B   **36** D

Part 6

> **Task type:**
> A text from which six sentences have been removed and placed in a jumbled order after it.

Training

Lead-in

Before you ask students to do Exercise 1, check that they understand the linking words and how they are used, for example which ones add a similar point (*what's more, besides this*), and which add a contrasting point (*however, on the other hand, although*). Then ask them to do the exercise individually and compare answers in pairs.

1 This aims to help students think about the kind of words that help to hold a text together, such as time words, linking expressions and pronouns for backward and forward reference.

> 1 What's more 2 Then / Next 3 She / one 4 At first / then
> 5 On the other hand / However 6 currently 7 This 8 Although

2 Ensure that students understand the purpose of the words in sentences 1–8, and get them to answer the questions in pairs.

> a 2, 4, 6 b 3, 7 c 1, 5, 8

3a/b This exercise is similar to the kind of task that students will have to do to complete the exam questions in Part 6. Ask them to read the base text very carefully and then choose the best sentence to fit the gap. Remind them that they have to look at the text both *before* and *after* the gap. What does *that* refer to in the text following the gap?

> Correct option: A
>
> B is wrong. A country home is unlikely to suit anyone who enjoys shopping. Also the sentence is quite positive, but the *And* coming after the gap adds a negative point rather than another positive one.
>
> C is wrong. *What's more* suggests that the sentence should follow a negative sentence about the city. And *that can be hard to achieve* in the following sentence doesn't refer to anything in sentence C.

Exam practice

Encourage students to skim through the text first of all to get the general sense of it. What does *Diamonds in the Sky* refer to? What sort of diamonds are they? Are they really in the sky or out in space? How did they get there? There may well be some vocabulary questions that arise with this text, but these are best tackled after students have completed the task. They should look carefully through the options. They may tackle each question in turn, or prefer to fit in answers that they can identify more easily first, and then go back to try and fill in the harder ones. However, ask the students to tackle the first question and check this together, so that they all clearly understand what to do. Remind students to use the *Advice* section for more help.

> 37 G 38 B 39 D 40 A 41 E 42 C

Extension

CLIL Students find out more information on this story from the Internet. Ask them to check which planets are involved, the process involved, and whether any progress has been made on bringing the diamonds back to earth.

Part 7

> **Task type:**
> A text or several short texts, preceded by 10 multiple-matching questions.
> Candidates must match a prompt to elements in the text.

Training

This prepares students for the kind of skimming and scanning that they will have to do in order to find the keys in Part 7.

Lead-in

Ask if any students in the class have been on a skiing holiday and what they thought of it. What level are they in skiing? Is it something their family does regularly? Is it a popular sport where they live? Have they seen any Olympic skiing on television? Do they think skiing is a dangerous sport?

1 Ask the students to quickly look through the paragraph first and then focus on the questions. Ask them to work individually and underline in the text where they find the answer, and then compare answers with a partner. Check they understand the vocabulary in the questions, e.g. *optimistic, overlook, calculate, subsequently,* and in the text: *chilly, cope, put off, touched.* Remind students to record any new words in their vocabulary notebooks.

> 1 … determined not to be put off … hoping our enthusiasm would grow …
> 2 … some practice on the dry ski slope … which we were all glad we'd done, in the event
> 3 … he'd reckoned without all the extra expense involved … ski-lift pass
> 4 … we've never actually been very keen … average ski resort!

2a/b Ask students to look carefully at the four options and decide which one reflects what Maisie says. The key is in the word *touched* so it is important that students understood this from Exercise 1. Then ask them to work in pairs to explain why the other two are wrong. This is an important skill, as students will be presented with ten different options in Part 7, which they have to choose from, and four or more texts.

> Correct option: A (… we were all touched by the fact that he really wanted to give us a special treat …)
>
> B is wrong. They weren't very keen on holidays in cold places, but they did make an effort to enjoy this one by going to dry ski slope classes beforehand.
>
> C is wrong. They were glad they'd been to the ski slope, but they didn't then find that skiing was easier than they'd thought.

3 Students read quickly through the text. Then pause for a moment to allow them to discuss in pairs what it is about. Check they understand vocabulary items: *virtually, gliding, ankles, burning, twisted, unforgiving, promoted.* Remind them to record new items in their vocabulary books. Then ask some comprehension-checking questions: *What were Marko's first experiences of going out on the slopes to ski? Did he manage to glide or jump? Were people gasping in admiration? Why were his ankles **burning with pain**? What was the **amazing thing** that happened?*

> 1 I spent most of the first hour or so down on the ground, ankles burning with the pain of being twisted …
> 2 … gliding skilfully down the slope, doing an amazing jump or turn at the bottom, and hearing gasps of admiration from everyone watching.
> 3 … something amazing happened and I actually experienced what it felt like to ski a short distance without crashing over.
> 4 Of course, nobody had told me what it would really be like to be on skis, had they?

4a/b Once students are familiar with the text, ask them to look at the three options and identify which most closely matches what Marko says. Check they know the meaning of all the vocabulary, e.g. *a natural skier, put off, instructor's response.*

> Correct option: B (But I was determined to keep going …)
>
> A is wrong. He didn't conclude that he wasn't a natural skier; in fact *it wasn't long before something amazing happened* and he was able to ski a short distance.
>
> C is wrong. He'd already begun to perform much better by the time his instructor promoted him, so it wasn't a surprise.

Exam practice

Lead-in

Ask whether any students in the class have taken part in swimming competitions of any kind, especially open-water ones. Have they ever been open-water swimming? Can they describe the experience? In which ways is it different from swimming in a pool?

Ask students to skim-read through the task so that they have a good idea of what each text is about. Set a time limit for this – check on progress after two minutes. Then get them in pairs to summarise what is in each text – ask them to talk about two texts each. Take any questions on vocabulary and check a few unfamiliar words together as a class, but stress that they may not need to understand every word to complete the task. You could ask comprehension-checking questions here, but it might be more useful to get on with the task.

Get students to read through paragraph A slowly and then look at the questions, putting an A next to the ones they think belong with paragraph A, underlining the parts of the question and text that tell them. Give them time to all find the answer, then check in pairs, and as a whole class. Make sure everyone understands what they have to do. They should then continue with B, C and D. They may find that they have two or three they have not matched up. They should then go through the texts again looking for matches. Remind them to refer to the *Advice* section for some further help.

43 B	44 D	45 A	46 C	47 A	48 D	49 B	50 C	51 D	52 B

Extension

Students could write a short paragraph about any positive swimming experiences, such as: learning to swim, open-water swimming, competitions, or just fun at the swimming pool, so that people who aren't strong or competitive swimmers also have something to write about.

Extension

CLIL Ask students to do a little research on open-water swimmers, and whether there are any famous ones in their home countries. Open-water swimming is now an Olympic sport – what can they find out about it? Ask them to prepare a short, informal presentation / discussion to be done in pairs. This can be followed up by a piece of writing to consolidate what they have learnt.

Test 1
Writing
Part 1

Task type:
An essay of 140–190 words giving an opinion and providing reasons for the opinion.

Training

Lead-in

This question is about good places to go for class trips. Ask students to talk in pairs about class trips they have been on, or places they would like to go. Ask around the class for a few examples to share with the whole class.

1 This exercise is aimed at helping students to develop strategies for tackling a Part 1 question. Ask students to read each part of the question carefully. The first part tells them what the general

topic is. This is then followed by the focus question on the same topic, which tells them exactly what to write about, with notes on ideas they must include.

2a/b Ask students to look at the adjectives in the list and make sure they understand them. Refer them to an English–English dictionary, but be prepared to take any further questions on them. Then get students to work individually to match each adjective with a definition, and then compare their answers in pairs.

Possible answers
1 urban
2 exhausting
3 picturesque, breath-taking, dramatic, impressive, fascinating
4 coastal
5 peaceful
6 memorable, impressive, outstanding, thrilling, remarkable
7 accessible
8 original
9 educational
10 interactive

Extension

Students spend a few minutes in pairs making definitions of the adjectives not already used and then swap with another pair to see if they can find the answer.

3 Ask students to talk about a trip they have done to one of the places in the list – not necessarily on a class trip. Give them time to prepare and make a few notes, and remind them to make use of some of the adjectives from Exercise 2. Then ask them to give a mini-presentation to their partner. Set a time limit, say 90 seconds. While the partner is listening, they should be thinking of two questions they can ask the speaker at the end. To round up, ask one or two people in the class what their partner talked to them about. Ask students to keep their notes.

Extension

Students can use their notes to write a short piece about their trip for homework. Set a word limit, e.g. 150 words. Tell them they can also include pictures if they have any.

4 Ask students to look and decide which places are in the city or in the countryside. This is preparation for the sample exam question that follows. The students are then given the focus question of the task.

5a–c Ask students to discuss the first two notes in pairs. They should already have some ideas from the work they have done. Remind them that they must give a reason for their answers. They can note down some brief ideas at this point.

6 Ask students to read through the sample answer carefully, and pay particular attention to the introduction, which they will also have to add in their answers. Which adjectives has she used from the list?

7 Students should look at how Sarah has tackled the first two points in the notes. Which one does she think is more interesting? Does she make a choice about the convenience point?

She thinks that the countryside could be more interesting, especially if you have an expert with you to explain things.
She thinks that deciding how convenient it is to visit the city or the countryside depends on where you live, and how far you are from each one.

8 Now students should look at the idea of their own that they have to come up with. Ask them to look at Sarah's answer and decide what aspect of the trip she is writing about *(how enjoyable)*.

> Sarah is talking about how enjoyable the countryside might be compared with the city.

9 This gives students additional ideas that they can include in their essay. Ask them to think about what they could say about each of these, e.g. *cost: the cost of transport, food, entrance tickets; weather: countryside locations not so good in winter, and bad weather at any time may ruin the trip; equipment: may be needed for outdoor pursuits – walking, climbing, cycling will all need weather-proof clothes and suitable footwear; age of teenagers: if they are young they may need more supervision.*

> **Possible answers**
> *Cost:* what might teenagers have to pay for on a city trip? Transport? Food? Entrance fees? How would that compare with the countryside? They might not have entrance fees to pay.
> *Weather:* in the city this wouldn't be so important as students are more likely to be doing something inside. But bad weather could ruin a trip to the countryside.
> *Equipment:* this really applies more to the countryside. Students might need good walking shoes, warm weather-proof clothes, and special equipment if they do a sport. In the city, they might need things like a camera, a guidebook and perhaps notebooks and pens.
> *Age of teenagers:* younger teenagers might appreciate outside activities more? Would older teenagers get more from a theatre or museum trip?

10 Remind students that they need to round off their essay in some way, not just end abruptly when they have covered all the points. One sentence may be enough to summarise what has already been said.

11a/b Students should look back at how Sarah used these linking phrases in her essay, and then complete the exercise in pairs. Remind students that they should keep a note of this type of phrase so that they can use them correctly in their own answers.

> **1** that's especially true if **2** That's why **3** Even though
> **4** If **5** it depends **6** Another point to consider

Extension

Students could write their own answer, either in class or for homework. If they do it in class, consider these two approaches: *either* they write their answer and check it, say within a 30-minute time limit. Then if students feel comfortable enough with each other, they work in pairs and edit each other's work. Remind them that they must not be too negative about their partner's work. This can work well provided classmates trust each other – but don't attempt it unless they are likely to handle it well. *Or* students could be put in pairs or small groups to produce a part of the essay each. This could be done on flipcharts or computers. Then display the results to the whole class, and get everyone to look at the work and suggest corrections. Remember to emphasise the positive aspects of the work and remind students to do the same.

Exam practice

Ask students to look at the *general* topic: sport. Have a brief discussion about, e.g. who does sport on a regular basis? Why? What are the benefits? Team sports or individual sports? Outside sports or inside ones? Then look at the focus question – outside *v* inside sports, and which is better.

Move on to the notes – enjoyable and cheaper, plus another idea of their own. Run through some ideas as a class for the last point, e.g. better for health, more convenient, cheaper. Give students about 30 minutes to produce an answer and check their work, then collect in for correcting.

> **Sample answer**
> Most people would agree that doing any kind of sport is important. However, some people will opt for outside sports, whereas others might enjoy inside sports more. So which is better?
> Outside sports can be fantastic to do in the summer when the weather is good, provided it is not too hot. But once the chilly weather of winter arrives, inside sports definitely seem more attractive to many people. However, there will be people who still want to play sports such as football outside and are not put off by the weather.
> A disadvantage of inside sport, though, is that there is usually a cost involved, such as entrance fees or equipment hire, while many outside sports can be enjoyed for free. This may influence some people's decision about which is better.
> I would say that whichever kind of sport people choose, the important thing is that they actually participate, as there is no doubt that sport is good for our health. And if more people take part and start to demand sports facilities, we will have a wider range of sports available to us.
> (185 words)

Part 2 (letter / email)

> **Task type:**
> Writing one task from a possible selection of five text types (article, letter / email, essay, review, story) based on a contextualised writing task *or* a question related to a set text in 140–190 words.

N.B: From 2015 onward, the revised *Cambridge English: First for Schools* exam will have only one set text and one set text question on the paper, rather than the two texts and two questions as previously. Candidates should not attempt the optional set text question in Part 2 unless they have the necessary understanding of the text to answer the task set. Teachers are best placed to judge which, if any, of the set texts and/or film versions may be appropriate and stimulating for a given teaching situation. The suggested editions are Graded Readers which have been adapted to the level and are suitable for *Cambridge English: First for Schools* candidates. Other editions of these books may be available. Teachers and candidates should be aware that the language level in other editions may be less accessible.

Training

1 The list helps students to learn some set phrases they can use to put into their letters and emails to open and close them, without wasting too many words. Remind students that they should not write too much in their introduction, however, as they need to devote the majority of their response to answering the question. Get them to complete the exercise individually and then compare their answers in pairs. Please note: Letters and emails in the *Cambridge English: First for Schools* Writing paper will require a response which is consistently appropriate in register and tone for the specified target reader, for example, a school principal, an English-speaking friend, a magazine editor or a classmate.

> **1** O **2** C **3** O **4** C **5** C **6** C **7** C **8** C **9** O **10** C **11** C **12** O

2a/b Ask students to read carefully through the exam task and then in pairs start thinking of some points to include. Remind them that Dan has asked for some advice, which they must give in their answer.

3a/b Students read Max's letter, then close their books and see what they can remember. What does Max suggest that Dan should do? Ask students to look at the list of functions and decide which ones Dan has included.

> **Functions in order of the text:**
> (4) saying thanks (Thanks for your last letter.)
> (1) apologising (... sorry I haven't replied sooner.)
> (9) agreeing (... sounds fantastic, doesn't it?)
> (6) being sympathetic (... I'm sorry to hear ...)
> (8) giving advice (If I were you, ...)
> 5 paragraphs, including close

4a/b Before looking at the exercise, elicit from the students different ways of making suggestions. Then ask them in pairs to come up with different suggestions for the problems in Exercise 4b.

> **Possible answers**
> **1** If you use the camera on your phone, you'll probably get some good shots.
> **2** Why don't you ask the teacher if he's got some spare kit you can borrow?
> **3** If I were you, I'd ask people in the class if they've seen it.
> **4** I think you should ask your mum if she'll give you a lift instead.

Extension

You could try writing different problems on cards and give students one each. Then they move around the room and explain their problem to someone. The other person has to make suggestions to help out. They then exchange cards, and move on to talk to someone else. This is a good activity for improving group dynamics, and gets students who don't normally talk to each other to interact. Then when they are sitting down again, ask for a few examples around the room of what their last problem was and what advice they were given.

5a/b Remind students how question tags work, i.e. positive sentence with a negative tag, and negative sentence with a positive tag. Put a few examples on the board, e.g. *You can see him, can't you? You can't see him, can you?* Ask students to complete the exercises in pairs and check together as a class.

> **1** won't you? **2** wasn't it? **3** is it? **4** shouldn't you?
> **5** didn't we? **6** don't we?

Extension

Ask students to write about six question tag sentences on different pieces of paper – sentence on one, tag on another. Tell them they must use a range of tenses. Check each pair's sentences. Then swap their sentences with another pair and see if they can solve each other's.

6a/b Remind students of how to write indirect questions and statements. Put one sentence on the board as an example, e.g. the one given: *Will they change their minds? I don't know if ...*

> **1** if / whether Mark is / 's at home today
> **2** what homework our teacher gave us
> **3** if / whether there's a party tomorrow night.
> **4** this answer is / 's wrong.
> **5** if / whether teenagers in your country watch a lot of TV
> **6** if / whether your sisters are going on holiday with you

Exam practice

Remind students to read the question carefully and maybe make a few notes before beginning to write.

> ***Sample answer***
> Many thanks for your letter – it was really nice to hear from you. The party sounds great, doesn't it? But I'm sorry you feel you've got nothing to wear, and that your sister won't help you. My sister's like that, too! Unfortunately, though, whenever she borrows my clothes, they often come back with a hole in or a mark on them, so I don't let her borrow them anymore!
> But perhaps if you explain to your sister why you really need something to wear, she might be more willing to help you. If that doesn't work, why don't you ask your parents if they could give you a little money to buy something new? Do you know if they would agree to that? Alternatively, maybe you could ask a close friend if they have something nice you could wear. I'm sure they wouldn't mind – that's what friends are for, after all!
> Well, Maria, I really hope you solve your problem, and that you have a great time at the party. Don't forget to write and tell me all about it!
> All the best.
> (183 words)

Part 2 (story)

> **Task type:**
> Writing one task from a possible selection of five text types (article, letter / email, essay, review, story) based on a contextualised writing task *or* a question related to a set text in 140–190 words.

Training

1a/b Students need to look carefully at the rubric to see who they are writing for. In this case, it is the readers of a magazine for teenagers – people roughly their own age, in other words. There is no right or wrong answer as to who Sam and Henry are, but it helps the students to imagine the story if they can visualise the people in it. It's also a useful reminder that the story is not about themselves but two other people, so they shouldn't accidentally slip into the first person *I* halfway through their answer. It's also important that they refer consistently to the people throughout the story, with no accidental name or gender changes. The remaining bullet points should get them to start thinking about what their storyline will be. This is important, as in the exam they should have a general idea of how the story will progress to the end, rather than running out of ideas halfway through.

1c Ensure that students know the meanings of all the words before they begin. They could work in pairs or groups, and then take a number of words each, checking unknown words in an English–English dictionary and reporting back to their partner or group. Encourage them to record any new ones in their vocabulary notebook. Discuss any words that students have categorised differently from the suggestions below.

Sample answer

the letter	the road / countryside	the weather	your feelings
mysterious	rough	stormy	optimistic
confusing	picturesque	bright	eager
surprising	stunning	damp	enthusiastic
astonishing	bumpy	frosty	puzzled
	wild	bitter	confident
	coastal	mild	nervous
	muddy	misty	determined
	unfamiliar		uneasy
		wild	
		rough	

2   Students could try doing this exercise on their own, and then compare their answers with a partner. Ask them to look carefully at any answers where they disagree, and think which answer might be correct. Can they retell the story to each other in their own words? They could also practise writing it from memory as a timed piece of writing.

> **1** had / arrived **2** got **3** had been raining **4** was **5** walked
> **6** took **7** laid **8** went **9** was making **10** wandered
> **11** were sitting **12** chatting **13** handed **14** had brought
> **15** had got **16** was looking **17** were **18** saw **19** was **20** cried

3   Again, students work by themselves and then compare. Can they make their own sentences using the remaining three time expressions?

> **1** finally **2** as soon as **3** while **4** gradually / until
> **5** by the time **6** during

4   Discuss any alternative answers that students have put in. Check that they fully understand what each of the adverbs means. Can they suggest another context when they might speak or behave in these ways? If appropriate to the class, students can mime or act out the adverbs by speaking in the manner of the adverb.

> **Possible answers**
> **1** confidently / enthusiastically / cheerfully
> **2** peacefully
> **3** crossly
> **4** jealously / miserably / crossly
> **5** nervously / anxiously / miserably
> **6** calmly

5   Ask students to compare the words and expressions they have underlined, and discuss any differences they have.

Students should underline the following:

Descriptive adjectives: puzzled, eager, rough, bumpy, determined, bitter, picturesque, difficult

Time words: that morning, at first, almost immediately

Adverbs that describe the way people said or did things: anxiously, confidently

Verbs in the past simple: read, climbed, set off, were, was, didn't, asked, replied, worked out, came across, announced, cycled, opened,

Verbs in the past continuous: was going on, were heading into

Verbs in the past perfect: had been, had cycled

Extension

Bring in objects for students to write stories about, e.g. make a pile of apparently unrelated items on a table – a watch, a piece of wood, a photo, some money, an invitation, a mobile phone, etc. Ask students to choose two items and write a short story about them.

Exam practice

The candidate's answer is within the word limit and continues from the prompt sentence. It also includes the two ideas at the end of the exam question. It uses good descriptive language and is well-organised.

> **Sample answer**
> The photo slipped to the floor, and Nicholas picked it up carefully. It was a picture of an old house surrounded by trees along a rough, bumpy road, with a dark and stormy sky in the background. As Nicholas looked more closely, he could just see an old man gently leading a horse. Nicholas felt uneasy just looking at it – it seemed a wild and mysterious place.
> Somehow, he needed to find the owner, as he was sure the photo was precious to them. He put a notice on the school board, and waited for the owner to contact him. Sure enough, the following day a girl he knew came to his classroom. 'I can't tell you how happy my family are to get that photo back!' she said excitedly. 'It was the last photo of my great-grandad's farmhouse before it was sold, so thanks for trying to find out who it belonged to. And look – my dad's sent you something! We're so grateful, Nicholas!'
> When she'd gone, Nicholas opened the envelope. Inside was enough money for him to buy the new computer game he wanted! A happy ending!
> 189 words

Test 1
Listening
Part 1

> **Task type:**
> One multiple-choice question per short monologue or exchange, each with three options.

Training

1   This is aimed at encouraging students to look carefully at the different parts of the question, and to confirm where the answer comes from. They also need to think about the attitudes and opinions of the speakers, which may be implied rather than stated in the audioscript.

Question 1

Ask students to read the rubric for the first context-setting sentence, and then ask: *Who is talking? What are they talking about?* Ask students what they know about wildlife parks. What would they expect to see there? How big would it be? Who in the class has been to one? Look at the questions, and the three options. Are they positive, negative or neutral? Ask students to read the audioscript, and underline where they think the answer came from. They can work individually for this and then compare in pairs. As consolidation, one of the pair can read the audioscript to the other to confirm where the answer lies.

Question 2

Take students through both parts of the question. Read the context-setting sentence – *Who is talking? What about?* Then look at what they are being asked – they have to identify *which class* the friends have just had. Look at the options. Ask students to think about what words they might expect to hear when students are talking about these subjects, e.g:

maths – *sums, add, subtract, calculator, work out, fractions*
geography – *countries, world, rivers, mountains, lakes, globe*
history – *time, dates, ancient, past, years ago*

Which words did they hear? What gave them the clues that A was the answer? Again, ask students to underline in the text where the answer came from. Then they could also read out the dialogue in pairs to confirm they are happy that A is the answer.

Question 3

Students look at both the context-setting sentence and the focus question. Check that they know what they are listening for. Before they look at the options, get them to speculate – *why* might a customer in a shop be talking to an assistant? To pay? To complain? To ask for something? To talk about the price of something? Check they know *refund* before they listen.

This time, one pair of students could read the dialogue while another pair tries to answer the question. When they have got their answer, the first pair must confirm from their reading whether it is correct. Check the answer as a class. Check vocabulary after they have completed the task, e.g. – *try on, changing room, in stock, hole, sleeve, faulty.*

Question 4

Go through the same procedure as above with the context-setting sentence and the focus question.

Make sure students understand that this is about the boy's *opinion* of the film. Before they begin, check students know *soundtrack.* Ask students to work in pairs. One can read out the audioscript while the other listens, then they can compare answers. Check as a class. Ensure students are familiar with the vocabulary in this audioscript, e.g . *publicity, hype, in some respects, storyline, kept you on the edge of your seat, a letdown.*

Question 5

Students have had some practice now at how to tackle Part 1s, so treat this one as if it were a real Part 1 question. Give students time to read through the question, and then play the recording. Get students to answer in pairs and check as a class.

> **1** B (… especially having driven for miles to get there … much-needed rest and drink)
> **2** A (… I don't remember doing fractions in that way … now we've got calculators …)
> **3** C (… there's actually a hole in the sleeve … I don't really want to get something that's faulty …)
> **4** A (… the whole storyline kept you on the edge of your seat – until the final few minutes. What a let-down!)
> **5** B (… but are they big enough? … these aren't really made for people our age I don't think … these are the only ones left)

2 It is important when listening to Part 1 recordings that students understand what the speaker's attitudes and opinions are, even when they are not directly stated. Ask students to cover the audioscript, and then look through the sentences and decide whether the speaker is being positive or negative. Are there any which could be positive or negative depending on the context? Don't supply the answer until the students have answered the exam question.

> **a** positive
> **b** negative
> **c** This can depend on the context, although here the girl intends it as a positive comment.
> **d** positive
> **e** negative
> **f** negative

3a/b Ask students to tackle this as they would an exam task – but also to think about why the options they didn't choose are wrong. Ask them to compare their answers in pairs and then look at the audioscript before you check as a class. They should also look at the sentences from Exercise 2 and decide whether they were correct, or if they would revise any of their answers after reading the audioscript, particularly c.

> Correct answer: B
> A is wrong – the girl says her friends are *really thoughtful … always thinking what you'd really like.*
> C is wrong – she doesn't really like the images of dogs. She prefers *simple designs.*

Exam practice P 48

Students have now had practice in looking closely at the context-setting sentence and the focus question – but remind them that this is necessary for each of these tasks. If students are not very experienced at listening tasks, it might be useful to try the first question, listen two or three times to the recording and then stop to allow students to consider their answers before comparing in pairs and checking as a class. Then work through the rest of the tasks, playing each question twice. Students should be ready to move on to the next question after the second listening even if they haven't identified a key for the last one.

Depending on the level of the class, pre-teach any vocabulary that might be problematic, e.g. *spectators, conservation, pass on, relieved, canoeing, risky, paddle.* At this stage, this is not a test of their vocabulary but practice in how to deal with the individual listening tasks. Remind students not to panic if they see a word they don't recognise, e.g. in Question 7, *difficult* gives an important clue.

> **1** C **2** A **3** B **4** A **5** C **6** B **7** A **8** C

Extension

Encourage students to listen to short clips of native speaker English, to give them practice in *tuning in* to what the speakers are talking about. This is an important skill for this part of the test.

Part 2

> **Task type:**
> Complete 10 sentences with information heard on the recording.

Training

You usually need to write between one and three words in the gap.

Point out that although the answer is *usually* between one and three words, candidates can actually write more than three words, so long as the answer is correct.

1a/b The aim of this exercise is to familiarise students with listening to a recording at the same time as they are reading through sentences and trying to identify the missing word(s). Ask students to look carefully at the question in 1a. It's about family trips to the beach. What are their experiences of this kind of trip? What do people do? Which members of the family go? They should then look at question 9. What *kind* of word is likely to go in the gap? Ask students to look at the audioscript in 1b, and underline the answer. Point out to them that a number of family members are mentioned in the passage – but only *one* is correct. Ask them to discuss in pairs why the other people mentioned aren't the correct answer.

> 9 (little) sister (My little sister's amazing, though … splashing about in the sea, with a huge smile on her face.) Sally also mentions her Dad, Mum, older brother and Grandma. They are incorrect answers because:
> Dad just sleeps on the beach.
> Mum looks for unusual things for her work if she's got the energy but there's no mention of whether she's having fun.
> Sally's older brother has to look after their younger sister.
> Grandma complains that it's too hot.

2a/b Ask students to cover the audioscript before they begin this section. Look first at the question. What kind of word is likely to fit? Once you've established that it's an activity of some kind, get students to think about the different activities that people do at the beach, e.g. swimming, diving, paddling, surfing, sailing, playing volleyball, sunbathing. Write them on the board then listen to the recording for 2b. Give all students time to decide on an answer, and check the answer with the class. Then get them to listen again and pick out other watersports mentioned in the recording, and note them down. Ask them to decide which is linked to weather conditions in the recording. Now let students look at the audioscript to confirm their answers. Ask them to pay particular attention to the spelling of the activities they have written down, as correct spelling is essential for Part 2.

> 10 sailing
> diving, swimming, surfing, sailing

3a–c The question is asking about something Sally's sister found on the beach. Students think of as many objects as they can in one minute that might be *found* on a beach. They might come up with things like: *fish, starfish, seaweed, bucket, spade, clothes, towel, blanket, chair, shoes, sunglasses, book, sun cream, food, drink, stone, rock, shell, shellfish, crab, bag*. Ask students to listen to the recording and identify the answer, then compare with a partner. What other objects did they hear mentioned? Why were they wrong? If necessary, read the audioscript back to them and discuss why the other objects mentioned were not keys.

> The word that fits the gap is a noun, as there's an article before it. A number of words might fit, all connected with the sea, e.g. *stone, fish, rock, starfish, shell, piece of seaweed or wood*, or things that people have left behind, such as buckets and spades.
> 11 (small) crab
> Other items are mentioned in the audioscript. Things like a *piece of wood* or *jewellery* are what the sister sometimes finds. The family thought she had found a stone. And after she'd had found the crab, the family went to collect seashells in a bucket that the brother had found.

Exam practice

Lead-in

Ask students to read the rubric carefully, then ask them these comprehension- checking questions – *Who is talking? Who to? Where did she go? What did she see there?* Check that students know what a *meerkat* is. If possible, find a colour picture. What do the students know about meerkats? Where do they live? *How* do they live? Now get students to read quickly through the sentences and think about the missing words. Deal with any words or sentences that students find a problem.

To make sure that students all know exactly what to do, play them the first part of the recording that relates to the first question, and then check students' answers by discussing them. Let students do the rest of the task without stopping and check answers at the end. Give students the chance to compare answers in pairs before checking together as a class. Ask them to compare spellings. Have they spelt the same words in the same way? Encourage them to check any they are not sure of in a dictionary.

> **9** relatives   **10** lake cat   **11** captivity   **12** blankets   **13** voice
> **14** balancing   **15** bark   **16** stripes   **17** small birds   **18** posters

Extension

Ask students to work in teams and see who can remember the most about it.

Extension

CLIL Tell students to find out more about meerkats and write a short piece about them for homework. They can use some of the information from the recording and add their own information. Ask them to add any pictures, maps of where they live or other graphic information they can find.

Part 3

> **Task type:**
> Multiple-matching.
> Five questions which require the selection of the correct answer from a list of eight.

Training

1   This section looks particularly at people's feelings, which may be tested in the options in Part 3.
Students look through the adjectives in the list and identify any that they are not sure of. They then do the exercise individually and check their answers in pairs, before checking as a class.

> **2** relieved / thrilled / grateful
> **3** impressed / surprised
> **4** discouraged / annoyed / shocked / disappointed / embarrassed / discouraged
> **5** thrilled / surprised / grateful / shocked
> **6** grateful

Extension

Students cover the exercise and leave just the list of adjectives visible. They describe examples of situations where they experienced one of these feelings (these can be invented), and ask their partner to guess the adjective they are referring to.

Lead-in

The students are going to listen to two people talking about a long train journey. Ask students what their own experiences of long train journeys have been. *Are they generally positive or negative? Have they ever spent the night on a train? Where were they travelling from and to? Who with? Have they had meals on a train? What did they take with them to pass the time?*

2a/b Look through the list of options. Which ones are positive?

Which are negative? Which could be either? Play the recording without letting students look at the audioscript. Tell students they should note down any key words that led them either to the correct answer, or to other options which they then discounted. Get students to discuss their answers in pairs. They confirm their answers from the audioscript.

> **Correct answer: D**
> The audioscript also refers to options A, E, F and H.
> A is wrong, because the family left in plenty of time to avoid missing the train.
> E is wrong because he knew he wouldn't be impressed by the view, as he'd seen it before from the car.
> F is wrong – he'd got a seat by the window, but he doesn't say how he felt about it.
> H is wrong – he wasn't going to be bored, as he'd brought lots of magazines.

3 Now students will hear another person talking about a long train journey. Students should look at the same list of options for the answer. Ask them to cover the audioscript again. Ask them to try taking notes of key words as they're listening, as this can help to identify clues. Then give them time to compare answers, including which other options they considered. Let them check their own answers in the audioscript and see which part of the text provided the correct answers. Draw their attention to the fact that the same words weren't used in the audioscript as in the options. Then confirm answers all together as a class.

> **Correct answer: B**
> Maria says she was *getting more and more excited, and couldn't wait to get started*. She doesn't use the word *thrilled*, which is in the option.
> The audioscript also refers to C, D, E, F and G.
> C is wrong, as she was the one who had to be quiet. She's not referring to the train.
> D is wrong – she'd brought her own food, and doesn't mention being given any.
> E is wrong – her journey was at night, so she couldn't see the view.
> G is wrong – the word *disappointed* is in the recording, but she *wasn't* *disappointed*, either by her seat or the trip.

Extension

Ask students to write a short piece about the longest overland journey they've done – by car, bus or train – or cycle! Ask them to include information like a brief map of the route, together with information about why they were travelling and what happened during the journey.

Exam practice

Lead-in

Ask students to read the rubric carefully. Who will be talking? What about? What is the focus question asking them? Before you begin the task, ask students about their hobbies – what do they do in their spare time? Do any of them collect anything? What kind of things do people tend to collect? (e.g. stamps, coins, model cars, dolls, figures from films). Did their parents or grandparents ever collect things when they were younger? What kind of things? Now ask students to read through the options.

Check they understand what *it* refers to in some of the options. Again, identify which are positive and which are negative. Then play the recording and give students time to compare their answers afterwards before you confirm them to the class. Try asking them if they can remember what each speaker was talking about. They may

not recall much detail, but some students will have committed a surprising amount to memory.

> **19** D **20** F **21** E **22** G **23** H

Extension

Ask students to find out about teenagers who have amazing collections of, for example, computer magazines, film figures, model cars, etc. They can look on the Internet and report back with a short presentation to the class or a small group. Can they also find any collections, for example of coins or stamps, that go back hundreds of years in history and are now very valuable?

Part 4

> **Task type:**
> Multiple-choice.
> There are seven three-option multiple-choice questions.

Training

1 This section is aimed at helping students think about what they might be about to hear, based on the information they get from the rubric and the questions that follow.

Ask students to look at the four topic areas and imagine what they might hear if these were the topic areas stated in the rubric. They should then look at the box below and choose which key words they might be likely to hear for each topic. They should work in pairs. Ask students to be prepared to give reasons for their answers.

> ***Suggested answers***
> **1** look forward / credit card / thrilled / uncertain
> **2** weather conditions / creatures / weather forecast / look forward / equipment / identify / thrilled
> **3** nervous / look forward / thrilled / uncertain / action / equipment / wetsuit
> **4** weather conditions / weather forecast / spectators / lens / action / shot / equipment / wetsuit

2 Look at the photo of the boy wakeboarding (a surface water sport which involves riding a wakeboard over the water. It was developed from a combination of water-skiing, snowboarding and surfing techniques. The rider is usually towed behind a motorboat). Ask students if they have ever tried this or any other watersport – especially waterskiing or surfing – which share some techniques with wakeboarding. Get them to describe what it is like: *How do they feel when they're doing it? Where do they do it? What kind of equipment do they need?* Look at the question and focus on the feelings that it is asking about – worried, curious, content. Ask students to listen to the recording and then decide which option best fits how he feels. Read the audioscript aloud to students if they need further help.

> **Correct answer: C**

3a/b Students look carefully at the question. Check they understand what they're listening for – it's his *first* attempt to stand. Then play the recording without letting students read it first. They can check their answers together afterwards by reading through the audio script and underlining where the answer came from.

> ***Suggested answers***
> He hadn't been prepared for the pressure on his legs when the boat took off, so he fell in.

4   Now ask students to approach this section as they would an exam question. Allow them time to read the question and the options and play the piece twice if necessary. Give everyone time to decide on their answer and then check all together. If students are still not sure, be prepared to read out the audioscript slowly to confirm answers. Focus on any new vocabulary introduced in the unit and the audioscripts, ready to be tested in the following lesson, e.g. *spectators, credit card, crouch down, roar off, pressure, immense, shift (your weight).*

Extension

Ask students to produce a short piece of writing about a watersport they have done or would like to do. Ask them to describe why they do / want to do the sport, where they can do it, and what equipment they need / would need. Ask them also to write about any difficulties they have found / might find when doing the sport.

Exam practice

Lead-in

Ask students whether anyone in the class has been climbing. Where did they go? Who with? What equipment did they need? What was it like?

Ask students to look carefully at the rubric. Who is talking? What about? They then read the questions and options. Give them about 45 seconds to do this, and then play the recording twice, as in the exam. If you prefer to check progress halfway through, get students to compare answers with a partner, and then encourage them to listen especially carefully for any keys they haven't got during the second listening. Remind students to use the *Advice* section for some extra help.

Extension

CLIL Ask students to find out about the stories of some famous climbers, e.g. Hillary and Tensing climbing Everest, or famous climbers in the past in their own countries. Ask them to compare a few things about how they climbed then and now, e.g. their clothes, their equipment, their tents, their means of communication, to show what an achievement this kind of climb was then.

Test 1
Speaking
Part 1

Training

Make sure students understand they will be taking the speaking test in pairs (or a group of three – though this only happens right at the end of the exam session if there is an uneven number of candidates, and students cannot choose to be examined in a group of three). Tell them there will be two examiners in the room: the interlocutor, who asks the questions, and the assessor, who writes down their marks. The interlocutor will also give them one overall mark at the end of the session.

1   Students decide which sentences belong with which photo.

2   Tell students that they should avoid giving very short answers (one or two words only). They need to expand a little on their answers and give reasons. If they don't say enough, the examiner has follow-up questions to prompt them to say a little more. However, they should also avoid giving extremely long and detailed answers to every question. They will have plenty of opportunity to talk for longer in Parts 2, 3 and 4 of the test. It is also very important that students do not learn answers in advance for this part of the test as this will sound unnatural, and they will lose marks if they have obviously prepared answers and learned them by heart. Students work in pairs to decide which are the best answers to the three questions.

Students should put a X by 1, 4, 7 and 8. 1, 4 and 7 are not full answers, and 8 does not have grammatical structures or link the ideas.

3   Tell students they will not lose any marks if they ask the examiner to repeat a question. Students put the words in the correct order to form sentences and check their answers with a partner.

4   Tell students that throughout the test, in Parts 1–4, the examiner will be listening out for stretches of language which use a range of discourse markers such as linkers. Students should use as wide a range as possible in the test. Remember, however, that they should not prepare and learn their answers in advance.

Exam practice

Students ask each other and answer these questions in pairs. Monitor students while they are doing the task, and make a note of good answers and suggestions for improvements. Remind students that they need to expand on their answers and give reasons, rather than give short responses. If they don't say enough they could be prompted by the follow-up question in the exam. Then discuss the questions with the whole class. Pairs of students could model good examples of replies in front of the whole class. Tell students it is not a good idea to learn pre-prepared answers by heart or it will sound unnatural.

Students now hear some different Part 1 questions. Put the students into small groups and ask them to listen to each question, then pause the recording. One student in each group answers the question, while the others listen and make notes of good language or suggestions for improvements. Every student should have the chance to answer a question. Discuss possible answers with the whole class at the end.

Extension

Pair work: Put students in pairs and ask them to think of one or two topics connected with everyday life (e.g. music, holidays, sport, TV) and write four questions on each topic that they might be asked in Part 1 of the test. Remind them to use present, past and future tenses.

Students then work with a different partner to ask and answer the questions.

Group work / Whole class activity: Students role-play being famous people at a party and ask each other questions about their everyday life. Again, remind them to ask about the past, the present and the future. Monitor the students during the activities, and note down the questions that are most appropriate for Part 1 of the test. Write these questions on the board and decide what would be the best answers.

Part 2

> **Task type:**
> An individual one-minute 'long turn' for each candidate, with a brief response from the second candidate lasting about 30 seconds. Candidates are assessed on their performance throughout the 14-minute test.
> If the second candidate's response is too short, the examiner will ask a back-up question.

Training

1 Students decide which sentences belong with which photo.

> 1 c, d   2 e, a, f   3 b, g

2 In pairs, students complete the sentences. Tell students they don't have to describe every detail in the photos. They have to compare them, which means saying what is similar and different about them.

> 1 both   2 while / whereas / but   3 look / seem / appear, perhaps / maybe   4 could / might / may

3 Students fill in the gaps and check their answers with a partner. Tell students that after Candidate A's 'long turn', when Candidate B answers a short question, they have about 30 seconds to answer. If Candidate B's answer is a bit short, the examiner might ask a follow-up question to encourage Candidate B to say a bit more.

> 1 more enjoyable   2 it would be   3 I prefer to / I'd rather   4 would choose

4a/b Elicit the answers from the class as a whole.

> **a** Candidate A has to compare two photographs and answer a question about them.
> **b** Candidate B has to answer a short question about the photographs.

5 Students listen, tick the expressions they hear, and compare their answers with a partner. If necessary, let them listen again, and stop the recording just after each expression. N.B. the expressions are underlined in the audioscript on page 184, along with the answers to Exercise 6.

> both, whereas, seem, look, appear, while, could, I'd rather, more enjoyable, may

6 Students write down expressions they have heard. Write these expressions on the board. Then let the students listen to the recording while they read the audioscript on page 184. Ask them to underline any other words or phrases they think are useful, and then write these on the board as well.

> **Suggested answers**
> show, the first photo is of people..., in the second picture, in contrast, like the people in the first picture, in my opinion

Exam practice

Candidate A's photos

Both photos show people singing, but in one picture, there are two girls singing in their living room for fun, with just one person listening to them. In the other, in contrast, there's a pop star singing on a stage, with a lot of people in the audience listening to him. Whereas the girls look quite young, and are probably at home after school, the pop star is older, and he may be a professional singer. The girls appear to be having fun and enjoy singing together and look very relaxed whereas people have paid to listen to the singer in picture B and he will feel he needs to sing really well and will be very tired after the show.

Candidate A's question

The girls might be practising for a school concert or party, and they have a microphone, which means they could be recording themselves. They look as if they are taking their singing seriously, even if they don't have the pressure of an audience watching them. In contrast, the man singing is probably quite famous in his town and he is singing with his band for people who have paid to come and listen. He will be hoping that lots of people come to listen and then buy his music.

Candidate B's question

Say where you would prefer to be singing, and why (e.g. It's more enjoyable to sing with other people in a relaxed situation because if you don't really sing that well, it doesn't matter) or give a reason why you'd like to perform for other people by singing on stage (e.g. I'd love to be a singer and maybe even become famous. I think it would be a great way to earn a living and I like performing in front of other people.) I think being on stage like the singer in the picture and singing for an audience who really appreciate what you're doing would be incredibly exciting. And when you are under pressure like that, in my opinion it can make you perform better because you don't want to let people down. So you really have to push yourself, which is something I enjoy. And if you want to get better, it's a good idea to ask your friends to listen to you and tell you what they think. If you record yourself, as the girls seem to be doing, then you can hear yourself and see where you can improve.

Candidate B's photos

There are teenagers working in both the pictures, and I imagine they're doing part-time jobs, at the weekend or in the evening after school. The people in both pictures look as if they're enjoying themselves, but whereas the girl in the supermarket probably doesn't talk to the customers very much, the person working in the café as a waiter will have to speak to the people he's serving. Although the boy in the café is dressed quite smartly, I imagine the atmosphere there is actually quite relaxed. The café looks like a pleasant place to work, and the customers look friendly. The girl in the supermarket also appears to be wearing some kind of uniform.

Candidate B's question

I think the girl in the supermarket may be quietly working on her own. I don't imagine she has to concentrate too hard while she's doing this job, so it must be quite relaxing and very different from schoolwork. She probably also likes being able to earn some extra money after school or at the weekend. The person working in the café probably enjoys interacting with the customers, and it might be interesting to meet different types of people. Maybe he gets to know some of the people who come in to eat regularly, and if the café's busy, then he'll never get bored.

Candidate A's question

Say which of the two jobs you'd prefer to do, and give reasons why you'd prefer to do it (e.g. *I'd rather work in the supermarket because after a long day at school I don't want to have to think too hard, and I'm often too tired to talk to other people much.* **or** *I think it would be better to be a waiter, because it's more interesting and I could learn useful things. I like cooking and food, so that's the kind of place I'd like to work in in the future.*)

Extension

Brainstorm a list of topics in class, and ask your students to find pictures related to the topics for homework. In the next class, put the students into groups and ask them to choose pairs of pictures on similar themes. Ask them to write a question for each pair of pictures. (E.g. *What do you think the people are enjoying about ..? How do you think the people in these situations are feeling? Why do you think the people are taking part in these activities?*) Then put the students into groups of three. One student is the examiner, and the other two are Candidate A and Candidate B. The three students role-play Part 2 of the test. While they are not speaking, students can note down good vocabulary and phrases their partners use. When the groups have finished one role-play, move the students into different groups and ask them to talk about a different set of pictures, making sure that everyone has a chance to be one of the candidates.

Part 3

> **Task type:**
> A two-way conversation between the candidates.
> Candidates receive spoken instructions and written stimuli.
> There is a two-minute discussion followed by a one-minute decision-making task.
> Candidates are assessed on their performance throughout the 14-minute test.

Training

1 Students put the sentences next to the correct photo and check their answers with a partner.

> **1** b, f, d   **2** a, c, e

2 Explain to students that they will get a better mark if they have a conversation and take into account their partner's thoughts, rather than waiting for their partner to finish speaking and then making their own completely separate point. In pairs, students choose the correct headings.

> **A** Starting the discussion
> **B** Expressing an opinion
> **C** Agreeing
> **D** Disagreeing politely

3 Students add the expressions to the table and check their answers with their partner.

> **A** Shall I go first?
> **B** I believe …
> **C** Good point.
> **D** Yes, that's true, but …

Extension

Ask students to add other expressions to the table in Exercise 2.

4 Students discuss the questions with a partner. Then check the answers with the whole class. Tell the students that the decision they have to make is always very closely related to the topic they have just discussed.

5 Students do the task and then check their answers in pairs.

> **1** T
> **2** F (They don't discuss having the opportunity to compete.)
> **3** T
> **4** T
> **5** T
> **6** F (They agree on one thing only – that being outside is not a good reason to do sport. They disagree about doing sport and having a break from school work. Fernando thinks it is a good reason to do sport but Jana disagrees. This is fine and good candidates will not have time to discuss all the prompts in detail.)

6 Write the expressions they have ticked on the board. Then, if necessary, play the recording again, stopping after each expression they should also have ticked. N.B. the expressions are underlined in the audioscript on page 184.

> Students should tick the following answers: Shall I start?, Personally, I think, Good point, I believe, I know what you mean, but..., In my opinion, Yes, I think that's true]

Exam practice

Before they start, remind students that, in the exam, they must listen carefully to the question telling them what decision they have to make, because they won't see this question written down. It will be on a topic which is closely linked to the discussion they have just had. Also remind them that it doesn't matter if they don't actually reach a decision. Finally, remind them again to always give a reason / reasons for their opinion / suggestion, and to listen and respond to what their partner says during the conversation. They shouldn't rush through their answers superficially. Students do the exam practice exercise in pairs or groups of three

Part 4

> **Task type:**
> A discussion on topics related to the Part 3 collaborative task.
> Candidates are assessed on their performance throughout the 14-minute test.

Training

1 Students fill in the gaps in the sentences under the photos, and then check their answers with a partner.

> **1 1** topic   **2** first   **3** see   **4** list   **5** three   **6** agree   **7** different

2 Tell students they should try to use a range of function words to express their opinions. They should try not to use *I think* at the beginning of every sentence. Students complete the exercise in pairs.

> **2 1** actually   **2** way   **3** reckon   **4** seems   **5** point

3 Remind students that they should always extend their answers by justifying their opinions. Tell them that the responses they can see in 1–6 are not sufficient, and that they need to be extended with a reason (a–f). Do the first item with the whole class, then ask the students to do the rest of the exercise in pairs.

> 1 b   2 f   3 a   4 d   5 c   6 e

4 Tell the students they are going to hear two students answering the first three questions in the exercise, and they must listen and decide in each case whether the students have similar or different opinions to the ones they have just read.

> 1 similar opinion   2 different opinion   3 different opinion

Exam practice

Students should do this exercise in groups of three, with one student in each group acting as the examiner. Before they start, tell them that in the test, if they are asked questions individually, they should answer them individually. They only speak together if the examiner indicates that they want them to do so.

Test 2
Reading and Use of English
Part 1

> **Task type:**
> Multiple-choice cloze containing eight gaps. There are four multiple-choice options for each gap.

Training

- You have to answer eight questions in Part 1.
- You have to choose from four options in each question.

1 This section focuses on encouraging students to build their knowledge of common collocations, which may be tested in Reading and Use of English, but can also be useful to students when they are tested in Writing. Please note that in this section some of the exercises may need extra support in the form of a teacher, dictionary, or reference book. Students may come up with other answers than the ones given in the exercise, e.g. 3 *pay attention to / draw attention to / get attention* but this is also helping to build their knowledge of collocation.

> 1 At   2 take   3 attracting   4 of   5 subject   6 common   7 take
> 8 extent   9 keep   10 got   11 goes   12 other

Extension

Students need to be reminded of what they've learnt, so some revision of these collocations needs to be built into subsequent lessons. For example, a quick exercise that can be used as a warmer is to give each student in a pair a list of the collocations and then ask them to give an example of the phrase for the other student (who has a different list) to identify, e.g. *take advantage of – What do you call it when someone treats someone else badly, say, just to get what they want?* Ensure that students have access to reference material where they can check meanings if they need to – but they shouldn't rely on this. This kind of exercise can be adapted for all sorts of vocabulary revision, and is very useful for settling students with a useful activity as they arrive in class.

2 This section looks at the differences between the kinds of words that students will meet in Part 1. It encourages students to look at the words and decide on significant differences in meaning, correctly identifying collocation and whether different words will fit in the context, depending on, for example, any prepositions that might come before or after the gap.

> 1 planted   2 uncovered   3 establish   4 settled   5 tell
> 6 mentioned   7 consider   8 said   9 influence   10 link   11 touch
> 12 contact   13 bear   14 order   15 spite   16 view

3 Check that students know what each phrase means, and the differences between similar phrases, e.g:

> in time / on time
> out of order / in order
> at once / for once
> on my own

Can students add any more phrases that use these prepositions? Encourage them to only suggest phrases that they can supply a meaning or an example for.

> | at speed | on my own | by chance | by accident |
> |---|---|---|---|
> | under control | in a hurry | in time | out of control |
> | for nothing | on time | in control | on purpose |
> | in order | for once | out of order | at once |
> | for a change | | | |

Extension

Encourage students to get into the habit of recording any prepositional phrases that they're not familiar with. Ask them to look up phrases that they don't know in an English–English dictionary.

4 Ask students to complete the exercises individually and then compare answers in pairs. Check as a class. Where students disagree in their pairs, check that they can see why their answer is wrong – or can someone else in the class explain why?

> 1 on my own / by myself   2 on time   3 by chance / by accident
> 4 in time   5 for a change   6 by accident   7 for nothing
> 8 out of order

Exam practice

Students look first at the title. Do they know a song with this in the title (e.g. David Bowie). What do they know about life on Mars? They should then read the text quickly, and be ready to ask some comprehension-checking questions, e.g. *What plans are there for life on Mars? How many people want to go? What would the successful astronauts have to do? What would they have to go without?* (explain this if they're not sure of the meaning). Then ask students to do the exercise individually and compare answers when they have finished. Set a time limit in preparation for the exam, say ten minutes, but be prepared to extend it if students are struggling. Encourage students to look carefully at any differences they find between their answers. Who has the correct answer? Why is the other one wrong? Remind students to look back at Exercise 2, as some of the answers are dealt with there. Then check together as a class and be ready to explain any answers that have caused difficulty.

> 1 B   2 C   3 B   4 C   5 D   6 A   7 C   8 D

Extension

Ask students if they would like to go on this trip. Why? Why not? What would they enjoy about it? What would they miss the most?

Extension

CLIL Students may already know something about this project. Ask them to contribute anything they do know, and then for homework, get them to look up information about it on the Internet and report back on any progress that has been made with it. They could also find out more about Mars itself, e.g. how far away is it? How easy would it be to live there? What is the atmosphere like there?

Part 2

Task type:
Open cloze test containing eight gaps.

Training

Lead-in

This section deals with the kind of prepositions that students may need to know in order to complete gaps in Part 2. This is an area of language that students need to work on regularly. They should get into the habit of recording these phrases in a vocabulary notebook and then revising them. As a lead-in, write up the following prepositions on the board: *by, out of, at, in, on* and supply a couple of examples from the exercise – perhaps the ones students are less likely to come up with themselves – to show the kind of phrases you are looking for, e.g. *in favour of, at all costs*. Give students about five minutes to find a few more and record them on the board.

- No – unlike Part 1, you have to come up with the words yourself in Part 2.

- It's a good idea to know what the text is generally about before you begin, as it helps you to get the answers – but don't spend too long reading it.

1   Ask students in pairs to fill in as many of the examples on the page as possible. They should then use a reference book, such as *Grammar and Vocabulary for First and First for Schools* (Cambridge University Press) to check further answers.

according *to*	*at* least
in turns	*in* due course
on account of	*in* favour of
thanks *to*	*out* of petrol
at risk	*by* far
in general	*at* all costs
by heart	*in* other words
in brief	*in* place of

2   Students complete Exercise 2 individually as a consolidation exercise and compare answers with a partner. Check together.

1 In other words   **2** by heart   **3** at least   **4** by far   **5** in brief
6 in turn(s)   **7** in due course   **8** According to   **9** out of
10 at all costs

3   This section focuses on passives, as filling the gap in Part 2 may depend on knowledge of these, particularly identifying and forming the different tenses of passive sentences. Introduce the section by quickly reminding students of how passive sentences are formed. Take one example sentence, e.g. Question 1: *Someone cleaned the windows at school yesterday.* Then give students different contexts in which to come up with the same sentence in a suitable tense:

now *the windows are being cleaned now*
yesterday *the windows were cleaned yesterday*
next week *the windows will / are going to be cleaned next week.*
when I arrived yesterday *the windows were being cleaned when I arrived yesterday*
since last Monday *The windows have / haven't been cleaned since last Monday.*
just *The windows have just been cleaned,* etc.

Remind students that unless the agent is someone specific, e.g. *the window cleaner*, they don't really need to include it in the answer by writing *by someone*. Remind them that in the passive, the action is often more important than *who* is doing it.

1 were cleaned	**5** is being fixed
2 tell you	**6** delivers the letters to
3 have been destroyed by	**7** mustn't be taken
4 must have been left	**8** hasn't / has not been seen

It's important that students keep a personal record of their own individual spelling mistakes. Encourage them to record the correct form of their spelling mistakes in a notebook. This should be used for studying when they have spare time during the lesson, e.g. if they have finished an exercise before the rest of the class. Test key words such as the above on a regular basis, e.g. five minutes at the start of each lesson.

4 | **1** which   **2** than   **3** because   **4** believe   **5** beautiful
       6 interesting

Exam practice

Lead-in

The text is about solar-powered cars. Before students start reading the text, ask them what they understand by the title. What does *solar* mean? How would solar-powered cars work? Why would they be a good idea? What other things can they think of that are solar powered?

Ask them to read quickly through the text, then ask them some comprehension-testing questions – or, depending on the level of the group, get them to ask each other in pairs. For example, *How does the car get its power? Does it only work on sunny days? How far can it travel? How does this compare with electric cars? What does the writer predict as the future for solar-powered cars?* Ask students to complete the exam task and then get them to compare answers. Set a time limit, e.g. ten minutes, but be prepared to extend this if necessary. Encourage students to use the Advice section if they can't think of an answer.

9 been   **10** which   **11** there   **12** than   **13** the   **14** before / until
15 being   **16** no / little

Extension

CLIL Solar power is becoming increasingly popular in some countries. How popular is it in the students' home countries? Ask them to think about the types of things they have seen in their towns / villages that are solar powered, e.g. houses – solar panels on roofs, lights in people's gardens, lights to illuminate pedestrian pathways. Ask them to look up on the Internet any other examples of things that are powered by solar energy and discuss them in the next lesson. What are the benefits of solar energy? (e.g. *less reliance on fossil fuels, reducing pollution.*) Are there any disadvantages?

Part 3

Training

- You will need to form nouns, verbs, adjectives and adverbs from base words that you are given.

- You need to look carefully to decide what kind of word is needed, and whether it is positive, or negative, singular or plural, depending on the context.

1a/b This section focuses on the kinds of changes that students need to make to the base words they are given in Part 3 of Reading and Use of English. Support from a teacher or dictionary may be needed. Exercise 1 looks at different suffixes that can be added to words to change the type of word, in this case changing verbs or nouns into nouns that relate to people. Put the suffixes on the board and ask students to think about job titles that might end in these suffixes. Give a couple of examples first, such as *design → designer, science → scientist*, to illustrate what you are looking for – not just job titles that end with these suffixes, but titles that come from a base noun or verb. If this is too difficult for students to do, accept any job titles in the first instance and then move on to a couple of examples of the kind of transformations you are looking for. However, limit the amount of time spent on this, and move on to the examples in the exercise. Students complete Exercise 1b as consolidation.

1 relative **2** assistant **3** photographer **4** economist **5** politician **6** supplier **7** inhabitant **8** detective **9** dealer **10** competitor

1 economist **2** competitors **3** photographer(s) **4** assistant **5** politician **6** relatives / relations

2 This exercise looks again at suffixes, but this time also considers the kind of changes that might need to be made to base words when suffixes are added. Write a couple of examples on the board to show what you are looking for, e.g. *independent → independence* – remove final *t*.

1 mysterious **2** continuous **3** Japanese **4** athletic **5** southern **6** densely **7** difference **8** priceless **9** tourism **10** patience

3 This exercise includes examples of nouns that aren't formed just by adding a suffix to the adjective or verb that they come from, e.g. *hot → heat*. Ask students to work through the list in pairs and check answers around the class.

1 width **2** strength **3** length **4** heat **5** destruction **6** behaviour **7** anxiety **8** freedom **9** division **10** admiration

4a/b One key skill that is needed for Part 3 is identifying the part of speech that is needed to fill the gap, i.e. is it a noun, verb, adjective or adverb? In order for students to be able to work this out, they need to have understood the surrounding context. Get students to complete this exercise in pairs and then think about which words could possibly fit the gaps. Then ask them how they decided on the kind of word that is missing. Which words provided the clues? Some suggestions as to possible answers are supplied for the missing words.

1 verb **2** noun **3** adverb **4** adjective **5** noun **6** adjective

Possible answers

1 fly, migrate, go	**4** exhausted, tired
2 reserves , places, areas	**5** people, visitors
3 absolutely, completely	**6** amazing, strange, incredible

These longer words are often misspelt by students. You could begin a wall display and add words that the class are frequently getting wrong. The more that students see them, the easier they may find them to remember when it comes to writing them. Regular spelling tests will also be useful.

5 **1** accommodation **2** advertisement **3** suddenly **4** environment **5** definitely **6** disappointed

Exam practice

Lead-in

Look at the title with the students. What do they already know about swans? Are they common birds in the students' home countries? Where do they live? What do they feed on? Then ask students to read quickly through the text, and ask them some comprehension-checking questions, e.g. *What does **migration** mean? Why do birds **migrate**? When do swans begin to migrate, according to the text? Where from? Where do they go? Why? What effects does such a long journey have on them? When do they return to their home countries? Why?*

17 sight **18** arrival **19** combination **20** steadily **21** successfully **22** recovery **23** feeding **24** Unfortunately

Extension

CLIL Ask students to find out a bit more about bird migration. Encourage them to look on a map and see exactly how far some of these birds fly by locating the countries at the start and end of their journeys. Tell them, for example, that swallows fly up to Europe from Africa during the start of summer, and return in the autumn. Swallows also tend to return to the same nesting sites year after year – but how do they find their way? Swallows also feed *on the wing* and rarely land on the ground – so how do they feed and rest during their incredible journeys? Ask students to find out more about swan and swallow migrations, and report back in a future lesson.

Part 4

Training

Lead-in

Ask students to respond to these examples using *I wish … didn't, I wish … wouldn't*, or *I wish … hadn't*:
I went to the party on Saturday, but it was really boring.
Possible response: *I wish I hadn't gone. / I wish it hadn't been so boring.*
I have loads of homework to do tonight!
Possible response: *I wish I didn't have so much to do. / I wish I hadn't left it all until this evening.*
My brother keeps playing really loud music late at night!
Possible response: *I wish he wouldn't keep doing that.*

Now ask them to look at *I'd prefer* and *I'd rather*. Students should provide a suitable alternative response:
Could we go to the cinema on Friday, instead of Saturday? That would be better for me.
Possible response: *I'd rather go / we went to the cinema on Friday than on Saturday. / I'd prefer to go / it if we went to the cinema …*
Exercises 1 and 2 are aimed at helping students to revise ways of expressing wishes and regrets, and raising awareness of the differences in meaning between structures that may look very similar.

- You need to rewrite six sentences.

- You need to check that your answer means the same as the first sentence.

1 Students now work in pairs to look at the differences in the sentences. Can they explain the meanings without looking at the possible answers?

1 a 2 b 3 a 4 a

2 This exercise focuses on the use of different modals, which may be tested in Part 4 transformations. Do some brief revision with students on conditionals. Ask them to finish the following statement appropriately: *If I lived in a different country, … .* Possible continuations: *… I might not have had to learn English. / … wouldn't be in this class now. / … wouldn't have met all my friends here / … might speak a different language.*

Now practise some deductions with *must, might* and *can't*. The teacher says: *John isn't in class today – and he never misses a class!* Students then make deductions about why he isn't in class and where he might be, e.g: *He must be sick. / He can't have forgotten. / He might have got up late. / He might be on his way here now.* Finally, look at – *didn't need to* and *needn't have*. For example:
*I ran all the way to the bookshop, but it was already closed when I got there, so I **needn't have run**.* (Meaning: Although I did run, it wasn't necessary.)
*I set off for the bookshop at 3 p.m. – it didn't close till 5, so I **didn't need to run**.* (Meaning: I didn't run because it wasn't necessary.)

1 hadn't / would be	6 can't have forgotten
2 might have been	7 must be
3 couldn't have	8 should have
4 wouldn't have gone	9 wouldn't have been able
5 needn't have hurried	10 didn't need to

Before doing the exercise, quickly revise the meanings of the different conditionals if you think students are having problems. Put on the board:
If I see him, I'll tell him. (I might see him)
If I saw him, I'd tell him. (but it's unlikely I will)
If I'd seen him, I would have told him. (I didn't see him, so I didn't tell him.)
Also remind students of the tenses that follow:
You'd better …
If I were you ...

3	1 would 2 would 3 will 4 can 5 should 6 would

Exam practice

Try getting students to look at the first sentence of Questions 25 and 27. Write the beginning of the second sentence on the board, without the prompt word, and see if they can supply the answer,

based on the work they have just done. Remind students to use the *Advice* section if they need help.

25 needn't have run	28 were blown down by
26 changes the subject	29 wouldn't have been able
27 can't have forgotten	30 rather you didn't / did not

Part 5

Task type:
A text followed by six four-option multiple-choice questions

Training

- There are six questions to answer for Part 5.

- They are multiple-choice questions – either with a complete question or a sentence to complete.

- There are four options to choose from.

1a Check that students have read and understood the question. Who is the text about? Students read quickly through and then think about where they might find this kind of text. A novel? An article in a magazine? A short story? Is it fact or fiction? Or perhaps we don't know from the extract we're given? Ask students to skim-read the text and then answer some comprehension-checking questions, e.g. *What had been organised for Jack's class? How did Jack feel about it? When had he been into the countryside before? What were his interests?* Check the vocabulary with students and get them to record new words in their notebooks, e.g. *alarmed, suspicion.* Then ask them to cover the text and talk about what they remember of it with a partner.

This looks like an extract from a novel or a short story.

1b/c Ask them to look at the four options individually and decide which option best answers the question, and then compare their answer with a partner. Encourage them also to discuss why the other options are wrong. This can help any students who have actually chosen the wrong option as their answer.

Correct answer: A
B is wrong. The text does mention Jack's interests – computers and technology – but this option doesn't answer the question. It's always important to look back at the question – you may find reference to the options in the text, but if they don't answer the question, they can't be correct.
C is wrong. The text does mention that Jack lives in a city, but he had nature trips in the parks, so he did have the opportunity to get involved with wildlife.
D is wrong. The option doesn't answer the question, and also the plan was welcomed by the rest of the class, so it clearly was a successful plan as far as they were concerned.

2a/b Make sure students understand that whichever option they choose must take the incomplete stem into account, in this case how Jack *felt* when he got to the countryside. There is some vocabulary in this section that students may not know, but encourage them to guess by using clues in the context. Then look at some of the possible unfamiliar words: *reluctant, a stretch of water, darting about, the shallows, a ripple, hostility, absorbing.* Ask students to look at the task in pairs and then check as a whole class. Discuss any differences in opinion over the key.

Correct answer: B
A is wrong. The text mentions that he reluctantly agreed to go, but it doesn't suggest he wanted to prove them wrong.
C is wrong. Camping next to water isn't always a good idea if it's damp, etc, but Jack seems positive about it. He *couldn't help wandering down to the water's edge.*
D is wrong. The campsite is in a forest next to a lake rather than on the coast, and there is no suggestion that Jack is surprised.

3   In this question, students are asked to work out the meaning of a word which they probably won't know – *skittering*. Ask them to look carefully at clues in the surrounding context, e.g. *wingless insects, making barely a ripple, on the surface of the water.* These all help to tell you more about what the insects were doing.

Correct answer: D
When you are faced with working out the meaning of an unknown word, look carefully at the rest of the paragraph. There will almost certainly be some clues there to help you.
A is wrong. The insects only touched the surface of the water; they didn't dive in and out.
B is wrong. We're told that the insects are wingless, so they couldn't be flying.
C is wrong. They are skittering over the water, not moving through it.

Extension

To help students with these types of questions for Part 5, get them to read short passages of English where you take out key words and replace them with nonsense words. Students can also make their own to give to each other. This can help to raise awareness of the kind of clues they need to leave in the text in order for their partners to work out the missing word.

Extension

Ask students to talk about any trips into the countryside they have done. Ask them to say where they went, why, and whether or not they enjoyed it.

Extension

CLIL What kinds of creatures live in the water? Ask students to find a cross-section of a pond or a river and label what they see e.g. *fish, insects, surface of the water, waves, ripples, pond weed, bottom of the pond, snails, beetles, frogs.*

Exam practice

Lead-in

Has anyone in the class ever been to a desert? What would they expect to find there? What would the temperature be like?

Ask students to read through the rubric. Ask them who it is about and where she went then ask them to skim-read the text quickly. Give them a time limit, say two minutes. Deal with any vocabulary that students want to ask about, and then ask them to do just Question 1. Give everyone time to answer, and then check the answer together, discussing any other options that students have chosen. Then let them finish the rest of the test. Give them ten minutes, but be prepared to extend this if necessary. Remind students that the *Advice* section is there to give them some extra help with getting the answers.

| 31 D | 32 C | 33 B | 34 A | 35 C | 36 A |

Extension

CLIL Which are the main desert areas of the world? Ask students to do a little research and find out. Get a world map to show students where they are, then give students an area to find out about. Ask them: *Which people live there, and also what wildlife?* They can report back in a future class.

Part 6

Task type:
A text from which six sentences have been removed and placed in a jumbled order after it.

Training

- You have to fill a gap with a sentence that you choose from seven different options. There is one sentence that is the distractor – it won't fit in any of the gaps.

- Look carefully at any *vocabulary* that might link a sentence to the general theme of the paragraph. Then look at any *linking words, pronouns, tenses* and *other references* both in the sentence and in the text on either side of the gap.

1   Check how many students in the class have a real interest in art, and whether they create art themselves and go to galleries to see exhibitions. Ask them to look at the words in the lists and check that they all know the meanings of them. If not, give them a short time to look up unfamiliar words in an English–English dictionary, and then record any new words in their vocabulary books. Then get them to do the vocabulary exercise, describing the meanings of the words to each other.

2   Students read quickly through the text about a visit to an art gallery. Ask some comprehension-checking questions, e.g. *Where did the writer's teacher take him/her?; What were they going to see there?; Had the writer been to this kind of exhibition before?; How do you know?; How was the writer feeling about the trip?; What was a surprise?* Now get students to look at the gap, the words either side of it, and the options. Remind them that the option they choose must fit with what goes before and after the gap. Discuss any wrong answers with the class.

Correct answer: C. The writer hadn't expected it to be well attended, but in fact *they actually had to queue round the block.* The *actually* emphasises that this isn't at all what they expected.
A The sentence doesn't really follow on from *I also wondered what to expect.* And *imagine my surprise, then* definitely rules out A. The text goes on to talk about the queue, not about seeing real paintings.
B At first, the sentence looks quite attractive – the text before the gap has mentioned abstract art. But *'Imagine my surprise, then'* after the gap signals that what goes in the gap should be a contrast to having to queue round the block. (You would expect there to be a large queue to see very famous artists.)

Extension

Get students to describe a visit to an art gallery that they have been to, either talking in groups or in a piece of writing.

Extension

CLIL Ask students to go on the Internet and look at the website of a major gallery in their town/area or country. Many websites of international galleries now have virtual tours. Ask students to try out a virtual tour, and to choose one painting from the tour that they particularly like. They don't need to know a lot about the painting, but just be able to say why it particularly appeals to them.

Exam practice

Students read through the rubric and make sure they understand what the text is about and what they have to do. They then read the text quickly and prepare to say a little bit to their partner about it. Do the first gap together, and then let students do the others. Suggest to them that they may find it easier not to fill the gaps in order. Some items will seem easier to them than others, so they should fill those gaps first and then go back to the others. This will help them get more of an idea of the meaning of the text as it comes together and thus the remaining gaps may be easier now that they have eliminated some of the possibilities. Give students a time limit, say ten minutes, but be prepared to extend this. Then check answers in pairs and as a whole class. Discuss any wrong answers that students got. If students finish early, they should identify the key words that helped them choose the correct sentence and share this information with students who may be struggling with one or two gaps. Remind students that the *Advice* section is there to give them a little extra help.

| 37 C | 38 F | 39 D | 40 A | 41 G | 42 B |

Part 7
Training

Task type:
A text or several short texts, preceded by 10 multiple-matching questions.
Candidates must match a prompt to elements in the text.

- You could be asked to read a number of different texts all on the same theme, or one text that has been split into sections.

- You need to answer 10 questions in this part.

- For each question, you have to look through the texts to see which section provides the correct answer.

1a/b Students read quickly through the text and decide what Nathan is talking about. Once they have decided it is his birthday party, get them to think about their own birthday parties. What's the best one they have ever had? Ask them to talk with their neighbours and then ask for a few examples around the room. Then ask them to work through the comprehension-checking questions in 1b.

a a birthday party
b in a hall in Nathan's village
c his relatives and family, and also all of his friends
d cold / colder than they'd expected

2 Ask students to look through the text for evidence of Nathan's feelings. These aren't always stated in the text, so ask how Nathan might feel at various points. Then ask them to look at the options and choose which one they have encountered in the text. They then compare their answers with a partner.

Correct answer: C (I couldn't help thinking that my party had somehow been taken over …)

3a/b Again, ask students to read quickly through the text to get an idea of what it is about. Then they do the comprehension-checking exercises in pairs.

a beach holidays
b taxi and plane
c They leave everything until the last minute.
d They're a nightmare.

Extension

Ask students whether the departure for the family holiday that Sarah describes is like their own experiences or very different! Are their preparations well-organised or chaotic? Where do they tend to go on family holidays? Where do they stay? Who goes with them?

Exam practice
Lead-in

Ask students to read through the rubric. What are they going to read about? Quickly ask a few students what their favourite family meals are.

Students read through the four texts. Ask students in pairs to summarise two texts each. Then do the first question together to make sure everyone knows what to do. After that, let students scan through the list to see if there are any they know the answers to as a result of the summarising exercise. Then get them to go back and look in more detail for the answers they are unsure of. After an allotted time, say ten minutes, get students to compare answers and discuss any differences, then check as a whole class.

| 43 D | 44 B | 45 A | 46 C | 47 B | 48 D | 49 C | 50 A | 51 B | 52 C |

Extension

Students could bring in the recipes for their favourite family dish, which could be put in a display or a small booklet and given to each member of the class.

Extension

CLIL What is the most popular dish / meal in the student's home country? Get them to do some research on the Internet and report back to their class.

Test 2
Writing
Part 1 (essay)

Task type:
Writing an essay of 140–190 words giving an opinion and providing reasons for the opinion.

Training

- You have to write an essay.

- You are writing it for your teacher.

- You have to include the ideas given in the question, and add another idea of your own.

- You have to write between 140 and 190 words.

1 Ask students to read what the general topic is. Once they have established that it is about protecting the environment, elicit some thoughts from the students on this topic. *Is it important? Why / Why not?; What sort of things have been in the news about the environment?; What have they learnt about it at school?*

You have to write about the environment.

2 Before students look at the list, elicit as many environmental issues as you can from the students. Put one on the board as an example. How many do they already know? Then get them to look at the list and check they are familiar with all of them.

They should explain what each one means and see if they can add more examples, e.g. the ones suggested in the key.

Possible answers
air pollution – the damage that is done to the air by toxic substances such as smoke or fumes coming from vehicles
plastic waste – the problem of what to do with all the plastic items we throw away, such as supermarket carrier bags or packaging and the threats they cause to wildlife
food waste – the amount of food we buy and then throw away
flooding – the problem of (e.g.) rivers overflowing and covering large parts of the surrounding area
water pollution – toxic substances entering the water supply and making it unhealthy or impossible for humans to use. It can also have major effects on wildlife.
wildlife conservation – monitoring and assisting different types of creatures to make sure they are surviving in good numbers and not becoming endangered or even extinct.
global warming – the gradual increase in world temperatures that is caused by gases polluting the atmosphere.
climate change – the way in which the weather on Earth is changing.
Other examples of environmental issues might be:
changes in the atmosphere
acid rain
endangered species
threats to the countryside
green energy
poor harvests
organic food

3a/b Students read through Ben's answer, then close their books and try to remember what he said in the main part of his essay.

4   Students look again at Ben's answer individually and find which two points he had to include. Tell students they must give reasons for their answers. Then ask them to compare with a partner.

Ben had to write about:
how important the environment is as a topic
how enjoyable it is to study

5   Follow the same procedure as above for Ben's own idea – which point did he include? Tell students to give a reason for their answer.

In this paragraph, Ben wrote about:
other ways of learning about the environment

6/7 Get students to find the phrases in Ben's essay and look carefully at how he used them. Then ask them to complete the sentences individually and compare their answers in pairs. Be prepared to discuss any differences the students may have in their answers.

Young people are usually taught about protecting the environment at school – but is school really the best place to learn about it?
There is no doubt that we need to learn about protecting the environment. In fact, many people think it's an essential topic to study at school. We have teachers who may be experts in areas such as climate change or wildlife conservation, so they're the perfect people to teach us about the environment.
Learning about the environment can also be fun. Many schools have up-to-date technology to help us, and there are hands-on experiments we can do such as monitoring weather changes or plastic waste.
On the other hand, although schools are good places to learn about the environment, there are other things we can do to find out more. There are huge amounts of information available on the Internet, for example. Personally, though, I feel the best way is just to go outside, whether you live in the city or the countryside. That way, you can see for yourself any changes taking place, for example with wildlife or weather, and then think about what you might do to help protect the environment.
1 There is no doubt
2 for example
3 Many people think
4 On the other hand
5 although
6 Personally

Extension

CLIL Give pairs or groups of students one environmental issue each, either from the list or the further ideas they suggested, to find out about and present to the rest of the class. They could include information from the Internet or the school library, or TV programmes they have watched. They could produce a short Powerpoint presentation with photos and maps, which could be done in class over a number of lessons.

Exam practice

Students read the general topic, the focus question and the notes very carefully. Before students begin writing, ask them to talk in pairs about the two points in the notes and to get some ideas about what to write. Then give them 30 minutes to produce the essay in class. Remind them that they have to write an introduction and add a third idea. They must also finish off the essay in some way, not simply stop writing. Remind them to use linking words and a good range of vocabulary. They must also check their work before they submit it to you for correcting.

Sample answer
Many people say that recycling is very important if we want to keep our environment clean and reduce pollution. But is recycling really so effective?
There is no doubt that recycling is encouraged in many countries. And because of that it is much easier now to take waste plastic and paper, for example, to a recycling centre so that they can be made into other things. What is more, many schools now have their own recycling programmes. That way, students learn to recycle their waste such as plastic water bottles.
Besides this, recycling means that waste plastics and paper are disposed of safely and not left to create litter in our cities and countryside. Plastic waste in particular can be very harmful to wildlife, so recycling is useful as it protects them.
On the other hand, there are many other things we can do to improve our environment, such as reducing our car use, cutting down on how much energy we use, and generally being less wasteful. Although recycling is useful, I personally think these are just as effective.
(179 words)

Part 2 (review)

Task type:
Writing one task from a possible selection of five text types (article, letter / email, essay, review, story) based on a contextualised writing task *or* a question related to a set text in 140–190 words.

Training

Lead-in

Ask students whether they have ever read any reviews of anything. Where do we tend to find reviews? What can they be about? If they wanted to buy something, e.g. a new laptop or a mobile phone, or go to see something, e.g. a film or a concert, would they read a review of it first? Why / Why not?

1 Write the categories on the board first, then get students to suggest points they might want to talk about in a review of these things. Then compare with the list on the page and see which ones they didn't think of.

shop	music venue	film
prices	music	story
staff	musicians	actors
range of goods	sound quality	ending
service	location	music
location	atmosphere	atmosphere
atmosphere	prices	location
	instruments	sound quality

2 Ask students to go through the list of adjectives in pairs and make sure they understand them all before they decide which are positive or negative. If one of the pair doesn't know a word, the other should explain it by using an example in English, rather than offering a translation.

Positive:	Negative:
original	weird
fast-moving	awful
impressive	dull
fashionable	confusing
dramatic	limited
helpful	
up-to-the-minute	**Either** (depends on context, e.g.
welcoming	whether you enjoy scary movies):
colourful	scary
friendly	complex
absorbing	outrageous
efficient	
good value for money	

3a/b This is to help students structure their review. They should choose a topic from the list to talk about and then start making some notes. Remind them to look back at the points and the vocabulary in the exercises they have already done, and to ensure that they clearly include positive and negative opinions. They should also write a conclusion, which should include some kind of recommendation for other people their age. A superlative sentence is also useful when writing the conclusion.

4a/b Remind students that they will need to make use of linking devices when making their points. Write the four sentence beginnings on the board, and elicit possible endings for them. You can also try swapping positive and negative linkers to give more practice in the answers.

Possible answers
1 they were very friendly to everyone in our group.
2 they were a bit limited in number.
3 the atmosphere there was fantastic.
4 the snacks in the coffee bar cost quite a lot.

5a/b Ask students what it is they have to write about for this question, and then ask them to read Jodie's answer. In pairs, they should close the book and try to remember as much as they can of Jodie's answer. Can they also remember any examples of describing words or linking phrases? Then get them to look at the review again and underline examples.

My parents love classical music, <u>so</u> we sometimes go to concerts at City Hall near my home. The Hall is by the river, with a <u>beautifully decorated</u> ceiling, and <u>massive</u> glass lights shining like diamonds. At the concerts, there's an orchestra, and <u>a conductor I always find absolutely fascinating</u>. <u>What's more</u>, the audience always dresses up in <u>amazing</u> clothes, so it's a very <u>colourful</u> event.

<u>However</u>, my musical tastes have recently developed a bit and, <u>although I still love classical music</u>, I go to City Hall now to watch rock concerts – which are very different! No-one dresses up or sits in the lovely red velvet seats. Everyone dances and, <u>because</u> the hall is specially built for music, the sound quality is <u>amazing</u>. <u>Besides that</u>, there's a <u>wonderful</u> café that serves <u>delicious</u> food – which we often don't have time to eat, sadly!

<u>On the other hand</u>, the Hall does get very crowded during popular concerts, which <u>I'm not keen on</u>. But the atmosphere there is so amazing and <u>welcoming</u> that I know people of any age would just love to go there!

Examples of:

opinions
a conductor I always find absolutely fascinating.
I still love classical music
I'm not keen on ...
describing words and phrases
beautifully decorated   massive   amazing   colourful   wonderful delicious   welcoming
linking words and phrases
so   what's more   however   although   because   besides that on the other hand

Extension

Ask students to find some reviews of their favourite bands, films, music CDs and so on in English on the Internet. They should be written for teenagers ideally, as the language of reviews can be very difficult. Ask them to find a couple of reviews for the same film / music / book / computer game, etc. and see if the reviewers agree. And do they agree with what the reviewer is saying?

Exam practice

Ask the students to look at who their target reader is, and what it is they are writing about – favourite websites that help them learn. Ask them to check how many points they have to cover.

Give them a few minutes to write down brief notes for their review. Remind them to make use of the language they have covered in the exercises. Give them 30 minutes to write their answer and check their work. If they are comfortable with peer correction, ask them to swap answers at the end and see if there is anything they can suggest that might improve their partner's answer, together with any language that they think is really good. Alternatively, collect the work for correcting – but only underline the mistakes and don't put in the corrected form. Leave the students to see if they can work this out for themselves. However, you could introduce some abbreviations to help the students, e.g. *sp* for a spelling error, *gr* for grammar. Students can find self-correction very difficult, and this can help to focus them. Also, if the class is not too big, you could photocopy their answers. Then in the next lesson ask them to edit their original version, and then present them with the one you have underlined. After an interval of a few days, students can often see errors more clearly than when they have just written something.

Sample answer
My teachers at school often give us homework to do that involves researching particular topics, either by using books in the school library or looking on the Internet.
And whenever I need to research a particular subject, I always go to my favourite site – www.faktz.en. It's fantastic! I discovered it when I was browsing one day, trying to find some information about dinosaurs! So now it's the first one I turn to when I want to know more. It has some great images, and links to other useful sites, too, so I can always find what I'm looking for. What's more, it covers a huge range of subjects, so I don't think it will ever let me down!
The only slight problem with it is that it's sometimes a bit slow when you want to move to another page on the site. But that certainly hasn't put me off, so I'd happily recommend it to anyone my age – especially someone like me who often needs help with their homework!
(169 words)

Part 2 (article)

Task type:
Writing one task from a possible selection of five text types (article, letter / email, essay, review, story) based on a contextualised writing task or a question related to a set text in 140–190 words.

Training

1a/b Ask students to look at who they are writing *for* – an international teenage magazine, so their article doesn't need to be in formal language. They should try to make it as lively and engaging as they can. Then ask them to look through what their article must be about, and the questions in the announcement that they have to answer. How many points do they need to address? Ask students to start thinking about the people they might help in their daily lives, and what they do. Section b shows students how to start planning their article by asking them to make brief notes.

Possible answer
my teacher   in class, after school

2a/b This exercise shows students how to add more detail to the notes they have made – to expand on their points. Once they have done this, they should have a good amount of material for their article. Ask them to work in pairs to add more ideas, and check as a whole class. Write examples of ideas on the board.

money	lending money to friends if they need it
being a good listener	listening when friends have problems
my teacher	– in class giving out books
	– after school tidying up in the classroom

3 Now students have to answer the final question in the announcement – what they find difficult about helping other people. There are three examples given, but ask if they can come up with any more.

Possible answers
I need to do my homework instead
I promised I'd go out with my friends.

4 Ask them to read through Rosemarie's answer, and then cover it and go back to the original question. Can students remember what she said about each of the points?

Rosemarie has covered all the questions in the announcement.

5 Ask students to look carefully at where these phrases are used in Rosemarie's answer, and the context in which they are used. Then get them to work individually on the exercise before comparing their answer in pairs, and finally checking as a whole class.

1 exactly the opposite	**5** Personally speaking
2 get round to	**6** I can't be bothered
3 in need of some help	**7** I've no idea where
4 it goes without saying	**8** better than it sounds

6 Give students an example of a *which* sentence on the board, e.g. *The weather forecast said it will be sunny tomorrow, which …* and elicit suggestions for the answer. Then ask them to look just at the sentences and cover the possible keys. In pairs they should come up with suggested solutions of their own before doing the matching task.

1 was annoying for her.
2 was really thoughtful of them.
3 meant it got soaking wet!
4 often happens in his village.
5 they found a bit scary.
6 he was very happy about.

Exam practice

Ask students to look at where the announcement comes from, i.e. who their target readers will be.

Allow them time to look carefully through the announcement. What kind of people have they got to write about? How many points do they need to cover? Then ask the class for some examples of people they could write about and put them on the board, to get them started. Give them a few minutes' thinking time before they share their ideas with a partner. Advise them to make sure that if they choose a famous person they must be able to find enough to say to be able to write 140–190 words. Once they feel they have got enough to write about and they are ready to start, set a time limit of 30 minutes to write their article. Remind them to check their work before they submit it to you for correcting. When correcting, you might find it useful to highlight any repeated errors that you notice in students' work. This can also help them in the checking process as they then have something specific to check for.

Sample answer
Young people like me often like to find someone who they think provides them with a good example of how to live their lives – the way they dress, the things they do, and even the decisions they take. Personally speaking, I'd say the person who has been the best example for me, and has acted as a great role model, has been my father. He's always been there for me when I've needed him, and never made me feel bad about things I've done or mistakes I've made, even if he thought they weren't always the best things to do. And if ever I've been in trouble and in need of some help, he's always been ready to help me out.
He does lots of youth work in our village, and also runs the local teenagers' cricket team. He's completely dedicated, and goes every week even when he's tired. I've no idea where he gets his energy from sometimes. So it goes without saying that all the team have a great deal of respect for him. I think all young people need someone like him to be their role model.
(190 words)

Test 2
Listening
Part 1

> **Task type:**
> One multiple-choice question per short monologue or exchange, each with three options.

Training

- There are eight short recordings.
- You listen to each recording twice.
- The questions are multiple-choice with three options. The question can be either a full question, or a sentence completion.

1a–c Encourage students to look at the question. Ask students *Whose feelings do they need to focus on – the boy's or the girl's?* Get students to read through the dialogue in pairs and briefly summarise what they've understood. Then ask some comprehension-testing questions, e.g. *Where are they planning to go on their trip?; What do they want to do there?; Who else is going, apart from the boy and girl, do you think?; What does the boy think the place will be like? Why? ; How does he respond to the girl's suggestion of swimming?*

> Correct answer: C

Extension

Ask students to discuss in pairs any visits they've made to local sports centres and/or skate parks. How did they feel about their trips? Then get one person in the pair to summarise what their partner told them and then say what their partner's feelings were. Were they: *satisfied? disappointed? glad they went? thrilled? exhausted afterwards? excited?* Write up some possible adjectives and expressions on the board for students to use.

2a/b This time, the students can't see the audioscript, so they should listen carefully. Ask them to focus first on the context-setting sentence. What will the dialogue be about? Have any students in the class climbed trees? What do you need to be careful of when climbing? Encourage them to look at the options while they listen, and identify which one is the answer. *What sort of sentences are these?* Answer: *Imperatives.* So what would you be doing if you used this type of sentence to tell someone something? Elicit answers as to the possible question from around the class. Discuss the fact that the question asks students to focus on what both speakers would say.

What do they agree is important when climbing trees?

> Correct answer: C

Extension

It's useful for students to listen to all kinds of short conversations and then identify what's happening – who's speaking, what they're talking about, their attitudes and opinions, and whether they agree. Students need to learn to understand not just what is stated in a conversation, but what is implied or indirectly stated too. Small snippets of native-speaker English such as from a radio or TV, or from course book recordings, can all help students tune in quickly to conversations.

Exam practice

Encourage students to read carefully through the questions and options as they are waiting for the recording to begin. It's essential to make the best possible use of this time.

To begin, you could work through a couple of the tasks and then check them before moving on to play the other six without stopping. This helps you to make sure students know what they have to do before you work through all of the tasks.

To give extra support, you could read through the questions and options with the students first, and discuss briefly what they can expect to hear, particularly if they haven't done this kind of exam task before. Remind them that the *Advice* section can give a little extra help if they need it.

Ask students to compare answers in pairs and then check as a class. Can students say why they chose the answers they did? If any proved particularly difficult, be prepared to read out relevant sections of the audioscript.

> **1** B **2** B **3** A **4** C **5** C **6** A **7** B **8** A

Part 2

> **Task type:**
> Complete 10 sentences with information heard on the recording.

Training

- You will hear one person in this part of the test.
- You usually write between one and three words to complete each gap.

1 The aim of this exercise is to help students tune in to the topic they are going to hear about, and think about the kind of information they might expect to hear. Ask students to talk in pairs or groups about the different trips they have had to any of these places. Before they begin, ask them to think about likely vocabulary they might need when talking about these topics, and put these on the board to help them.

Extension

Students could follow up their discussion about trips to different places by writing a short piece for homework about a trip they have been on.

2a/b Before students listen to the recording, get them to think about the word that might fit and consider the context. The recording is about a theme park, and the sentence is talking about a *ride*. How many different words do they know for rides at a theme park? (E.g. roundabout, big wheel, rollercoaster, big dipper, waltzer, slide, swing, boats.) Then ask students to listen and compare their answers in pairs.

> Correct answer: (massive) roundabout
> Harry wasn't keen to go on the roundabout as it was going at great speed, which he didn't like. The section also mentions a *big wheel*, which he **was** keen to go on, and he persuaded his brother to join him. From there, they saw their parents on the *swings*.

3a/b Point out that students are listening for the name of some type of flavoured drink. Ask them to think about what the word could be – apple, orange, lemon? Encourage students to get into the habit of speculating on missing words on the gaps in Part 2. Then ask students to answer the question in pairs, and explain why the other flavours they heard were wrong.

pineapple
The recording includes the words *orange* and *strawberry*, both of which would fit the gap. But it was Harry's brother that wanted orange, and Harry's dad brought Harry a strawberry favoured drink - although Harry had hoped for pineapple.

4a/b This is aimed at raising students' awareness of the importance of correct spelling in Part 2. This exercise practises ten common spelling mistakes, but students should be encouraged to monitor and record their own mistakes.

1 newspaper   2 exhibition   3 museum   4 library   5 journey
6 clothes   7 accommodation   8 environment   9 mountains
10 Wednesday

Extension

Encourage students to get their own notebook, divide it up into a few pages for each letter of the alphabet and then use it as a place to record spellings. Students can then keep these to practise – encourage them to work on their spellings if, for example, they have finished their work ahead of other students and have nothing to do. The notebook is also useful when students are producing a piece of writing in class and ask you for spellings. These can be recorded in the notebook, as can any words that a student consistently spells wrongly.

Exam practice

Ask students to look at the rubric and title: Who is talking? What about? Where did she go? What did she do there? What does *dog-sledding* mean, do you think? Take a few minutes to read through the sentences with the students. Encourage them to talk in pairs about what they think the words might be, and then see if they were right once they've listened and checked with the recording. Encourage students to pay particular attention to sentences where they are asked about the speaker's feelings, e.g. Karen was *grateful, alarmed (positive or negative?), disappointed (positive or negative?)*. Remind students to make use of the *Advice* section at the end.

9 ski resort   10 valley   11 sociable   12 safety lesson
13 15 / fifteen   14 frozen lake   15 stand (up)   16 wolves
17 winter boots   18 ice sculptures

Extension

CLIL The dogs in the text are called huskies. Ask students to find out more about them. *Where do they live?; What do they look like?; What do they do?; Why are they so good at pulling sleds?; And are the sleds and huskies only used by tourists, or are they used for work purposes, too?; If so, where? What sort of work?* Ask students to bring in a few pictures of huskies and sleds. Huskies are also kept as pets in some countries. Have the students ever seen one in their country? They are quite demanding to keep as pets. Get students to think about why this might be.

Part 3

Task type:
Multiple-matching.
Five questions which require the selection of the correct answer from a list of eight.

Training

- You listen to five short extracts in Part 3.

- You have to choose from eight options.

1 This is aimed at getting students to look carefully at the list of options they will be presented with in Part 3. Students will find it helpful if they are familiar with the options before the recording starts, and have had the chance to think carefully about any options they are not entirely certain about. Ask students to talk in pairs about what they understand by each of the options A–H. The common theme is a party; ask them to talk about each option in turn and think of examples, perhaps from their own experience, for example:

What kind of clothes might you wear to a fancy dress party? What might the wrong kind of clothes be, e.g. at a smart party? Why might you turn up too late at a party? How would you feel?
Who might you meet at a party? An old friend? A new friend? What's an embarrassing thing you might do at a party? Forget someone's name? Fall over?
Why might you be saying goodbye to someone at a party? A teacher? A student who is moving to another town or country? How would you feel?
How might you end up at the wrong party?
What might you be given at a party? A present? Special food or drink?

To avoid the activity going on for too long, give a couple of options to each pair, and then ask for a few ideas at the end of the discussion.

2a/b Ask students to read through the text in pairs and then summarise what the speaker said. They should identify the answer and then close their books and listen to the recording. Ask them to listen carefully to any of the other options that also seem to be suggested in the recording, as this will help them prepare for the exam. Parts of each recording may seem to be referring to other options, but students have to decide which one is a complete match.

D '... ran into a person ... best mates ever since!'
Students might consider Option A and B, as clothes are mentioned – *an expensive dress*. Option H might also seem attractive – *the family were giving out drinks.*

3a/b Students now have to rely only on the recording to find the answer. They might find it useful to note down any key words or phrases that give them clues. Ask them to compare their answer, and also any other options that they considered and then rejected. Then ask students to summarise in pairs what the speaker said. You could read sections of the audioscript aloud for the class at the end, to confirm answers, and help with any sections that they didn't catch.

Correct answer: G
1 ... didn't know anyone there at all ... our party was actually in another room next door'
2 Students might also consider Option C – they were in a rush, and Option A – *Everyone was in fancy dress, including us*

4 This provides a bit more practice for the students in identifying what the speaker is talking about. The student's partner should try to guess which option the student is talking about.

Extension

For homework, the students could write a short story about their experience of one of the situations in the options. They can use what they discussed in Exercise 1 in their story. Ask them to write down a few short notes before they forget what they discussed.

Exam practice

Give students a few moments to look at the rubric, and then ask them: *Who is going to be talking?* and *What are they going to be talking about?* Ask a few people in the class to talk briefly about their experiences of surprise parties. Are these parties always successful? If this is the first time the class has tried this type of listening task stop the recording after each speaker and give the students time to consider the options. You can also ask them to discuss their answers in pairs, and then give them the answer after each speaker instead of right at the end. This helps to familiarise them with the task type. Remind them that there are three options they won't use. Encourage students to refer to the *Advice* section for extra help.

19 D	**20** C	**21** F	**22** G	**23** A

Extension

CLIL Ask students to do some research on the topic of fancy dress for parties and carnivals, e.g. the carnivals in Rio and Venice, or special festivals and parties in the students' home countries, when it's traditional to dress up in costumes. Ask them to find photos of people wearing costumes. Students could also draw pictures, make masks and take photos to make a wall display. The artwork could be accompanied by short explanatory texts written by the students.

Part 4

Task type:
Multiple-choice.
There are seven 3-option multiple-choice questions.

Training

- There are two speakers in Part 4.

- You have to answer seven multiple-choice questions, each with three options. They are either whole questions or sentences to complete.

1 In Part 4, the options may focus on identifying how the speaker feels, so students may come across the kinds of verbs given in the exercise. Check with students that they understand the meanings of these verbs, and then ask them to do the exercise in pairs, and check the answers around the class.

Possible answers
1 encourage / persuade
2 advise / warn
3 criticise / advise
4 prefer
5 praise / approve / encourage
6 intend / describe / claim / insist
7 advise
8 plan / intend

Extension

Once students have finished the exercise, ask them to close their books. Write the verbs on the board and then ask students to work in pairs. One student should give an example of the verb, similar to the type of examples given in the exercise, and the other student in the pair should guess the verb. Write up the first sentence from the exercise as an example if students are still unsure what to do.

2a/b This section prepares students to answer a multiple-choice listening task. Ask students to read the question and the options before they begin listening. Are there any students in the class who are interested in photography? Is it a difficult or an easy hobby to take up? Is there anything they have found *discouraging* about it? Would they say they have a natural

talent for it? Ask students to close their books and just listen to the recording. Ask them to summarise what Dan said about his experience of doing photography. They might find it useful to note down key words and expressions. Then ask them to look at the audioscript, and the letters that show where each option came from. Ask them to try and explain why B and C are wrong.

Correct answer: A
B is wrong. He didn't think his brother was better, as he hadn't done much photography either. But Dan accepted that his brother's criticism was correct and he was just trying to help. Dan feared his brother was better than him. C is wrong – it wasn't that he thought he had no talent. His mother thought his work was great, and he also thought his own work wasn't too bad. In fact he later went back to it when his school began photography classes.

Exam practice

Ask students to look at the rubric, and then ask them: *Who is the interview with?; What is his hobby?; What does pottery mean?; How do you make pottery?; What do you need to make it?* (The material that is commonly used is called clay). Then get students to look at the first question and the options. If students are not very experienced at this type of exercise, try doing the first two questions, then stopping and checking the answers after each one, before going through the rest of the task without stopping. Encourage students to use the *Advice* section for extra help.

24 C	**25** A	**26** C	**27** B	**28** A	**29** C	**30** A

Extension

Ask students to talk about any hobbies they have involving arts and crafts, such as painting, drawing, pottery, photography, film-making, knitting, sewing or printmaking. Students could be encouraged to bring in a piece of their work and give the class, or a small group, a short presentation on it.

Extension

CLIL Get students to find out a bit more about pottery. What does a potter's wheel look like? Is there anywhere in the school that they could try one? And what is a *coiled* pot? Ask students to find out, or even make one. Are there any particular types of pottery that are very traditional in their home countries, or even their home area? Ask them to find photos. The local museum might even have a display of pots that have been found in their area and date back thousands of years. What type of shapes were they? What patterns did they use to decorate them? What might people have eaten out of them?

Test 2
Speaking
Part 1

Task type:
A conversation between one examiner and each candidate.
In Part 1, candidates are asked questions on a variety of topics related to their everyday life.
They are not asked for their opinions on these topics, because that happens in Part 4 of the Speaking Test.
Candidates are assessed on their performance throughout the 14-minute test.

Training

- The questions are about everyday life.
- You speak to the examiner / interlocutor.

1 Remind students that the Speaking Test is taken in pairs, but if there is an odd number of candidates, at the end of the session, there will be one group of three. Students cannot choose to be in a group of three. Students answer the questions in pairs, and then go through the answers with the whole class.

For a group of three taking the test, then
Part 1 lasts 3 minutes instead of 2 minutes
Part 2 lasts 6 minutes instead of 4 minutes
Part 3 lasts 5 minutes instead of 4 minutes
Part 4 lasts 6 minutes instead of 4 minutes.
So the test lasts 20 minutes instead of 14 minutes.

The students should look at the questions and decide on the answers in pairs. Don't give them the answers to questions 1 or 2 at this stage, because they will be able to check their answers in the next exercise.

> 1 two   2 different   3 don't see

2 Tell the students that they don't see the questions in Part 1. Ask them to time the recording, and listen to hear whether the students are asked the same questions or different ones. Check the answers with the whole class.

3 Before they listen again, ask the students what the topic was. Then ask them which of the expressions they think they heard in the recording. Play the recording again.

1 The topic was school.
2 Students should tick the following words and expressions:

> a so; also; as well as; and
> b like; such as
> d I'm sorry, I didn't quite catch that

Exam practice

1 Students ask each other and answer these questions in pairs. Monitor students while they are doing the task, and make a note of good answers and suggestions for improvements. Then discuss these with the whole class. Pairs of students could model good examples of replies to each question in front of the whole class.

2 Tell students they are now going to hear some different Part 1 questions. Put the students into small groups and ask them to listen to each question, then pause the recording. One student in each group answers the question, while the others listen and make notes of good language or suggestions for improvements. Every student should have the chance to answer a question. Discuss possible answers with the whole class at the end.

Part 2

> **Task type:**
> An individual 1-minute 'long turn' for each candidate, with a brief response from the second candidate lasting about 30 seconds. Candidates are assessed on their performance throughout the 14-minute test.

Training

- You talk about two pictures.
- You have to compare the pictures and give your opinion in reply to a question about the pictures.
- You talk about and answer questions about your own set of pictures, but you also answer a quick question about your partner's pictures after your partner has finished talking about them.

Remind students that they have to *compare* the two photographs, i.e. talk about the similarities and differences between the two, and NOT describe the photographs in detail. They also have to answer the question they will see above the two pictures.

1 Students complete the exercise in pairs, and use the Useful language in Test 1 on page 57 if they need to.

> 1 both   2 Both   3 first   4 second   5 whereas / whilst

2 Students fill the gaps in the sentences with a partner, using the Useful language in Test 1 on page 57 if they need to.

> ***Possible answers***
> 1 seems to / appears to   2 looks   3 seems to   4 Maybe / Perhaps
> 5 like   6 impression / feeling

3 Remind students that the 'listening' candidate will be asked a short follow-up question after the candidate with the 'long turn' has finished talking about their two pictures. This question will be about one or both of the same pictures, and they will have about 30 seconds to answer the follow-up question. Students complete the sentences and check the answers with their partner.

> 1 it would be   2 I'd / I would   3 so

4/5 Look at the example with the whole class. Students then do the rest of the exercise in pairs. Tell students to listen to the recording to hear whether the sentences they wrote were correct. Check the answers with the whole class. Then play the recording again as they read the audioscript on page 189.

> 1 It's sunny in both (the) pictures.
> 2 The girl in the second picture looks as if she's feeling very happy.
> 3 I have the impression (that) the boy is / 's enjoying the book he's reading.
> 4 The girl's doing something thrilling, whereas the boy's just relaxing.
> 5 In my opinion, it would be more enjoyable to read on the beach, because I don't like sport very much.

Exam practice

Candidates do the exam practice in pairs or groups of three.

Part 3

> **Task type:**
> A two-way conversation between the candidates.
> Candidates receive spoken instructions and written stimuli.
> There is a two-minute discussion followed by a one-minute decision-making task.
> Candidates are assessed on their performance throughout the 14-minute test.

Training

- You speak to your partner.
- Part 3 lasts about 4 minutes.
- You see a question and five prompts in the booklet, but you **don't** see the summary question that the examiner asks you after you have discussed the question and prompts for about two minutes.

1 Remind the candidates that the stimuli are all written prompts in this part. There are no photos or pictures. Tell students they can use the words in the prompts when they are speaking, but they will get extra marks for using their own words where possible. Also remind them that they don't need to discuss every single idea. Students listen to the recording and number the prompts according to the order in which they hear them, and then compare their answers with a partner. When checking the answers with the whole class, you could ask students which words or phrases helped them decide which idea was being discussed.

> **1** school subjects
> **2** the best clothes to buy
> **3** how to cook
> **4** how to behave well
> Not discussed: the latest technology

2 Students need to practise working together to keep the conversation going. They shouldn't rush and only discuss the ideas in the prompts superficially. Instead, they should address each prompt together, listening to each other and agreeing and disagreeing politely with each other to move the conversation forward. Students listen to the recording again and tick the expressions they hear.

> **Students should tick the following:**
> What do you think about...? _
> What about this idea here? _
> This suggestion looks good, doesn't it?

3 Students listen to the next part of the discussion in Part 3, in which the candidates are asked to make a decision. Students check their answers with a partner. Remind them that they don't lose marks if they don't actually reach a decision.

> **1** Which two things would be most useful to learn from older people?
> **2** They don't make a final decision: they agree on one thing, but not two.

4 Students listen again and note down the expressions.

> **1** That's true
> **2** Yes, but ... ; I know what you mean, but ...; Hm, maybe

Exam practice

Go through the tips on the page with the whole class, and then students do the task in pairs or groups of three.

Part 4

> **Task type:**
> A discussion on topics related to the Part 3 collaborative task. Candidates are assessed on their performance throughout the 14-minute test.

Training

- No, you don't see the questions in part 4.
- You may be asked some of the same questions as your partner, but not necessarily.

It is not easy for teens to keep a conversation going but, as interactive communication is well rewarded in the exam – it is worth 25% of the marks given, students should be encouraged to interact with their partner, for example by involving them when initiating the discussion, e.g. *Shall I start?* and also by responding when their partner addresses them.

1 In pairs, students try to predict two or three questions the examiner may ask them, related to the topic of the Part 3 task. Possible ideas: *how older people and younger people get on together, whether they should spend more time together, whether older people can learn things from younger people.*

> **1** Do you think young people spend enough time talking to older people?
> **2** Can young and old people enjoy activities together?
> **3** Is it a good idea for several generations in a family to live together?

2 Students listen to the recording and write down the three questions the examiner asks. N.B: usually the questions in Part 4 start off very close to the topic in Part 3, and have a more personal focus, then they widen out. Here, they move from younger and older people talking together, and then the questions deal with wider issues, such as whether it is a good idea for different generations to live together.

Extension

Ask the students to ask and answer in pairs the questions they have just written down. Remind them to give reasons for their answers.

Exam practice

Students do the exam task in groups of three, with one student acting as the examiner. Monitor the students while they are doing the task, and when they have finished, ask a group who have done the task particularly well to ask and answer the questions in front of the whole class.

Key

Test 3

Reading and Use of English

Part 1

1 A 2 C 3 D 4 C 5 B 6 A 7 D 8 C

Part 2

9 something   10 be   11 at   12 no
13 if   14 All   15 as   16 one

Part 3

17 disagreement   18 runners   19 (un)surprisingly
20 preferable   21 enthusiasm 22 sickness
23 importance   24 consideration

Part 4

25 only | did Nadia / she leave
26 allowed to cycle | here unless
27 cancelled | even though it
28 spent | the whole evening playing
29 reminds her | of
30 giving us | a lift

Part 5

31 D   32 A   33 B   34 C   35 C   36 C

Part 6

37 E   38 C   39 G   40 A   41 F   42 D

Part 7

43 B   44 D   45 C   46 A   47 C   48 B   49 A
50 D   51 C   52 A

Writing

Part 1

Sample answer

Most people would agree that cooking is a useful skill. However, not everyone believes that it is necessary for teenagers to be able to cook their own meals.

On the one hand, many teenagers can manage perfectly well without being able to prepare their own food. Their parents can do it for them, and they can focus on things like homework and other activities in their free time. They may also feel that cooking is a boring thing to do, and that they can learn it later in their lives if they need to.

On the other hand, most people will need to be able to cook for themselves at some point in their lives, so why not learn to do so at an early age, either at home or at school? It can be great fun, and people who know how to cook can eat more healthily, without relying on fast food or ready meals which are often bad for you.

On balance, I think we should all learn to prepare a few dishes, so we find it easier to look after ourselves when we leave home.

(188 words)

Part 2

Sample answers

Question 2

Hi Tom,

Thanks for your email. It sounds like an interesting project. In my country, Brazil, the most popular dance is the Samba.

There are a variety of Sambas, including Samba Reggae and Samba Rock, but I'd say the most popular type is called Samba no pé. Have you seen videos of the famous Rio de Janeiro Carnival? That's what the people you see in those are dancing. It's a solo dance and the way people dance it varies slightly from region to region.

It's enjoyed by all sorts of people, of all ages. My grandparents still dance it, and I like it too. Samba music has a special rhythm, which comes from a mixture of African and Brazilian music. It has its roots in music brought to Brazil from Africa in the sixteenth century, when Brazil was a Portuguese colony. I think it's special because as soon as I hear Samba music I want to get up and dance, and so do most people I know!

I hope this helps you with your project. Let me know how you get on with it.

Write soon,

Marta

(187 words)

Question 3

Café Verdi

If you're looking for a café in Copenhagen to go and relax with your friends, then Café Verdi is a good place to choose. It's in the centre, just off the town hall square, just a few minutes' walk from the main station.

You can have all sorts of hot drinks there, including their absolutely delicious hot chocolate with cream. There's also a wide variety of soft drinks to choose from. They serve delicious cakes and pastries too, or you can have snacks like crisps or peanuts. They don't serve hot meals, but they do have sandwiches and salads on the menu.

The atmosphere there is very friendly, and they play great music from the 1970s and 80s. That doesn't mean to say it's a café for old people though – it's very popular with younger people too. The service is good and the staff polite and efficient.

I'd definitely recommend it to other people my age, but my friends and I can only afford to go there from time to time. I think most teenagers would agree that it's a little expensive, but definitely worth a visit!

(188 words)

Question 4

Jim knew it would be a long journey, but he couldn't wait to set off. He was going to visit his favourite uncle in the city. Jim hadn't seen him for ages, because he lived so far away. Jim's parents, who ran a small shop, were always too busy to take him, but they'd finally agreed he was now old enough to make the five-hour coach journey on his own.

He said goodbye to his parents and walked to the coach station, carrying everything he needed for the week in a small rucksack. When he got on the coach, the only free seat was next to a boy his own age, who looked very upset. Although Jim was quite shy, he asked him what the matter was.

It turned out that the boy, whose name was Billy, had promised to call his mother when he was safely on the coach. Unfortunately, he'd left his phone at home so had no way of contacting her. 'Don't worry, you can borrow mine,' Jim said kindly. By the time his uncle picked him up a few hours later, Jim had a new friend.

(190 words)

Question 5

In this book, most of the characters face challenges and have to cope with difficulties at some point. However, I believe that Susan has the worst problem to deal with in the story.

When she hurts her shoulder just before the most important swimming competition she has ever been in, Susan has to decide whether or not to tell her coach. The coach might tell Susan not to take part, which would be a huge disappointment for her. On the other hand, if Susan ignores her injury and swims, she risks doing badly and letting her team down.

Susan discusses the issue with her brother, William, and he persuades her to speak to her coach, because he is worried that Susan might have problems in the future if she swims while injured. Susan does so, and her coach sends her to see a physiotherapist. In my opinion, she makes the right decision: although she misses the race, by the end of the book she is swimming even better than before and has even managed to get into the national swimming team.

(181 words)

Listening

Part 1

1 A   **2** C   **3** C   **4** B   **5** A   **6** A   **7** B   **8** B

Part 2

9 history   **10** costumes   **11** programme / program
12 waiter   **13** garden   **14** sister   **15** cakes
16 shoes   **17** children   **18** director

Part 3

19 D   **20** E   **21** B   **22** F   **23** H

Part 4

24 B   **25** A   **26** B   **27** A   **28** C   **29** B   **30** C

Test 4

Reading and Use of English

Part 1

1 C   **2** B   **3** D   **4** B   **5** C   **6** D   **7** C   **8** C

Part 2

9 as   **10** have   **11** in   **12** nor / neither   **13** to
14 with   **15** are   **16** do

Part 3

17 interested
18 evidence
19 automatically
20 surroundings
21 majority

22 uncomfortable
23 strength
24 Consequently

Part 4

25 wish I hadn't / had not | eaten
26 succeeded in | fixing
27 in case | it's / it is
28 to take advantage | of
29 as soon as | she got / was
30 are / were | far / less

Part 5

31 B   **32** C   **33** A   **34** D   **35** C   **36** C

Part 6

37 C   **38** G   **39** A   **40** E   **41** D   **42** F

Part 7

43 C   **44** E   **45** D   **46** F   **47** A   **48** D   **49** C
50 F   **51** B   **52** E

Writing

Part 1

Sample answer

Some people think that if you want to talk to another person properly, you have to be face to face. Although there are reasons for believing this, there are arguments for and against this view.

On the one hand, there are great advantages to being able to chat to friends and family online at any time of day, whenever you feel like it. Even when you are at home you can stay in touch with all your friends. And you can also contact your parents if you need to from school.

On the other hand, it is true that if you want to talk to your parents or brothers and sisters about something important, you may need to sit down and talk face to face. Moreover, in order to get to know a new friend well, chatting online may not be enough. Keeping up a good friendship may not be easy if you rarely actually meet.

On balance, I think it is perfectly possible to communicate well with other people online. It is nice to be able to see people in person, but sometimes chatting online is just as good.

(190 words)

Part 2

Sample answers
Question 2

Laura realised the girl's bag was still on the café chair. The girl had walked out of the café and got on the bus without it and, for a moment, Laura couldn't think what to do. The bus moved off and the girl was chatting on her phone, so that's probably why she hadn't noticed that she'd left her schoolbag behind.

Laura was with her mum, and they decided to look inside the bag and see if they could work out who the girl was and where she lived. They found a small piece of card with a name and address on it. To their amazement, the address was that of a flat in their street.

Laura and her mum went to the flat and knocked on the front door. A woman opened the door and Laura's mum explained why they were there. 'Oh, that's typical of Anna! She's so forgetful!' said the woman, laughing. 'I'll call her and tell her straight away.' Later that afternoon, Anna called Laura and her mum to thank them.

(175 words)

Question 3

Dear Chris,

Thanks for your letter. I think it's a great idea to have a party for Ms Daniels. She's really lovely, and it would be good to do something nice for her before she leaves. If our teachers help us, it will be fantastic!

I have a few ideas that might be helpful. First of all, it would be great to hold the party in the garden, because the weather is very good here in summer. How about taking some tables outside and asking every student to bring a plate of food? We could also play some of the language games she likes. If we have it on the last day of term, then maybe we could have the party in the afternoon before we go home, if our teachers let us.

As for a present, I've thought about it quite a lot. I think Ms Daniels might like something that will remind her of us after she has left our school. How about giving her a photograph of our class? We could all sign it!

I hope you think my ideas are helpful.

Best wishes,

Mark

(188 words)

Question 4

Sport, sport, sport!

Do I like sport? That's a good question! I play football and volleyball at school, and I cycle to school every day. I'd say I like it, but am not obsessed by it. Some of my friends, however, watch sport and talk about it all the time. And when they're not watching a football match on TV, they're playing it themselves.

For me, playing a team sport like football is the ideal way to exercise. You have fun with your friends, you make an effort because you're in a team and trying to beat the other team, and you usually have a regular training and match schedule you have to stick to. Other people prefer to exercise more independently. Things like jogging work well for them, or going to the gym.

I generally prefer to play sport than passively watch it, but there are many sports I can't do well. I'm pretty bad at tennis, for example, so though I enjoy trying to improve, I also love watching international players on TV. I know I'll never be as good as they are, but I can always dream!

(190 words)

Question 5

The plot of [title] is complicated, involving a number of very different characters. Whether or not it ended well for all of these characters is an interesting question.

Alex and Frances, the brother and sister who are the heroes of the story, face a number of challenges. They deal with these successfully, and by the end of the story have managed to return to their family safely. However, Judy and Heather, the other main characters, are not so fortunate: they are still in the jungle, trying to get home. They have met Drin, though, who appears to be able to help them. The reader therefore feels that they will eventually overcome their difficulties and get back home.

If I had written this story, I might have been tempted to allow Judy and Heather to reach safety before the end. Nevertheless, I think that the author made the right decision when she left the reader in a little doubt about how things would turn out for them: it makes the story more exciting, and means that people will think about the book even after reading the final page.

(187 words)

Listening

Part 1

1 B 2 B 3 A 4 C 5 C 6 A 7 B 8 C

Part 2

9 aunt   10 English   11 logo   12 flowers   13 radio
14 chess   15 drawings   16 sweatshirt / sweat shirt
17 businessman / business man   18 basketball

Part 3

19 F   20 A   21 E   22 H   23 D

Part 4

24 A   25 B   26 A   27 C   28 B   29 B   30 A

Test 5

Reading and Use of English

Part 1

1 B   2 C   3 B   4 D   5 A   6 D   7 A   8 C

Part 2

9 who   10 from   11 part   12 sure / certain
13 been   14 like   15 though / when / if
16 them / themselves

Part 3

17 relationship
18 defence / defense (US spelling)
19 independently
20 economic
21 advantageous
22 movement
23 popularity
24 inexpensive

Part 4

25 let her go swimming / by
26 wishes he had spent / wishes he'd spent / less
27 may have / taken
28 is generally thought / to be
29 is unlikely / to go
30 at taking / care of

Part 5

31 B   32 C   33 A   34 C   35 A   36 D

Part 6

37 D   38 F   39 B   40 G   41 A   42 E

Part 7

43 B   44 C   45 A   46 E   47 B   48 D   49 A
50 C   51 D   52 E

Writing

Part 1

Sample answer

In my opinion, it is essential that schools should teach students about the importance of protecting the environment, and one of the best ways that they can do this is by setting pupils a good example.

The school can do so in a number of different ways. Firstly, it needs to have a good recycling policy. There should be bins in all the classrooms making it easy to dispose of recyclable products in an appropriate way. Teachers should make sure they use these bins themselves too and that they insist on their pupils doing the same thing. Similarly, the school needs to make a point of saving energy. Staff must take care always to switch off lights as well as computers and other electrical equipment whenever they are not in use. Students should also be encouraged wherever possible to walk or cycle to school rather than being driven by their parents and teachers must ensure they don't come to work by car either.

Although lessons are important, setting a good example is likely to be a more effective way of influencing pupil behaviour in the long run.

(187 words)

Part 2

Sample answers
Question 2

Feeling very excited, Gina picked up her bag and got on the train. It was the first time she had travelled on a train alone without her parents. She was going on a school trip to France. All her friends were going too and they were all talking and laughing as they settled down for the long journey.

It took them ten hours to get to the town where they would be staying but the time passed quickly as they played games and looked out of the window at the changing scenery. They were to be living in a small town beside a lake in the mountains. The sun was setting as they arrived and it looked very beautiful. Gina knew she was going to be happy there.

As they left the train they were met by the group of French students who they would be spending the next two weeks with. They were all carrying flowers to welcome Gina and her friends. A tall girl with dark hair and smiling eyes came to give Gina a beautiful bunch of anemones. It was the start of a wonderful fortnight.

(189 words)

Question 3

Hi Sam,

Lovely to hear from you.

My friends and I all listen to lots of music. We are all interested in different kinds of music, particularly rock and jazz. We listen to the radio a great deal in order to keep up with what's new. We tell each other if we've heard something we like. If something's particularly special then we buy it online and download it to our phones or MP3 players.

We listen to music whenever we have a spare moment. I'm typical, I think. I listen to my MP3 player, for example, on the bus on my way to school and when I go to the gym. I always have the radio on when I'm doing my homework. And, of course, I also listen to music when I'm just relaxing.

Probably about half of my friends can play a musical instrument. Several of them have piano lessons and three of them are learning the guitar. One of my best friends is a great drummer. He plays in a band and occasionally they've played gigs in public. He dreams of being in a famous band one day!

I hope this helps.

Love

Maria

[192 words]

Question 4

Last night there was an excellent documentary about elephants on TV. I watched it quite by chance. I felt like watching some television before going to bed so I flicked through the channels to see if there was anything interesting on. I was about to give up when I saw some amazing pictures of a group of elephants.

The documentary was made by a team of researchers who had been observing a group of elephants over a period of fifteen years. They had given each of the elephants names and were able to tell viewers all about the relationships between them. It was absolutely fascinating. I had no idea that elephants had such strong family relationships. In many ways they seem to support each other in the same ways as people in a human family do.

I would certainly recommend this film to my friends. We all enjoy nature programmes and like learning about animals. Like me, they would also enjoy the stunning African landscape shown in the documentary. There is going to be a second documentary about these elephants next week and I can't wait!

(186 words)

Listening

Part 1

1 A   **2** C   **3** B   **4** B   **5** C   **6** B   **7** A   **8** B

Part 2

9 4,000 / four thousand   **10** (the) wind
11 10 / ten months   **12** oysters   **13** sea
14 indigestion   **15** mosquitoes   **16** Mexico
17 meat   **18** apple pie

Part 3

19 H   **20** E   **21** C   **22** A   **23** F

Part 4

24 C   **25** A   **26** B   **27** C   **28** A   **29** B   **30** C

Test 6

Reading and Use of English

Part 1

1 D   **2** B   **3** A   **4** A   **5** C   **6** D   **7** C   **8** B

Part 2

9 up   **10** where   **11** be   **12** in   **13** it
14 enough   **15** which   **16** another

Part 3

17 commercially   **18** resemblance   **19** frequency
20 prohibition   **21** disagreement   **22** production
23 safety   **24** underestimated

Part 4

25 am supposed / 'm supposed / to be doing
26 would cost / would have cost / would've cost / less than

27 we had (some) difficulty / we experienced (some) difficulty / (in) staying
28 better goalkeeper / than anyone / anybody / everyone / everybody
29 old enough / to have / to take / for
30 it wasn't / was not worth / spending

Part 5

31 C **32** B **33** D **34** A **35** C **36** B

Part 6

37 F **38** B **39** G **40** C **41** A **42** E

Part 7

43 D **44** C **45** A **46** C **47** B **48** A **49** D
50 B **51** C **52** B

Writing

Part 1

Sample answer
Learning a foreign language is extremely important for young people today.

Languages can be very useful when someone is travelling in another country. You may be able to do a great deal with sign language but you can only get to know what a place is really like if you can talk to the people there in their own language. It is even more important to know foreign languages for study purposes. More and more students nowadays would like to do at least part of their higher education in another country. They will find it much easier to achieve this dream if they can speak the language of the country where they would like to study. When it comes to working, it is an enormous advantage to know another language as so many businesses these days are either international companies or have suppliers or customers abroad.

But the most important reason is that communication between young people of different nationalities means that the world is likely to become a more peaceful and a happier place in the future.

(178 words)

Part 2

Sample answers
Question 2
I went on a very special journey this summer when I visited St Petersburg. I went with my parents and my brother and our plan was to go to Russia by boat from Helsinki.

We decided to go by train to Helsinki so that we would be able to see more on the journey. That meant going by train from London to Brussels, then taking another train to Cologne. We looked at the famous cathedral and had a meal there before catching a sleeper to Copenhagen. From Copenhagen we took a train to Sweden and then from Stockholm we went on an overnight ferry to Turku in Finland. From there it was a short train journey to Helsinki. The journey was particularly interesting because I love travelling by train and boat. It was exciting to go through the Channel Tunnel and to cross the long bridge between Denmark and Sweden. Above all, it was beautiful sailing through the Finnish islands and arriving by sea in the historic city of St Petersburg. The journey took three days instead of three hours in a plane but it was well worth it.

(189 words)

Question 3
Hi Tom

Good to hear from you. There are quite a lot of films about Scotland but the one I'd recommend is called *The Angel's Share*. It's by a well-known director called Ken Loach and it's an excellent film, I think.

It tells the story of a new young father who's anxious to provide for his child and gets involved in an ingenious crime. It shows both sides of Scottish life – the magnificent scenery and the distilleries popular with tourists and the poverty in some urban areas. So it will help to give you an impression of the contrasts of Scottish life.

It will also help to get you used to the Glasgow accent, which can be quite difficult at first, even for native speakers of English!

A lot of films about Scotland focus on the romantic side of the country – its heather-covered mountains and beautiful sea lochs. This one is not typical in that it also shows the difficulties of life for many people here.

Anyway, do watch it and let me know what you think about it.

Iain

(180 words)

Question 4
When Chris woke up, he expected the day to be like any other one. He quickly put on his school uniform, had breakfast, grabbed his football kit and said goodbye to his parents as on any ordinary day.

However when he got to school, there was great excitement. There was a notice up to say that Warren Blake, the famous footballer, was coming to give a talk to all the students at the school that morning. Warren Blake had been a pupil at that school for a couple of years and he was Chris's hero. He played for one of the best teams in the country and had also represented his country in the last World Cup.

Warren gave the students a fascinating talk about his life as a footballer. He had lots of funny stories and everyone loved listening to him. At the end of his talk he said he had tickets for the school football team to come to his next match with an invitation to meet the team afterwards. As Chris was the goalkeeper in the school team, he couldn't believe his luck!

(186 words)

Listening

Part 1

1 C **2** B **3** C **4** A **5** B **6** B **7** A **8** B

Part 2

9 film / movie **10** 1895
11 ecology **12** penguins
13 sea **14** China
15 wind **16** playing chess
17 (bright / unpolluted / amazing) light **18** Snowstorm

Part 3

19 F **20** H **21** D **22** A **23** G

Part 4

24 C **25** A **26** C **27** B **28** B **29** C **30** A

Reading and Use of English

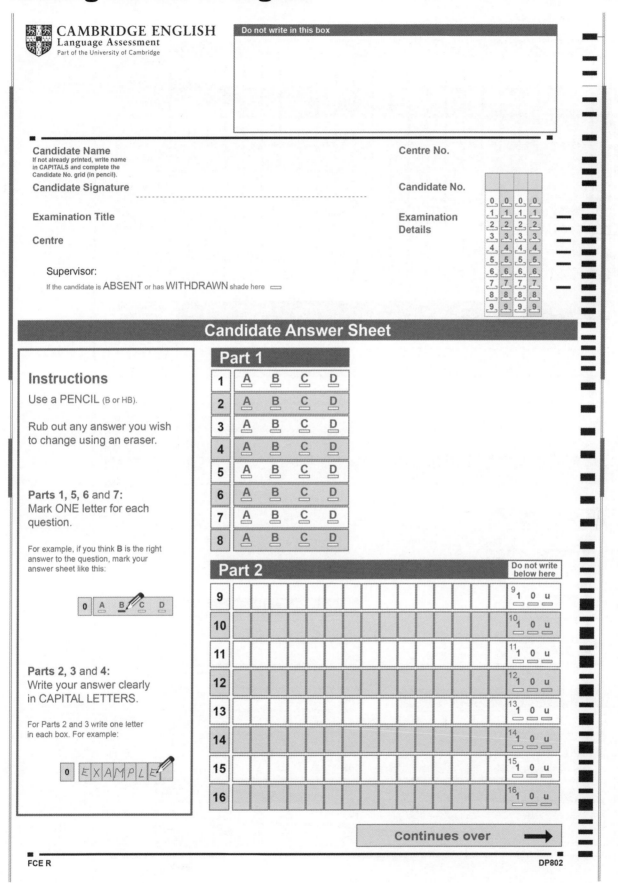

Photocopiable

Reading and Use of English

Part 3

		17
17		1 0 u
18		18 1 0 u
19		19 1 0 u
20		20 1 0 u
21		21 1 0 u
22		22 1 0 u
23		23 1 0 u
24		24 1 0 u

Do not write below here

Part 4

Do not write below here

25		25 2 1 0 u
26		26 2 1 0 u
27		27 2 1 0 u
28		28 2 1 0 u
29		29 2 1 0 u
30		30 2 1 0 u

Part 5

31	A B C D
32	A B C D
33	A B C D
34	A B C D
35	A B C D
36	A B C D

Part 6

37	A B C D E F G
38	A B C D E F G
39	A B C D E F G
40	A B C D E F G
41	A B C D E F G
42	A B C D E F G

Part 7

43	A B C D E F
44	A B C D E F
45	A B C D E F
46	A B C D E F
47	A B C D E F
48	A B C D E F
49	A B C D E F
50	A B C D E F
51	A B C D E F
52	A B C D E F

denote
Print Limited 0121 520 5100

© UCLES 2014

Photocopiable

Listening

Part 1

	A	B	C
1	⊂⊃	⊂⊃	⊂⊃
2	⊂⊃	⊂⊃	⊂⊃
3	⊂⊃	⊂⊃	⊂⊃
4	⊂⊃	⊂⊃	⊂⊃
5	⊂⊃	⊂⊃	⊂⊃
6	⊂⊃	⊂⊃	⊂⊃
7	⊂⊃	⊂⊃	⊂⊃
8	⊂⊃	⊂⊃	⊂⊃

Part 2 (Remember to write in CAPITAL LETTERS or numbers)

Do not write below here

		1 0 u
9		9
10		10
11		11
12		12
13		13
14		14
15		15
16		16
17		17
18		18

Part 3

	A	B	C	D	E	F	G	H
19	⊂⊃	⊂⊃	⊂⊃	⊂⊃	⊂⊃	⊂⊃	⊂⊃	⊂⊃
20	⊂⊃	⊂⊃	⊂⊃	⊂⊃	⊂⊃	⊂⊃	⊂⊃	⊂⊃
21	⊂⊃	⊂⊃	⊂⊃	⊂⊃	⊂⊃	⊂⊃	⊂⊃	⊂⊃
22	⊂⊃	⊂⊃	⊂⊃	⊂⊃	⊂⊃	⊂⊃	⊂⊃	⊂⊃
23	⊂⊃	⊂⊃	⊂⊃	⊂⊃	⊂⊃	⊂⊃	⊂⊃	⊂⊃

Part 4

	A	B	C
24	⊂⊃	⊂⊃	⊂⊃
25	⊂⊃	⊂⊃	⊂⊃
26	⊂⊃	⊂⊃	⊂⊃
27	⊂⊃	⊂⊃	⊂⊃
28	⊂⊃	⊂⊃	⊂⊃
29	⊂⊃	⊂⊃	⊂⊃
30	⊂⊃	⊂⊃	⊂⊃

denote
Print Limited 0121 520 5100

Speaking

Do not write in this box

Candidate Name
If not already printed, write name
in CAPITALS and complete the
Candidate No. grid (in pencil).

Centre No.

Candidate No.

Examination Title

Examination
Details

Centre

Supervisor:
If the candidate is ABSENT or has WITHDRAWN shade here ⊂⊃

Candidate No. grid:
```
0  0  0  0
1  1  1  1
2  2  2  2
3  3  3  3
4  4  4  4
5  5  5  5
6  6  6  6
7  7  7  7
8  8  8  8
9  9  9  9
```

Speaking Test Mark Sheet

Date of test:

Month 01 02 03 04 05 06 07 08 09 10 11 12

Day 01 02 03 04 05 06 07 08 09 10 11 12 13 14 15 16 17 18 19 20 21 22 23 24 25 26 27 28 29 30 31

Marks awarded:

	0	1.0	1.5	2.0	2.5	3.0	3.5	4.0	4.5	5.0
Grammar and Vocabulary	0	1.0	1.5	2.0	2.5	3.0	3.5	4.0	4.5	5.0
Discourse Management	0	1.0	1.5	2.0	2.5	3.0	3.5	4.0	4.5	5.0
Pronunciation	0	1.0	1.5	2.0	2.5	3.0	3.5	4.0	4.5	5.0
Interactive Communication	0	1.0	1.5	2.0	2.5	3.0	3.5	4.0	4.5	5.0
Global Achievement	0	1.0	1.5	2.0	2.5	3.0	3.5	4.0	4.5	5.0

Test materials used:

Part 2 1 2 3 4 5 6 7 8 9 10 11 12 13 14 15 16 17 18 19 20

Part 3 21 22 23 24 25 26 27 28 29 30

Assessor's number
```
A A 0 A A
B B 1 B B
C C 2 C C
D D 3 D D
E E 4 E E
F F 5 F F
G G 6 G G
H H 7 H H
J J 8 J J
K K 9 K K
```

Interlocutor's number
```
A A 0 A A
B B 1 B B
C C 2 C C
D D 3 D D
E E 4 E E
F F 5 F F
G G 6 G G
H H 7 H H
J J 8 J J
K K 9 K K
```

Test format

Examiners : Candidates

2 : 2

2 : 3

Number of 2nd Candidate
```
0 0 0 0
1 1 1 1
2 2 2 2
3 3 3 3
4 4 4 4
5 5 5 5
6 6 6 6
7 7 7 7
8 8 8 8
9 9 9 9
```

Number of 3rd Candidate
```
0 0 0 0
1 1 1 1
2 2 2 2
3 3 3 3
4 4 4 4
5 5 5 5
6 6 6 6
7 7 7 7
8 8 8 8
9 9 9 9
```

SMS 1

denote
Print Limited 0121 520 5100

DP749/307

Acknowledgements

Author acknowledgements

The authors would like to thank Jane Coates for her help in producing this second edition. Many thanks also to Lucy Edwards (production projects co-ordinator), Kay George (permissions clearance controller), Louise Edgeworth (freelance picture researcher), Leon Chambers (audio producer), Denise Cowle (proof reader).

Helen Tiliouine would like to thank Ahmed, Adam and Oliver for being so patient and supportive. Also thanks to Ann-Marie Murphy at CUP for all her help and encouragement.

Publisher acknowledgements

The authors and publishers are grateful to the following for reviewing the material during the writing process for both the previous edition and the new content for this edition:

Jessica Smith, Clare Tonks, Catherine Toomey: Italy; Laura Clyde: Spain; Bridget Bloom, Helen Chilton, Petrina Cliff, Sarah Dymond, Mark Fountain, Felicity O'Dell, Helen Tiliouine: UK.

Development of this publication has made use of the Cambridge English Corpus (CEC). The CEC is a computer database of contemporary spoken and written English, which currently stands at over one billion words. It includes British English, American English and other varieties of English. It also includes the Cambridge Learner Corpus, developed in collaboration with the University of Cambridge ESOL Examinations. Cambridge University Press has built up the CEC to provide evidence about language use that helps to produce better language teaching materials.

This product is informed by the English Vocabulary Profile, built as part of English Profile, a collaborative programme designed to enhance the learning, teaching and assessment of English worldwide. Its main funding partners are Cambridge University Press and Cambridge ESOL and its aim is to create a 'profile' for English linked to the Common European Framework of Reference for Languages (CEF). English Profile outcomes, such as the English Vocabulary Profile, will provide detailed information about the language that learners can be expected to demonstrate at each CEF level, offering a clear benchmark for learners' proficiency. For more information, please visit www.englishprofile.org

The authors and publishers acknowledge the following sources of copyright material and are grateful for the permissions granted. While every effort has been made, it has not always been possible to identify the sources of all the material used, or to trace all copyright holders. If any omissions are brought to our notice, we will be happy to include the appropriate acknowledgements on reprinting.

Wright's Media for the text on p. 109 adapted from 'You've Gotta See The Graduation Dress This Teen Made Out Of Her Old Homework' by Mandi Woodruff, *Business Insider*, 06.06.12. Reproduced with permission; Gyldendal Norsk Forlag AS for the text on p. 149 adapted from *Kon-Tiki Ekspedisjonen* by Thor Heyerdahl. Copyright © Gyldendal Norsk Forlag AS 1948. All rights reserved; ESPN for the text on p. 172 adapted from 'Japanese teen calmly takes on SNB pipe's best' by Wayne Drehs, *ESPN*, 27.01.13. Copyright © 2013, ESPN, Inc. Reprinted courtesy of ESPN.

Photo acknowledgements

T = Top, C = Centre, Be = Below, L = Left, R = Right, B/G = background

p. 53: Alamy/© David Wall; p. 94: Shutterstock/© Dragon Images; p. 115: Alamy/© Mark Conlin; p. 147: Alamy/© nagelestock. com; C1 A: Shutterstock/© oliveromg; C1 B: Alamy/© PeopleByDarrellYoung; C2 A: Corbis/© Daniela Buoncristiani/cultura; C2 B: Alamy/© H. Mark Weidman Photography; C3 A: Getty/© Blend Images/John Fedele; C3 B: Getty/© Joey Foley; C4 A: Getty Images/© The Image Bank/Yellow Dog Productions; C4 B: Thinkstock/© Photodisc/Jochen Sand; C8 A: Alamy/© Keith Morris; C8 B: Alamy/© Kumar Sriskandan; C9 A: Alamy/© Picture Partners; C9 B: Alamy/© Hangon Media Works Private limited; C13 A: Shutterstock/© Monkey Business Images; C13 B: Getty Images/© The Image Bank/Nivek Neslo; C14 A: Thinkstock/© Digital Vision/Ulrik Tofte; C14 B: Getty Images/© Photodisc/Rob Melnychuk; C16 A: Getty Images/© Iconica/Cavan Images; C16 B: Shutterstock/© Eugenia-Petrenko; C17 A: Shutterstock/© Aleksandr Markin; C17 B: Alamy/© Paul Gapper; C19 A: Alamy/© LOOK Die Bildagentur der Fotografen GmbH; C19 B: Shutterstock/© Wallenrock; C20 A: Corbis/© Wavebreak Media Ltd; C20 B: Corbis/© Hero Images; C22 A: Alamy/© Bubbles Photolibrary; C22 B: Corbis/© Katie Garrod/JAI; C23 A: Alamy/© Doug Houghton; C23 B: Alamy/© Juniors Bildarchiv GmbH.

Commissioned photography by Gareth Boden on p. 6, p. 60.
Commissioned photography by Trevor Clifford on p. 55, p. 57, p. 63.

Illustrations by:

Alasdair Bright (nb illustration) pp. 11, 15, 39, 49, 92, 128, 146; Fitz Hammond (nb illustration) pp. 22, 32, 68, 72, 164; Ben Hasler (nb illustration) pp. 16, 73, 127, 145; Clementine Hope (nb illustration) p. 158; Brett Hudson (Graham-Cameron Illustration) pp.14, 19, 47, 79, 96; Paul Hutchinson (Graham-Cameron Illustration) pp. 70, 169; Mike Lacey (Beehive Illustration) pp. 84, 103; Robin Lawrie (Beehive Illustration) pp. 10, 18, 21, 25, 30, 38, 42, 85, 89, 98, 100; Dan Lewis (Beehive Illustration) pp.26, 36, 87, 133; Andrew Painter pp.4, 67

Design, layout and art edited by: Wild Apple Design Ltd.

What are the people enjoying about taking photos in these different places?

A

B

Why have the people chosen to do these activities?

A

B

Why are the people singing in these situations?

A

B

What do the people enjoy about doing these jobs?

A

B

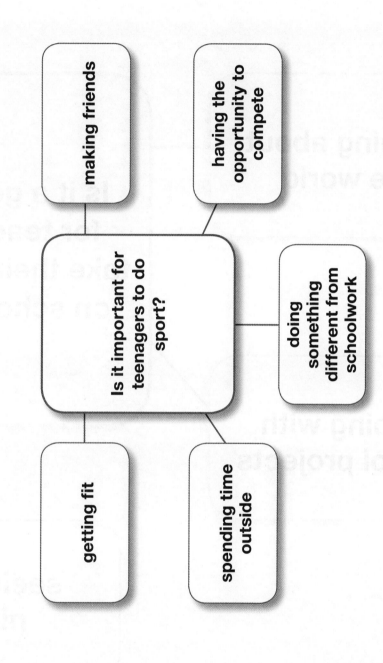

making friends

having the opportunity to compete

Is it important for teenagers to do sport?

doing something different from schoolwork

getting fit

spending time outside

learning about the world

Is it a good idea for teachers to take their students on school trips?

helping with school projects

seeing new places

time outside the
classroom

having fun

Why have the people decided to do these things in their spare time?

A

B

Why do people enjoy talking to friends in these ways?

A

B

how to cook

Is it always best to learn things from older people?

the latest technology

the best clothes to buy

school subjects

how to behave
well

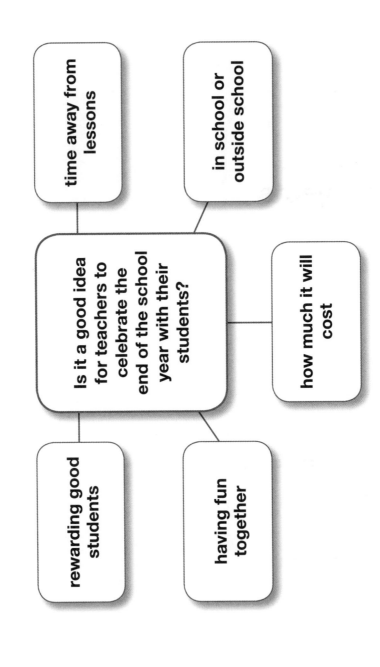

Is it a good idea for teachers to celebrate the end of the school year with their students?

- time away from lessons
- in school or outside school
- how much it will cost
- having fun together
- rewarding good students

Why might the people like watching films in these different places?

A

B

Why have the people decided to travel in these ways?

A

B

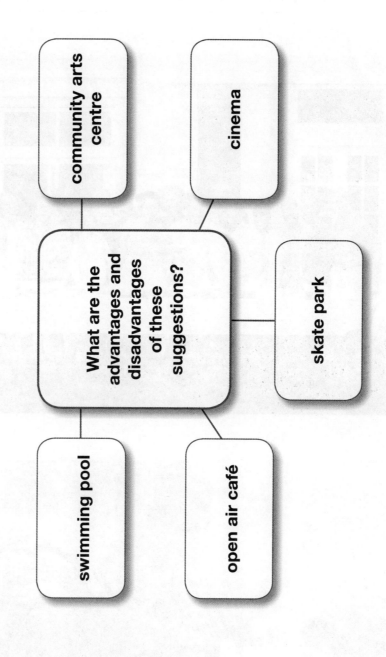

- community arts centre
- cinema
- skate park
- open air café
- swimming pool

What are the advantages and disadvantages of these suggestions?

Why have the friends decided to do these things together?

A

B

Why have the people chosen to exercise in these ways?

A

B

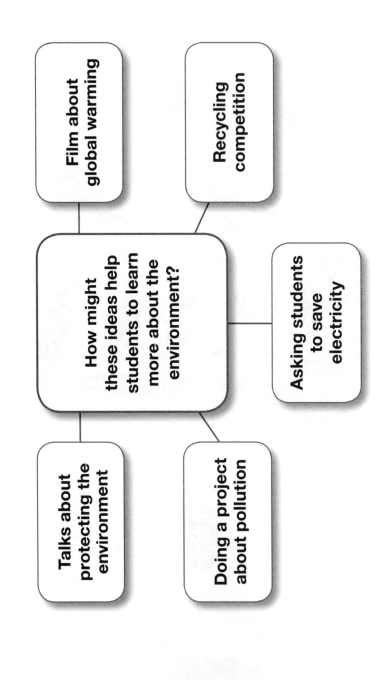

Film about
global warming

Recycling
competition

How might
these ideas help
students to learn
more about the
environment?

Asking students
to save
electricity

Talks about
protecting the
environment

Doing a project
about pollution

What are the people enjoying about these activities?

A

B

Why do you think the students are studying in these ways?

A

B

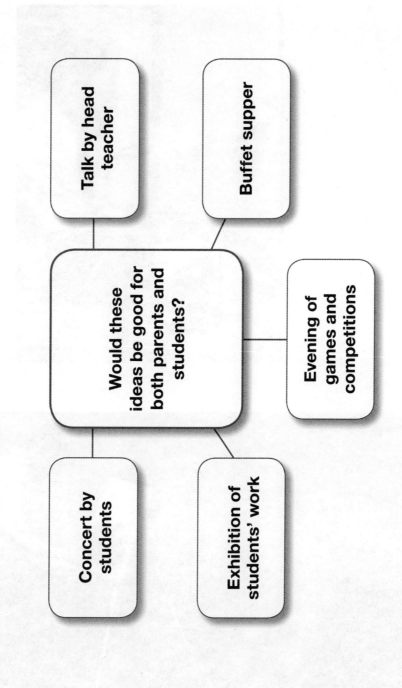

Talk by head teacher

Buffet supper

Would these ideas be good for both parents and students?

Evening of games and competitions

Concert by students

Exhibition of students' work

Why are the people painting in these situations?

A

B

What are the people enjoying about being with animals in these situations?

A

B

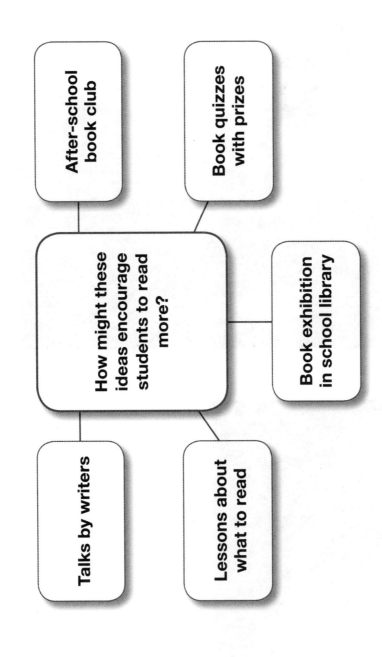

After-school
book club

Book quizzes
with prizes

How might these
ideas encourage
students to read
more?

Book exhibition
in school library

Talks by writers

Lessons about
what to read